40 Strategies for Guiding Readers through Informational Texts

Also from Barbara Moss

Exemplary Instruction in the Middle Grades:
Teaching That Supports Engagement and Rigorous Learning
Edited by Diane Lapp and Barbara Moss

Exploring the Literature of Fact:
Children's Nonfiction Trade Books in the Elementary Classroom
Barbara Moss

Teaching New Literacies in Grades K–3:
Resources for 21st-Century Classrooms
Edited by Barbara Moss and Diane Lapp

Teaching New Literacies in Grades 4–6:
Resources for 21st-Century Classrooms
Edited by Barbara Moss and Diane Lapp

40 Strategies

for Guiding Readers
through Informational Texts

Barbara Moss
Virginia Loh-Hagan

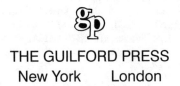

THE GUILFORD PRESS
New York   London

Copyright © 2016 The Guilford Press
A Division of Guilford Publications, Inc.
370 Seventh Avenue, Suite 1200, New York, NY 10001
www.guilford.com

Printed in the United States of America

This book is printed on acid-free paper.

Last digit is print number: 9   8   7   6   5   4   3   2   1

Library of Congress Cataloging-in-Publication Data

Names: Moss, Barbara, 1950– author. | Loh-Hagan, Virginia, author.
Title: 40 strategies for guiding readers through informational texts / Barbara Moss,
    Virginia S. Loh-Hagan.
Other titles: Forty strategies for guiding readers through informational texts
Description: New York, NY : The Guilford Press, 2016. | Includes bibliographical
    references and index.
Identifiers: LCCN 2016006013 | ISBN 9781462526093 (paperback)
Subjects: LCSH: Reading comprehension—Study and teaching—Activity programs. |
    BISAC: LANGUAGE ARTS & DISCIPLINES / Reading Skills. | EDUCATION /
    Teaching Methods & Materials / Reading & Phonics. | LANGUAGE ARTS &
    DISCIPLINES / Literacy.
Classification: LCC LB1573.7 .M68 2016 | DDC 372.47—dc23
LC record available at *https://lccn.loc.gov/2016006013*

About the Authors

Barbara Moss, PhD, is Professor of Literacy Education in the School of Teacher Education at San Diego State University. She has taught English and language arts in elementary, middle, and high school settings and has worked as a reading coach. Dr. Moss's research focuses on the teaching of informational texts at the elementary and secondary levels. She regularly presents at local, state, national, and international conferences and has published numerous journal articles, columns, book chapters, and books. Dr. Moss has served as the Young Adult Literature column editor for *Voices in the Middle*, a publication of the National Council of Teachers of English.

Virginia Loh-Hagan, EdD, is a full-time Lecturer in the School of Teacher Education at San Diego State University, where she is in charge of two teaching credential programs. She is also a curriculum designer, educational consultant, and former K–8 teacher. The author of several academic publications and more than 70 children's books, Dr. Loh-Hagan serves on several children's book award committees and is cover editor and columnist for *The California Reader*, a peer-reviewed journal of the California Reading Association. She is a frequent presenter at state and national conferences.

Introduction

Increasingly, teachers across the country have discovered the value of using authentic texts to supplement textbooks and basal readers. The Internet has made it possible to obtain a broad range of texts with the click of a mouse. Teachers use these texts in the classroom for a variety of purposes, including but not limited to guided reading, shared reading, independent reading, and/or content-related instruction. In the past, however, teachers have most often employed narrative texts rather than informational texts for these purposes. The increased availability of quality informational texts has led to greater teacher use of this text type. The ability to read informational texts is crucial to students' success, whether in college or career, since most texts they will be reading as adults will be informational.

The Common Core State Standards (CCSS) have placed the focus on informational texts as never before. They recommend that students in grades K–5 spend 50% of their time reading informational texts. By eighth grade that recommendation changes to 45% literary texts and 55% informational texts, and by 12th grade it is recommended that students spend 70% of their school day reading informational texts. These suggestions are based on the fact that students are living in an age of information, globalization, and digitalization. Today's students are constantly bombarded with and surrounded by information from a variety of sources beyond books and magazines. These texts have one important thing in common: Their purpose is to inform or persuade the reader. These sources include the World Wide Web, television/cable, radio/podcasts, social networking sites, texts, e-mails, and many more. Information can be accessed literally from the palms of our hands through smartphones. Today's students are at the forefront of advancing communication technologies. So what does this all mean for classroom teachers?

The need for today's teachers to involve students, even in primary grades, in reading informational texts is greater than ever before. As students move through the grades, the amount of expository text reading required increases significantly. As adults, too, most of what we read at work and at home is informational text. If students are to thrive in the workplace or university in the Information Age, they must develop the skills required to read the many different types of informational texts they will encounter. The ability to gain information from the Internet, for example, depends on the ability to read and understand informational texts. In addition, success on today's assessments depends on this ability. Much of the material found on the Partnership for Assessment of Readiness for College and Careers (PARCC) and Smarter Balanced assessments, for example, is informational. If students are going to succeed on these tests, they need exposure to and understanding of how informational texts work. If students are to become responsible citizens and future leaders, they must learn how to think about and use the information they receive. Simply being able to locate information is not enough. Whether in school or in the workplace, it is imperative that students be able to evaluate the truth value of the information they access. For these reasons, we would like to make a case for using critical literacy as a framework for learning through informational texts.

Because students are inundated with information, they may have difficulty differentiating between what's important versus interesting, what's "true" and what's "really true," and so on. Information can be biased and, as a result, students need the ability to critically examine data to determine their truth value. Teaching students how to read and comprehend critically will empower them to make better and more informed decisions and opinions, which is the ultimate goal of teaching informational texts. Critical literacy encourages us to examine how people and ideas are represented and to investigate embedded and/or implicit messages (Morgan, 1997). Boutte (2002) contends that even young children can learn to be critical readers, to "learn to identify and clarify ideological perspectives in books" (p. 147). Many of our biases may be the result of the accumulation of both subtle and overt messages in books, media, and instructional practices (Boutte, 2002); thus, learning how to recognize issues of power and perspective by assuming a critical perspective is necessary. In short, teachers would be remiss not to push students to think critically and constructively about all the information they receive.

Contrary to popular belief, however, learning through informational texts is not just a bitter pill that students must swallow in order to succeed in school. Studies indicate that many students actually *prefer* reading informational texts to fiction. With the incredible array of enticing informational resources available today, it is easier than ever to engage students in real-world reading. Regardless of a student's area of interest, whether it's video games, hip-hop, rocks, horses, tattoos, dinosaurs, medieval weaponry, outer space, or art, informational texts can fuel this curiosity and deepen comprehension and understanding. These are the materials that answer our questions about the universe—about the people, places, and things students encounter in their daily lives. Too often, though, we don't capitalize on our students' fascination with facts. Instead, we fill our classrooms with stories—fantasies and realistic tales—ignoring the excitement that reading information might ignite.

This newly revised and expanded edition of *35 Strategies for Guiding Readers through Informational Texts* (Moss & Loh, 2010) is designed to provide classroom teachers in grades K–12 with a practical resource for using informational texts in the classroom. Like the earlier volume, *40 Strategies for Guiding Readers through Informational Texts* is intended to help teachers guide students in learning about strategies for understanding these texts. It differs from the previous edition in several ways, however. First, we have expanded the total number of strategies to 40. In many instances, we have changed or updated the strategies that appeared in the earlier book. Sixteen strategies are completely new. In addition, we have tried to create a better balance between strategies appropriate for students across the grade levels. Most important, we have updated the examples to reflect the CCSS and other state standards by providing a listing of Anchor Standards pertinent to each strategy. These include Anchor Standards for Reading, Writing, and Speaking and Listening. In addition, we have added two categories of strategies: Reading Closely and Discussion. These two areas are of interest to teachers because of their emphasis in the CCSS and state standards documents. We have also updated the Appendix to provide teachers with more current informational text resources.

The strategies in the book are organized according to the following topics: Getting Started, Building Background, Vocabulary, Reading Closely, Comprehension, Discussion, and Writing. A shaded box beneath each strategy indicates the topic it addresses. Each strategy is also identified by its recommended grade levels. Anchor Standards pertinent to the strategy example are also provided.

A common format is used to explore each strategy. Each strategy is explained and described in the "What Is It?" section. A rationale for using each strategy is provided in the "What Is Its Purpose?" section, and specific, step-by-step procedures for using the strategy are described under "What Do I Do?". The "Example" section describes how the strategy might be implemented in a classroom with students at a specific grade level, and a list of references gives teachers more information on the strategy. Within the references, trade books described in the examples are coded by grade levels. Primary books are coded P and are intended for grades K–3; intermediate-level books are coded I and are intended for grades 4–6; middle-level books are coded M and are intended for grades 7–8; and books coded YA (young adult) are suitable for use with high school students (grades 9–12). The final section, "Your Turn!", provides directions for using the reproducible forms and templates designed for student use and, in some instances, teacher planning purposes.

At the end of the book is an updated Appendix of recommended materials, including trade books categorized according to level. The Appendix also includes a listing of informational magazines for children and young adults, as well as a list of useful informational text websites.

Most of the strategies included in this book are suitable for use with the many wonderful student magazines available today, including *Time for Kids, Kids Discover, Sports Illustrated Kids,* and *Cobblestone.* Most of the strategies can be used with newspaper articles, websites, or any other sources of informational texts. The strategies can also be used to teach textbook information in virtually every discipline, including science, social studies, and mathematics.

We hope that you will enjoy using *40 Strategies for Guiding Students through Informational Texts* and that it will be a useful resource as you begin to involve your students in developing and increasing their understanding of informational texts. We hope, too, that your students will develop an increased enthusiasm for informational texts that will prompt them to find pleasure and enjoyment in this type of reading.

References

Boutte, G. S. (2002). The critical literacy process: Guidelines for examining books. *Childhood Education, 78*(3), 147–152.

Morgan, W. (1997). *Critical literacy in the classroom: The art of the possible.* New York: Routledge.

Moss, B., & Loh, V. (2010). *35 strategies for guiding readers through informational texts.* New York: Guilford Press.

Contents

PART ONE

Getting Started Strategies

Strategy 1	Planning a Lesson with Informational Texts	3
Strategy 2	Understanding and Evaluating Informational Texts	12
Strategy 3	Assessing Text Complexity	19
Strategy 4	Shared Reading and Text Feature Search	31

PART TWO

Building Background Strategies

Strategy 5	Anticipation Guide	39
Strategy 6	KWHL	44
Strategy 7	KLEW	50
Strategy 8	Table of Contents Prediction	55
Strategy 9	IEPC	60

PART THREE

Vocabulary Strategies

Strategy 10	Word Map	67
Strategy 11	SLAP	71
Strategy 12	Root Wheels	77
Strategy 13	List–Group–Label	82
Strategy 14	Word Sort	87
Strategy 15	Semantic Feature Analysis	92

PART FOUR

Reading Closely Strategies

Strategy 16	Close Reading	99
Strategy 17	Close Thinking	109

Strategy 18 Text Annotation   *119*
Strategy 19 Text-Dependent Questions   *124*
Strategy 20 Thinking Aloud   *132*
Strategy 21 Sticky Notes Bookmark   *138*

PART FIVE

Comprehension Strategies

Strategy 22 Study Guide   *145*
Strategy 23 Four-Box Comment Card   *150*
Strategy 24 I-Chart   *158*
Strategy 25 CAATS   *165*
Strategy 26 Text Structures   *173*
Strategy 27 Interactive Notebooks   *184*

PART SIX

Discussion Strategies

Strategy 28 Discussion Web   *191*
Strategy 29 4–3–2–1 Discussion Guide   *196*
Strategy 30 Intra-Act   *202*
Strategy 31 Talking Points   *208*
Strategy 32 Three-Step Interview   *216*
Strategy 33 3-Minute Pause   *221*

PART SEVEN

Writing Strategies

Strategy 34 Readers Theatre   *229*
Strategy 35 Paragraph Writing Frames   *234*
Strategy 36 I Used to Think . . . but Now I Know . . .   *239*
Strategy 37 Summary Writing   *244*
Strategy 38 CLIQUES   *249*
Strategy 39 EPIC   *254*
Strategy 40 Two-Column Journal   *260*

Appendix Recommended Materials   *265*
Index   *273*

Purchasers of this book can download and print select materials at
www.guilford.com/moss2-forms for personal use
or use with individual students (see copyright page for details).

PART ONE

Getting Started

Strategies

Strategy 1

Planning a Lesson
with Informational Texts

GRADE LEVELS: K–12

Getting Started
Building Background
Vocabulary
Reading Closely
Comprehension
Discussion
Writing

CCSS Anchor Standards: Reading*

➤ **CCSS.ELA-Literacy.CCRA.R.1** Read closely to determine what the text says explicitly and to make logical inferences from it; cite specific textual evidence when writing or speaking to support conclusions drawn from the text.

➤ **CCSS.ELA-Literacy.CCRA.R.2** Determine central ideas or themes of a text and analyze their development; summarize the key supporting details and ideas.

➤ **CCSS.ELA-Literacy.CCRA.R.3** Analyze how and why individuals, events, or ideas develop and interact over the course of a text.

➤ **CCSS.ELA-Literacy.CCRA.R.4** Interpret words and phrases as they are used in a text, including determining technical, connotative, and figurative meanings, and analyze how specific word choices shape meaning or tone.

➤ **CCSS.ELA-Literacy.CCRA.R.5** Analyze the structure of texts, including how specific sentences, paragraphs, and larger portions of the text (e.g., a section, chapter, scene, or stanza) relate to each other and the whole.

➤ **CCSS.ELA-Literacy.CCRA.R.6** Assess how point of view or purpose shapes the content and style of a text.

➤ **CCSS.ELA-Literacy.CCRA.R.7** Integrate and evaluate content presented in diverse media and formats, including visually and quantitatively, as well as in words.

*The CCSS are available at *www.corestandards.org*. Copyright © 2010 the National Governors Association Center for Best Practices and Council of Chief State School Officers. All rights reserved.

> **CCSS.ELA-Literacy.CCRA.R.8** Delineate and evaluate the argument and specific claims in a text, including the validity of the reasoning as well as the relevance and sufficiency of the evidence.

> **CCSS.ELA-Literacy.CCRA.R.9** Analyze how two or more texts address similar themes or topics in order to build knowledge or to compare the approaches the authors take.

> **CCSS.ELA-Literacy.CCRA.R.10** Read and comprehend complex literary and informational texts independently and proficiently.

What Is It?

Because the Common Core State Standards (CCSS) call for more use of informational texts than ever before, it is essential that teachers develop confidence in creating lessons that address this text type. Effective lesson planning is central to good teaching, and nowhere is this more important than with informational texts. Lessons using informational text can take place in the English language arts class or in disciplines such as social studies, science, or mathematics. Research consistently indicates that informational texts are more challenging for students than narrative ones. For this reason, effective planning that includes scaffolding is crucial to student success with this text type.

The CCSS Anchor Standards provide a good starting point for identifying those reading abilities central to understanding informational texts that can form the basis for a variety of lessons. These Anchor Standards address key aspects of understanding informational texts including identifying main ideas and details, analyzing text structures, and identifying arguments and claims and citing evidence. Teachers may create lessons that address these standards by using shared reading, guided reading, read-alouds, or close reading, which requires a different format than the other three and is addressed later in this text (see Strategies 16–21).

Shared reading typically involves the teacher reading aloud with students following along, as she thinks aloud and models for students how to approach an informational text. Guided reading is typically a small-group reading activity in which a teacher guides a small group of children with similar reading abilities through a common text. Read-alouds typically involve the teacher reading to the students from an informational text at a level above student reading abilities.

What Is Its Purpose?

The purpose of informational text lessons is to expand students' knowledge, teaching them concepts and terms related to a variety of topics and people. In addition, they sensitize students to the patterns of exposition, which are far less familiar to students than stories. Informational texts provide tie-ins to many curricular areas, and provide opportunities for comparing texts, a skill that is required by the CCSS.

They can ignite student interest in a variety of topics, leading to silent, independent reading. This silent reading is a critical factor in the development of lifelong readers.

Informational text lesson plans can introduce, culminate, or provide new information about a topic explored in a cross-curricular unit that might incorporate a multiplicity of texts, such as novels, dramas, short stories, or other genres.

Please note that the lesson plan provided in this strategy is not appropriate for close reading. See Strategies 16 and 17 for lesson plan templates for close reading.

What Do I Do?

1. Identify the CCSS you wish to focus on. The Anchor Standards identify a variety of informational text reading skills that increase in sophistication across grades K–12. They specify the following areas of emphasis for both literary and informational texts.

Key Ideas and Details

- *CCSS.ELA-Literacy.CCRA.R.1* Read closely to determine what the text says explicitly and to make logical inferences from it; cite specific textual evidence when writing or speaking to support conclusions drawn from the text.

- *CCSS.ELA-Literacy.CCRA.R.2* Determine central ideas or themes of a text and analyze their development; summarize the key supporting details and ideas.

- *CCSS.ELA-Literacy.CCRA.R.3* Analyze how and why individuals, events, or ideas develop and interact over the course of a text.

Craft and Structure

- *CCSS.ELA-Literacy.CCRA.R.4* Interpret words and phrases as they are used in a text, including determining technical, connotative, and figurative meanings, and analyze how specific word choices shape meaning or tone.

- *CCSS.ELA-Literacy.CCRA.R.5* Analyze the structure of texts, including how specific sentences, paragraphs, and larger portions of the text (e.g., a section, chapter, scene, or stanza) relate to each other and the whole.

- *CCSS.ELA-Literacy.CCRA.R.6* Assess how point of view or purpose shapes the content and style of a text.

Integration of Knowledge and Ideas

- *CCSS.ELA-Literacy.CCRA.R.7* Integrate and evaluate content presented in diverse media and formats, including visually and quantitatively, as well as in words.

Formats for Informational Text Read-Alouds

- **Reading "bits and pieces."** Bits-and-pieces read-alouds can include book chapters, book sections, or short magazine or newspaper articles. Excerpts from collective biographies like *Lives of the Artists: Masterpieces, Messes (and What the Neighbors Thought)* (Krull, 2014), *or Lives of the Athletes: Thrills, Spills (and What the Neighbors Thought)* (Krull, 2012), for example, make excellent 5-minute read-alouds. These breezy thumbnail sketches of the lives of prominent artists and athletes teach today's students about outstanding achievers from the past and the present.

- **Reading picture captions.** This can whet student appetites for information and enhance visual literacy skills. Captions from *Anne Frank: Beyond the Diary* (Van der Rol & Verhoeven, 1993) connect artifacts back to the diary itself. They include maps of the secret annex, Nazi documents identifying the Frank family members, and more. Reading captions for *Surprising Sharks (Read and Wonder)* (Davies, 2008) creates reading motivation and heightens student interest in these amazing creatures.

- **Breaking up the reading over a period of days.** Identify logical breaking points and read a short section of text at one sitting rather than the entire work.

- **Linking informational texts with other genres.** For example, linking uniquely interactive titles like *The American Revolution (Letters for Freedom)* (Rife, 2009) with poetry like *Colonial Voices: Hear Them Speak* (Winters, 2015) helps teachers build students' schema about this important period in history.

- **Reading different books about the same person or topic.** For example, reading different biographies of Martin Luther King, Jr., such as *Martin's Big Words: The Life of Dr. Martin Luther King, Jr.* (Rappaport, 2001) or *MLK: The Journey of a King* (Bolden, 2008), can illustrate for students the varied points of view an author can take about a person or topic. These reading experiences help students develop a critical stance toward what they are reading, teaching them that different sources of information may contradict one another and that different authors can take different perspectives on the same person.

- **Planning before-, during-, and after-reading activities designed to scaffold student understanding.**

- *CCSS.ELA-Literacy.CCRA.R.8* Delineate and evaluate the argument and specific claims in a text, including the validity of the reasoning as well as the relevance and sufficiency of the evidence.

- *CCSS.ELA-Literacy.CCRA.R.9* Analyze how two or more texts address similar themes or topics in order to build knowledge or to compare the approaches the authors take.

Range of Reading and Level of Text Complexity

- *CCSS.ELA Literacy.CCRA.R.10* Read and comprehend complex literary and informational texts independently and proficiently.

2. Identify the lesson objective and the purpose.

3. Determine the format for your lesson (guided reading, shared reading, read-aloud, close reading, independent reading, or other).

4. Determine what you will do before, during, and after reading.

Example

Teacher Lorena Cortez engages her fourth-grade students in shared reading of informational texts on a regular basis. She selects shared readings that link to content-area topics like science and social studies and often uses these books to introduce or expand upon textbook content. She sometimes focuses students on a small section from a larger text, such as when she had students read the profile of Van Gogh from *Lives of the Artists: Masterpieces, Messes (and What the Neighbors Thought)* (Krull, 2014) to introduce an art lesson. On other occasions, she shares informational books that she knows will interest her students and that have the potential to motivate them to read on their own.

When planning informational book shared readings for her students, Lorena creates before-, during-, and after-reading experiences that maintain student engagement. The Informational Book Lesson Planning Guide included with this lesson provides guidelines for planning these experiences. Before reading *The Book of Stars* (Twist, 2007), for example, Lorena provided students with an Anticipation Guide (Strategy 5) designed to help her evaluate students' prior knowledge about stars. Lorena previewed the text with her students, noting the unique format of the book that included pages of different sizes, bold chapter titles such as "The Sun," "Red Dwarf," "Giant Star," and more; she also previewed the placement, types, and topics of the text boxes with her students. She pointed out to students that the book was organized topically, with each section focused on a different type or aspect of stars.

Because the text contained dense information, Lorena chose to complete a

7

Before Reading

The before-reading step establishes links between students' experiences and text materials. Use strategies like Anticipation Guides (Strategy 5), KWHL (Strategy 6), or Table of Contents Prediction (Strategy 8) to engage students in predicting the content of the text. Bring in props, pictures, or examples of things mentioned in the story to make information more concrete to students. For example, showing students pictures of the incredible gold artifacts found aboard the Spanish galleon ship *Atcham* could pique student interest and enhance children's enjoyment of Gail Gibbons's (1990) *Sunken Treasure*.

Before students read, help them to notice text features (see Strategy 4) like bold headings, text boxes, the table of contents, and the index. By pointing out text features, teachers can help students understand the cues the author provides to the text organization. In this way, students will find it easier to comprehend the information.

During Reading

The lesson objective and purpose will determine the focus of the during-reading step. During-reading activities are especially important with informational text, since students are less familiar with the academic vocabulary and structures of this text type. For this reason, teachers should find opportunities to model their own thinking through the use of think-aloud (Strategy 20). Students might answer text-dependent questions (Strategy 19), clarify terms (Strategies 10–15), annotate the text (Strategy 18), complete graphic organizers that reflect the text organization (Strategy 26), or record written responses to the text using two-column journals (Strategy 40). Through such activities, teachers can help focus student attention on making meaning from the text.

After Reading

Students should demonstrate their understanding of a text in some way after reading. This typically involves further reading, writing, speaking, or listening in ways that allow students to build upon what they have learned. Further reading, for example, might involve students in analyzing sources related to text content using CAATS (see Strategy 25), participating in discussions about the text (Strategies 28–33) or writing about the text (Strategies 34–40). All of these strategies provide meaningful ways to extend and enhance student understanding.

shared reading with only one section per day. As she read the text aloud, she helped students create a chart that allowed them to compare information about different stars, including their diameters, their temperatures, distances from earth, myths and legends, and so on. After reading, students compared the information in their science text with that found in the trade book. This furthered their ability to compare and critically analyze information.

References

Bolden, C. (2008). *MLK: The journey of a king*. New York: M. Abrams. (P)

Davies, N. (2008). *Surprising sharks (Read and wonder)*. New York: Candlewick. (P)

Gibbons, G. (1990). *Sunken treasure*. New York: HarperCollins. (I)

Krull, K. (2012). *Lives of the athletes: Thrills, spills (and what the neighbors thought)*. Boston: HMH Books for Young Adults. (YA)

Krull, K. (2013). *Lives of extraordinary women: Rulers, rebels (and what the neighbors thought)*. Boston: HMH Books for Young Adults. (YA)

Krull, K. (2013). *Lives of the musicians: Good times, bad times (and what the neighbors thought)*. Boston: HMH Books for Young Adults. (M, YA)

Krull, K. (2014). *Lives of the artists: Masterpieces, messes (and what the neighbors thought)*. Boston: HMH Books for Young Adults. (YA)

Rappaport, D. (2001). *Martin's big words: The life of Dr. Martin Luther King, Jr.* New York: Hyperion Books for Children. (P)

Rife, D. (2009). *The American revolution (Letters for freedom)*. New York: Kids Innovative. (I)

Twist, C. (2007). *The book of stars*. New York: Scholastic. (I)

Van der Rol, R., & Verhoeven, R. (1993). *Anne Frank, beyond the diary: A photographic remembrance*. New York: Viking. (M)

Winters, K. (2015). *Colonial voices: Hear them speak*. New York: Puffin. (I).

Your Turn!

Select an informational text to use as a read-aloud, shared, or guided reading, either from the Appendix at the back of this book, or one of your own choosing. Before you choose, however, consider what format you will use to engage your students with the book. Record that information on the form on pages 10–11. In addition, record notes about what you will do before, during, and after the reading.

Informational Text Lesson Planning Guide

Instructions: Complete the planning guide to prepare for teaching an informational text.

1. Which CCSS standard(s) do you plan to address and what is the purpose of your lesson?

_____

_____

2. What informational text do you plan to use? _____

_____

3. What format (shared, guided, read-aloud) do you plan to use for this lesson? _____

_____

_____

4. What will you do before, during, and after reading this book?

Steps in Lesson	Sample Strategies
Before Reading: How will you activate prior knowledge about the topic? _____ _____ _____ What new words will you need to introduce? _____ _____ _____ How will you teach students about the text organization (review headings, table of contents) and features? _____ _____ _____	Anticipation Guide (Strategy 5) KWHL (Strategy 6) KLEW (Strategy 7) Table of Contents Prediction (Strategy 8) Other: _____ _____

(continued)

Steps in Lesson	Sample Strategies
During Reading: How will you help students understand the readings? _____ _____ _____	Point out text structures and signal words (see Strategy 26) Explore vocabulary (see Strategies 10–15) Ask text-dependent questions (see Strategy 19) Have students annotate (see Strategy 18) Other: _____ _____

After Reading:
 	
How will students demonstrate what they have learned?
 	
_____
 	
_____
 	
_____
	Have students:
	• Ask/answer questions
	• Complete a graphic organizer such as:
	  Series of Events Chart (p. 180)
	  Venn Diagram (p. 181)
	  Cause–Effect Map (p. 182)
	  Problem–Solution Outline (p. 183)
	• Discuss the text (see Strategies 28–33)
	• Write in response to the text (see Strategies 34–50)
	Complete a multimedia project
	Other: _____
	
	_____

Strategy 2

Understanding and Evaluating Informational Texts

GRADE LEVELS: K–12

Getting Started

Building Background

Vocabulary

Reading Closely

Comprehension

Discussion

Writing

CCSS Anchor Standards: Reading

➤ **CCSS.ELA-Literacy.CCRA.R.1** Read closely to determine what the text says explicitly and to make logical inferences from it; cite specific textual evidence when writing or speaking to support conclusions drawn from the text.

➤ **CCSS.ELA-Literacy.CCRA.R.2** Determine central ideas or themes of a text and analyze their development; summarize the key supporting details and ideas.

➤ **CCSS.ELA-Literacy.CCRA.R.3** Analyze how and why individuals, events, or ideas develop and interact over the course of a text.

➤ **CCSS.ELA-Literacy.CCRA.R.4** Interpret words and phrases as they are used in a text, including determining technical, connotative, and figurative meanings, and analyze how specific word choices shape meaning or tone.

➤ **CCSS.ELA-Literacy.CCRA.R.5** Analyze the structure of texts, including how specific sentences, paragraphs, and larger portions of the text (e.g., a section, chapter, scene, or stanza) relate to each other and the whole.

➤ **CCSS.ELA-Literacy.CCRA.R.6** Assess how point of view or purpose shapes the content and style of a text.

➤ **CCSS.ELA-Literacy.CCRA.R.7** Integrate and evaluate content presented in diverse media and formats, including visually and quantitatively, as well as in words.

➤ **CCSS.ELA-Literacy.CCRA.R.8** Delineate and evaluate the argument and specific claims in a text, including the validity of the reasoning as well as the relevance and sufficiency of the evidence.

➤ **CCSS.ELA-Literacy.CCRA.R.9** Analyze how two or more texts address similar themes or topics in order to build knowledge or to compare the approaches the authors take.

➤ **CCSS.ELA-Literacy.CCRA.R.10** Read and comprehend complex literary and informational texts independently and proficiently.

What Is It?

The CCSS have placed informational texts in the spotlight as never before. A key recommendation of the standards is that 50% of elementary students' reading diet should include informational text, and that by the end of high school, 70% of the reading students do across the school day should be informational. There are at least a couple of possible reasons for this shift: (1) traditionally, students have had minimal exposure to informational texts in school, especially elementary school, and (2) school and workplace success depend on the ability to read informational texts. A large percentage of the reading we do as adults, whether at home or in the workplace, involves reading information.

According to the CCSS, "Students must read widely and deeply from among a broad range of high-quality, increasingly challenging literary and informational texts. . . . By reading texts in history/social studies, science and other disciplines, students build a foundation of knowledge in these fields that will also give them the background to be better readers in all disciplines" (NGA Center for Best Practices and Council of Chief State School Officers, p. 10).

What is an informational text? The term *informational text* is an umbrella classification for a wide range of nonfiction text types written to inform readers about topics in a variety of disciplines. Informational texts range from biographies, which often are written more like stories, to functional texts, like bus schedules and directions for downloading apps. The CCSS identify four broad categories of informational text:

1. **Literary nonfiction** combines information with a narrative format. Biographies, memoirs, and informational storybooks are all forms of literary nonfiction.

2. **Expository texts** include textbooks, informational trade books, news articles, and more. These texts provide information in a straightforward way, usually using third-person point of view and text features like tables of contents, headings, glossaries, maps, charts, and indices.

3. **Functional/Procedural texts** provide information on how to complete a task and include recipes, science experiments, and manuals.

4. **Persuasive and argumentative texts** have the purpose of convincing the reader of a point of view. Examples include opinion pieces, editorials, reviews, or advertisements.

Informational texts also include digital texts, e-books, audio books, websites, newspapers, magazines, and graphic texts. They don't usually have characters or plots, so selecting these materials on the basis of compelling characters or fast-paced plots does not work. Whether choosing materials for a whole class or for individual reading, teachers need to apply different criteria to the selection of informational texts than they would to the selection of literary texts. Informational texts can be chosen for (1) their relevance to the curriculum, (2) their appeal to students, (3) their overall quality, and (4) their appropriateness for teaching particular literacy skills. In addition, the CCSS call for students to read more complex texts, so text complexity (see Strategy 3) should also be a consideration.

What Is Its Purpose?

The purpose of carefully selecting informational texts is to provide students with rich experiences in reading quality materials that can inform or educate. Through such experiences students can develop disciplinary knowledge, gain exposure to non-narrative text structures, reinforce content learning, and learn to evaluate information for its "truth value," a critical skill in the 21st century. By teaching students to evaluate the quality of a text on their own, we provide them with critical literacy skills. By asking students to consider the five A's listed below, we help to ensure that they don't just accept information from a text, but also reflect on its meaning and point of view.

What Do I Do?

When evaluating informational materials, teachers and students should consider the five A's (adapted from Moss, 2002):

1. The AUTHORITY of the author:

- Who is the author of the book or article or publisher of the website?

- What are the author's or publisher's qualifications for writing the book or article or creating the website?

2. The ACCURACY of the text content:

- Are the text and visual matter accurate?

- Does the author explain where he or she got his or her information?

- Does the author cite experts or provide references or a bibliography that validates the information?

- Does the book or website explore more than one side of an issue or does it represent only one point of view? Does it appear to be biased? Is the information current?

3. The APPROPRIATENESS of the text for the age group of the audience:

- Is the level of difficulty and writing style appropriate to the audience?

- Are there headings and subheadings that help the reader move through the text?

- If it is a website, does it load quickly? Is it easy to navigate?

- Do the pictures and visuals support the text?

4. The literary ARTISTRY:

- Does the material read like an encyclopedia entry, or is it written in an engaging style?

- Does the author use a "hook" to get readers interested in the material?

- Does the author use examples, analogies, and/or metaphors, similes, and other literary devices to help readers better understand the information?

5. Kid APPEAL:

- Does the text include interesting visuals?

- Is the text one that appeals to students at your grade level?

- Would you pick up the book or go to the website on your own?

Example

Eighth-grade American history teacher James Hernandez decided to begin involving his students in selecting and reading more informational texts during independent reading time. He introduced his students to the five A's described above and modeled for students how to evaluate the quality and "truth value" of an informational text. To facilitate the development of these critical literacy skills, James showed students how to complete the Informational Text Evaluation Form using the website *www.martinlutherking.org*, a racist website that advocates abolishing Martin Luther King Day. He demonstrated for students how to identify the publisher of the site, how to evaluate the accuracy of the information, and how to recognize the bias of the site's creator. He then explained to students that they needed to locate at least one book or website related to their next unit of study, the civil rights movement. They would then evaluate this book or website. James consulted the school librarian to help him

Resources for Locating Informational Texts

The titles listed in the Appendix at the end of this book include trade books, magazines, websites and other online resources that meet the criteria listed above. Other excellent resources include:

- The National Council of Teachers of English's (NCTE) Orbis Pictus Award for Outstanding Nonfiction for Children (*www.ncte.org/awards/orbispictus*) is given annually by the NCTE for the most outstanding nonfiction book for children.

- The Robert F. Sibert Informational Book Medal (*www.ala.org/alsc/awardsgrants/bookmedia/sibertmedal*) is given annually by the American Library Association to the most outstanding informational book of the year.

- StarWalk Kids Media (*https://starwalkkids.com*) is an excellent online resource for teachers and students. It provides e-books available for home or classroom use for students in grades K–8, along with accompanying lesson plans based on the CCSS. A Lexile level for each title is provided. The collection contains many high-quality informational books, many by noted author Seymour Simon.

- NEWSELA (*https://newsela.com*) is a website that contains daily news articles suitable for students in grades 3–12. It provides Lexile levels for each article, and can also provide the same text at multiple Lexile levels, which can help teachers differentiate instruction to meet all students' needs.

- ReadWorks (*www.readworks.org*) provides short informational texts for classroom use on a variety of topics. These texts can be sorted by content area, Lexile level, and more.

For additional resources for informational texts, look at the Appendix at the back of this book.

identify some potential titles related to this topic. After students identified their texts, they completed the Informational Text Evaluation Form (p. 18) and shared their findings in small groups.

References

American Library Association. Robert F. Sibert Informational Book Medal. Retrieved May 20, 2015, from *www.ala.org/alsc/awardsgrants/bookmedia/sibertmedal*.

Martin Luther King, Jr.: A true historical examination. Retrieved May 20, 2015, from *www.martinlutherking.org*.

Moss, B. (2002). *Exploring the literature of fact*. New York: Guilford Press.

National Council of Teachers of English. Orbis Pictus Award for Outstanding Nonfiction for Children. Retrieved May 20, 2015, from *www.ncte.org/awards/orbispictus*.

NEWSELA. Retrieved May 20, 2015, from *https://newsela.com*. (M)

NGA Center for Best Practices and Council of Chief State School Officers. (2010). *Common Core State Standards for English language arts and literacy in history/social studies, science and technical subjects*. Washington, DC: Author.

ReadWorks. Retrieved May 20, 2015, from *www.readworks.com*.

StarWalk Kids Media. Retrieved May 20, 2015, from *www.starwalkkids.com*.

Your Turn!

Locate an informational text in the Appendix at the back of this book, or one of your own choosing. Use the rating sheet on page 18 to evaluate the text you have chosen, or you may have your students evaluate an informational text, print or electronic, as described in the example.

Informational Text Evaluation Form

Instructions: Evaluate the informational text you have chosen using the form below.

Title of Text: _____

Type of Informational Text: _____

Part 1: Authority of the Author	YES	NO
Is the author or website publisher identified?		
Does the author or publisher have expertise in the topic?		
Part 2: Accuracy	**YES**	**NO**
Are the text and pictures accurate?		
Are there references or a bibliography that validates the information?		
Does the book or website explore more than one side of an issue, or does it represent only one point of view?		
Does it appear to be biased?		
Is the information current?		
Part 3: Appropriateness	**YES**	**NO**
Is the level of difficulty and writing style appropriate to the audience?		
Is the book or website well organized and easy to navigate?		
Do the pictures and visuals support the text?		
Are there headings to aid the reader?		
Part 4: Literary Artistry	**YES**	**NO**
Did the author use a "hook" to get you into the text?		
Did the author use examples, analogies, or metaphors and similes to keep you interested?		
Part 5: Kid Appeal	**YES**	**NO**
Does the text have interesting visuals?		
Would you pick up the book or go to the website on your own?		

Strategy 3

Assessing Text Complexity

GRADE LEVELS: K–12

Getting Started
Building Background
Vocabulary
Reading Closely
Comprehension
Discussion Strategies
Writing

CCSS Anchor Standards: Reading

> **CCSS.ELA-Literacy.CCRA.R.1** Read closely to determine what the text says explicitly and to make logical inferences from it; cite specific textual evidence when writing or speaking to support conclusions drawn from the text.

> **CCSS.ELA-Literacy.CCRA.R.2** Determine central ideas or themes of a text and analyze their development; summarize the key supporting details and ideas.

> **CCSS.ELA-Literacy.CCRA.R.3** Analyze how and why individuals, events, or ideas develop and interact over the course of a text.

> **CCSS.ELA-Literacy.CCRA.R.4** Interpret words and phrases as they are used in a text, including determining technical, connotative, and figurative meanings, and analyze how specific word choices shape meaning or tone.

> **CCSS.ELA-Literacy.CCRA.R.5** Analyze the structure of texts, including how specific sentences, paragraphs, and larger portions of the text (e.g., a section, chapter, scene, or stanza) relate to each other and the whole.

> **CCSS.ELA-Literacy.CCRA.R.6** Assess how point of view or purpose shapes the content and style of a text.

> **CCSS.ELA-Literacy.CCRA.R.7** Integrate and evaluate content presented in diverse media and formats, including visually and quantitatively, as well as in words.

> **CCSS.ELA-Literacy.CCRA.R.8** Delineate and evaluate the argument and specific claims in a text, including the validity of the reasoning as well as the relevance and sufficiency of the evidence.

> **CCSS.ELA-Literacy.CCRA.R.9** Analyze how two or more texts address similar themes or topics in order to build knowledge or to compare the approaches the authors take.

> **CCSS.ELA-Literacy.CCRA.R.10** Read and comprehend complex literary and informational texts independently and proficiently.

What Is It?

Text complexity is the *degree of challenge* a text poses for students, based on three facets of a text: quantitative features, qualitative features, and reader/task factors. Anchor Standard 10 of the CCSS calls for students to read complex texts at every grade level from 2 to 12, and research supports this practice. Students become stronger readers by reading texts that require them to flex their reading muscles by reading increasingly difficult texts. They need daily, ongoing practice in closely reading challenging texts that will equip them to read more deeply. If students spend most of their time reading easy texts they won't grow as readers. Instead, teachers need to provide scaffolded support to students as they "ramp up" text difficulty in ways that will help students read appropriately complex texts independently by the end of each school year as required by Reading Anchor Standard 10. There are three components of text complexity that work in concert with one another: quantitative features, qualitative features, and reader and task concerns.

Quantitative Features

Quantitative features of text complexity can be counted with a computer. These include determination of sentence length, number of syllables, word length, word frequency, and other features. Lexiles are the readability formulae of choice for measuring quantitative text features of the texts recommended for use with the CCSS. Lexile text measures rank texts based on a number from 0L (the "L" is for "Lexile") to above 2000L (see *www.lexile.com*). The CCSS recommend specific Lexile level bands for different grade-level ranges, as well as "stretch" bands. Lexile level bands begin at grades 2–3 and range from 450L to 820L; from 640L to 1010L for grades 4–5; from 860L to 1185L for grades 6–8; from 960L to 1335L for grades 9–10; and from 1070L to 1385L for grades 11–12.

You can determine the Lexile level of a book by typing in its title on *www.lexile.com* or you can compute Lexile levels using the instructions at *www.lexile.com/analyzer*.

Qualitative Features

Qualitative text features can't be measured by counting. They require that teachers carefully analyze texts in relationship to student readers on a variety of dimensions. These dimensions are usually ranked as easy, grade-level, or challenging for student readers using a rubric like the one provided on pages 25–26. This evaluation is especially important with informational texts, because careful analysis can help teachers pinpoint specific areas of challenge that may be very different from those identified in literary texts. The rubric identifies three key questions teachers should consider carefully in terms of their students' abilities to comprehend a text: (1) *What does the text say?*; (2) *How does the text work?*; and (3) *What does the text mean?* (Kurland, n.d.).

What Does the Text Say?

This question focuses on the overall meaning of the text and key ideas and details.

How Does the Text Work?

This question refers to how the text is constructed in terms of organization, visual supports, layouts, relationships among ideas, author's purposes, and vocabulary.

- **Organization.** Informational texts work differently from literary ones. Often the comprehension of informational texts requires the knowledge of specific text structures like description, sequence, comparison–contrast, problem–solution, or cause–effect (see Strategy 26). These are very different from the typical story plot structure, and often require that teachers familiarize their students with these constructions.

- **Visual supports and layouts.** In addition, informational texts often contain visual supports like maps, graphs, charts, and tables that extend much of the text's meaning along with layouts that range from simple to complex.

- **Relationships among informational ideas.** Relationships among informational ideas may also be very clearly and explicitly stated or extremely complex, requiring readers to identify how ideas connect across a passage.

- **Author's purpose** examines why the author wrote the text.

- **Vocabulary.** Finally, informational texts contain discipline-related vocabulary, sometimes referred to as Tier Three words, that are essential to comprehending this text type. If a text is full of unfamiliar terms, students will require scaffolding designed to address this area.

What Does the Text Mean?

This question involves examining aspects of the text requiring more sophisticated levels of comprehension, including author's tone and style, theme, point of view, uses of language, and knowledge demands.

- **Tone and style.** Informational text authors' uses of tone and style range from casual and conversational to extremely formal and academic, especially in texts from specific disciplines.

- **Theme.** The theme of the text may be easy to identify or very complex, requiring inference on the reader's part.

- **Point of view** indicates the author's position in the text.

- **Uses of language.** The uses of language in informational texts may include familiar terminology, or highly sophisticated language that provides few supports for the reader.

- **Knowledge demands.** Knowledge demands relate to the background knowledge required for text comprehension. With some texts, students will possess the background knowledge they need, but with other highly technical texts on specific topics they may lack the requisite knowledge for successful comprehension.

Reader and Task Concerns

Reader and task concerns (see page 27) refer to the relationship between readers' abilities and the tasks associated with the text reading. It is impossible to determine text complexity without considering the crucial role of the reader. Teachers must consider students' reading/cognitive skills, background knowledge, motivation and engagement, and task concerns. This is most important with informational texts, since it often poses greater challenges for students than narrative text; it also often requires more background knowledge, especially with complex content area materials (Lapp, Moss, Grant, & Johnson, 2015).

What Is Its Purpose?

The purpose of determining quantitative, qualitative, and reader/task aspects of text complexity is for teachers to develop in-depth understanding of the text they are about to teach to their students. Through this immersion in the text and consideration of its relationship to their readers, teachers can effectively scaffold instruction in ways that ensure student success.

What Do I Do?

1. Select an informational text for use during shared, guided, or close reading.

2. Carefully read the text.

3. Complete the Evaluating Informational Texts for Complexity Form on page 25.

- Part One: Key Information. Complete the information required here and determine the text Lexile level and record on the form.

- Part Two: Rubric for Qualitative Evaluation of Informational Text. Read the text a second time and evaluate it in terms of each of the areas on the rubric. Circle the appropriate level for each area: easy text, grade-level text, or challenging or stretch text.

- Part Three: Reader/Task Evaluation Checklist. Check the items that represent areas of challenge for your students.

Example

Third-grade teacher Svetlana Cvetkovic's students are studying animal adaptations. Svetlana wanted to locate a motivating close-reading article for her students to learn about animal adaptations, and she found such an article, titled "Once Upon a Woodpecker," from *Ranger Rick* magazine reprinted in her science textbook, *Science: A Closer Look: Grade 3* (Hackett, 2011).

Svetlana began her analysis of text complexity by reading the article carefully and reviewing the Evaluating Informational Texts for Complexity Form on pages 25–27. She recorded the information for Part One and computed the Lexile level (900L) using *www.lexile.com*. She then completed the rubric in Part Two of the form, analyzing each dimension of the text by highlighting the appropriate column for easy, grade level, or challenging. Because her students were rather inexperienced with close reading, she wanted a text that was of moderate difficulty. In terms of What the Text Says, she felt that the meaning and key ideas of the text were at grade level in terms of difficulty. In terms of How the Text Works, she felt that the organization was easy. The text's visual supports and layout included photos and columns, but she felt that these features would not be overly difficult for her students. Relationships among ideas and vocabulary terms were also grade-level appropriate. In terms of What the Text Means, she rated style and tone as well as theme as easy, but determining the author's point of view would be challenging for her students. Uses of language and level of background knowledge might be more difficult for her students, but she still rated these text aspects as appropriate to students' grade level.

In terms of reader/task considerations, Svetlana was confident that her students had the reading and cognitive abilities, background knowledge, motivation, and ability to successfully complete the tasks she identified. As noted earlier, she was a bit concerned about their ability to infer point of view, and she identified this on Part Three of the form. Her completed Evaluating Informational Texts for Complexity Form is provided on pages 25–27 with circled items denoting her evaluations of rubric dimensions.

References

Hackett, J. K. (2011). Once upon a woodpecker. *Ranger Rick Magazine*. Reprinted in *Science: A closer look: Grade 3*. New York: Macmillan/McGraw-Hill, pp. 170–171. (P)

Kurland, D. (n.d.). Dan Kurland's www.criticalreading.com: Reading and writing ideas as well as words. Retrieved June 10, 2015, from *www.criticalreading.com*.

Lapp, D., Moss, B., Grant, M., & Johnson, K. (2015). *A close look at close reading: Teaching students to analyze complex texts K–5*. Alexandria, VA: ASCD.

Lexile.com. Text complexity bands and grade level bands. Retrieved June 6, 2015, from *www.lexile.com/using-lexile/lexile-measures-and-the-ccssi/text-complexity-grade-bands-and-lexile-ranges*.

Your Turn

Select an informational text from the Appendix or of your own choosing. Evaluate the text for complexity using the template provided.

Sample Evaluating Informational Texts for Complexity Form

Part One: Key Information

Title of Text: _Once Upon a Woodpecker_

Type of Text: Literary Nonfiction (Expository) Functional/Procedural Persuasive/Argumentative

Quantitative Evaluation: Lexile Level __900__

Part Two: Rubric for Qualitative Evaluation of Informational Text

Directions: Circle the best description for each text dimension.

Text Dimension	Notes	Easy Text	Grade-Level Text	Challenge or Stretch Text
What Does the Text Say?				
Meaning		Clear and obvious	Somewhat complex	Highly abstract
Main Ideas and Details		Explicitly stated	Some explicitly stated but some require inference	Most main ideas and details must be inferred
How Does the Text Work?				
Organization		Single, clear text structure	Multiple structures; may be discipline-specific, with a single thesis	Intricate with multiple structures, multiple theses, sophisticated organization
Visual Supports and Layout	Text contains columns and photos that students will enjoy	Text placement is consistent with readable font, simple charts, tables, etc., with easy-to-understand headings	Text placement includes columns, medium font size, text interrupted with visuals, complex charts, tables, etc., and headings and subheadings requiring interpretation	Inconsistent text placement, small font size, with intricate charts, tables, etc., and headings and subheadings requiring inference and synthesis
Relationships among Ideas		Clear and explicitly stated	Implicit and/or subtle	Intricate, deep, and subtle

(continued)

From *A Close Look at Close Reading: Teaching Students to Analyze Complex Texts K–5* (p. 42) by Diane Lapp, Barbara Moss, Maria Grant, and Kelly Johnson. Alexandria, VA: ASCD. Copyright © 2015 ASCD. Adapted by permission. Learn more about ASCD at *ww.ascd.org*.

Text Dimension	Notes	Easy Text	Grade-Level Text	Challenge or Stretch Text
Vocabulary	*Some terms like blow and shock absorbers will be difficult*	Some subject-specific vocabulary; many familiar terms supported by context clues	Subject-specific vocabulary with many unfamiliar terms with limited support from context clues	Highly academic subject-specific, demanding vocabulary that is context dependent
Author's Purpose		Simple, clear, concrete, and obvious	Subtle or abstract; requires interpretation	Very abstract; must be inferred

What Does the Text Mean?

Text Dimension	Notes	Easy Text	Grade-Level Text	Challenge or Stretch Text
Author's Tone and Style		Style is conversational with narrative elements	Style is objective, with passive constructions and compound sentences and a formal tone	Style is specific to a discipline, with dense concepts and complex sentences with an extremely formal tone
Theme		Obvious and clearly stated	Is not obvious, but easily inferred	Requires inference based on careful reading
Point of View	*This will be challenging for my students*	Clearly stated in the text	Easily inferred by the reader	Requires careful reading to infer
Uses of Language		Common, explicitly disciplinary language that can be literally interpreted	Less familiar disciplinary language with explanations that support interpretation of meaning	Highly sophisticated disciplinary language that does not include supports for interpretation
Knowledge Demands	*Students have not yet studied woodpecker adaptations specifically*	Content addresses common information familiar to students	Content requires some background knowledge that may be unfamiliar to students	Content is highly technical, requiring deep background knowledge about specific information

(continued)

Part Three: Reader/Task Evaluation Checklist

Directions: Check those items that represent areas of challenge for your students.

Reading/Cognitive Skills

☑ Do my students have the reading/cognitive skills to comprehend this text at the literal level? At deeper levels of meaning?

They may have some trouble with inferring point of view.

Background Knowledge

☑ Do my students have the background knowledge, genre knowledge, and academic vocabulary knowledge to understand this text?

Yes. We have been studying adaptations.

Motivation and Engagement

☑ Will this text be one that motivates my students to read and maintain reading stamina?

This is a motivating text for my students.

Reader and Task Concerns

☑ How challenging will this task be for my students?

Moderate level

☑ Have I matched the task to the text? In other words, if the task is challenging, have I used an easier text? If the task is easier, have I used a challenging text?

Yes.

Evaluating Informational Texts for Complexity Form

Instructions: Select an informational text and analyze it for text complexity using the form provided below. As you think about the text, consider what instructional scaffolds you will need to provide for your students to support their understanding.

Part One: Key Information

Title of Text: _____

Type of Text: Literary Nonfiction   Expository   Functional/Procedural   Persuasive/Argumentative

Quantitative Evaluation: Lexile Level _____

Part Two: Rubric for Qualitative Evaluation of Informational Text

Directions: Circle the best description for each text dimension.

Text Dimension	Notes	Easy Text	Grade-Level Text	Challenge or Stretch Text
What Does the Text Say?				
Meaning		Clear and obvious	Somewhat complex	Highly abstract
Main Ideas and Details		Explicitly stated	Some explicitly stated but some require inference	Most main ideas and details must be inferred
How Does the Text Work?				
Organization		Single, clear text structure	Multiple structures; may be discipline-specific, with a single thesis	Intricate with multiple structures, multiple theses, sophisticated organization
Visual Supports and Layout		Text placement is consistent with readable font, simple charts, tables, etc., with easy-to-understand headings	Text placement includes columns, medium font size, text interrupted with visuals, complex charts, tables, etc., and headings and subheadings requiring interpretation	Inconsistent text placement, small font size, with intricate charts, tables, etc., and headings and subheadings requiring inference and synthesis

(continued)

Text Dimension	Notes	Easy Text	Grade-Level Text	Challenge or Stretch Text
Relationships among Ideas		Clear and explicitly stated	Implicit and/or subtle	Intricate, deep, and subtle
Vocabulary		Some subject-specific vocabulary; many familiar terms supported by context clues	Subject-specific vocabulary with many unfamiliar terms with limited support from context clues	Highly academic subject-specific, demanding vocabulary that is context dependent
Author's Purpose		Simple, clear, concrete, and obvious	Subtle or abstract; requires interpretation	Very abstract; must be inferred
What Does the Text Mean?				
Author's Tone and Style		Style is conversational with narrative elements	Style is objective, with passive constructions and compound sentences and a formal tone	Style is specific to a discipline, with dense concepts and complex sentences with an extremely formal tone
Theme		Obvious and clearly stated	Is not obvious, but easily inferred	Requires inference based on careful reading
Point of View		Clearly stated in the text	Easily inferred by the reader	Requires careful reading to infer
Uses of Language		Common, explicitly disciplinary language that can be literally interpreted	Less familiar disciplinary language with explanations that support interpretation of meaning	Highly sophisticated disciplinary language that does not include supports for interpretation
Knowledge Demands		Content addresses common information familiar to students	Content requires some background knowledge that may be unfamiliar to students	Content is highly technical, requiring deep background knowledge about specific information

(continued)

Part Three: Reader/Task Evaluation Checklist

Directions: Check those items that represent areas of challenge for your students.

Reading/Cognitive Skills

☐ Do my students have the reading/cognitive skills to comprehend this text at the literal level? At deeper levels of meaning?

Background Knowledge

☐ Do my students have the background knowledge, genre knowledge, and academic vocabulary knowledge to understand this text?

Motivation and Engagement

☐ Will this text be one that motivates my students to read and maintain reading stamina?

Reader and Task Concerns

☐ How challenging will this task be for my students?

☐ Have I matched the task to the text? In other words, if the task is challenging, have I used an easier text? If the task is easier, have I used a challenging text?

Strategy 4

Shared Reading and Text Feature Search

GRADE LEVELS: K–12

Getting Started
Building Background
Vocabulary
Reading Closely
Comprehension
Discussion
Writing

CCSS Anchor Standards: Reading

> **CCSS.ELA-Literacy.CCRA.R.5** Analyze the structure of texts, including how specific sentences, paragraphs, and larger portions of the text (e.g., a section, chapter, scene, or stanza) relate to each other and the whole.

> **CCSS.ELA-Literacy.CCRA.R.7** Integrate and evaluate content presented in diverse media and formats, including visually and quantitatively, as well as in words.

> **CCSS.ELA-Literacy.CCRA.R.10** Read and comprehend complex literary and informational texts independently and proficiently.

What Is It?

The Shared Reading strategy teaches students how expository text works and how it differs from narrative text. Shared Reading is a strategy that scaffolds students' reading of books they may not be ready to read themselves. It can be particularly useful as a way to introduce the unique characteristics of informational texts. The Text Feature Search engages students in looking for and exploring those text features they have learned about during Shared Reading.

31

What Is Its Purpose?

Shared Reading with informational texts helps teachers demonstrate how this type of text works and how it differs from narratives. Demonstrations and discussions of the features found in these two types of texts can develop students' metacognitive awareness of the characteristics of the two text types and adds to prior knowledge about the nature and purposes of informational texts. Once teachers have shared these features with students through Shared Reading, they can use the Informational Text Feature Search form to locate and reflect on the purposes of those features.

What Do I Do?

Shared Reading can be done with big books for younger students or with textbooks or trade books for older students. To do a Shared Reading, the teacher should:

1. Set up an enlarged informational book on an easel, distribute multiple copies of an informational trade book or article, or project the text using an overhead or document camera. This allows everyone to see the text in order to follow along.

2. Involve students in making predictions about the text using the following questions as a guide:

- What kind of book/text is this?
- How do you know?
- What kind of information do you expect to find?
- What kind of illustrations do you expect to find?
- What do you know about the author?
- Who is the publisher and/or funding source?

3. Focus student attention on the various features of expository text, using the following questions as a guide:

- What do the headings and subheadings tell me?
- What parts of the book help me find information?
- How is the information organized?
- How do I read the diagrams (or maps, graphs, timelines)?

4. Next, demonstrate and explain how students can use text features like tables of content, indices, glossaries, and headings to help them locate specific information:

- What is the table of contents for? When and how is it used?

- What are the page numbers for?

- Why are the pages numbered?

- What is the index for? When and how is it used?

- Do all information books have contents and indices? Why? Why not?

5. Point out visual information, including charts, graphs, maps, diagrams, and timelines. Use the following questions as a guide:

- Why do authors include visual information in maps, graphs, or timelines?

- How are these maps, graphs, and timelines the same? How are they different?

- How is reading a "visual text" different from reading a regular text?

6. Point out to students that we never depend on one data source. We need to research topics using several sources in order to make an informed opinion about the topic. Point out the need to consider the accuracy and validity of the content. Use the following questions as a guide:

- Where did the author get his or her information?

- What sources are listed in the bibliography or references?

- What do you know about the topic? Is there anything that you want to explore or need more information about?

7. At this point, teachers should bring in fiction and informational texts for comparison. Focus on the differences between the two types of texts using the following questions as a guide:

- Do we read informational books the same way as stories? Why? Why not?

- What are some of the differences in the way we read the two text types?

- What do informational books have that stories do not?

- What do storybooks have that informational books do not?

- Why are the two text types different (Moss, 2002)?

Example

Teacher Evelyn Craig used Shared Reading to introduce her first graders to the similarities and differences between fiction and informational texts using two simple texts, *Frog and Toad Are Friends* (Lobel, 1979) and *Early Reader: Toad or Frog?* (Stewart & Salem, 2003). Using these two texts, she demonstrated for her students the differences between the two using the questions listed on page 33. She previewed an informational enlarged text, involving students in making predictions about the text. After that, she introduced students to the access features of expository text, like tables of contents, indices, and glossaries, by pointing them out in the enlarged text. She also pointed out visual information, including charts, graphs, maps, diagrams, and timelines. Following this, Evelyn allowed teams of students to select their own informational trade books. She involved students in completing an Informational Text Feature "scavenger hunt" by locating page numbers where each feature was found and recording the purpose of each feature on the line provided (an example is provided on page 35).

References

Lobel, A. (1979). *Frog and Toad are friends*. New York: Harper Collins. (P, fiction)
Moss, B. (2002). *Exploring the literature of fact*. New York: Guilford Press.
Reeder, T. (2005). *Poison dart frogs (Life cycle)*. Washington, DC: National Geographic. (P)
Stewart, J., & Salem, L. (2003). *Early reader: Toad or frog?* New York: Continental Press. (P)

Your Turn!

Plan a Shared Reading experience like the one described above, using an informational text from the Appendix or of your choosing. Focus students on identifying and comparing features of informational texts and fictional ones. Once you have completed this activity, provide students with an informational trade book and have them complete the Informational Text Feature Search provided on the facing page. The teacher will need to model how to do this by completing the first few items with the students.

Sample Informational Text Feature Search

Book Title: _Poison Dart Frogs_

Author: _Tracy Reeder_

Feature	☑	Page #	Purpose
Table of contents	☑	3	To tell where chapters are
Headings	☑	6, 8, 9, 10, 11	To tell you what is in that section
Bolded words	☑	9, 10, 11	To show you the new words
Glossary	☑	31	To define the new words
Index	☑	32	To help you look up topics
Sidebars	☐	none	
Fact box	☑	12, 13, 14	To give small bits of information
Captions	☑	22, 24	To tell what the picture is about
Photographs	☑	almost every page	To help you understand the information
Diagrams	☑	11	To show a poison dart frog's life cycle
Tables	☐	none	
Graphs	☐	none	
Maps	☑	7	Shows where grasslands are
Flowcharts	☑	19	Show how a frog sheds its skin
Webs	☐	none	
Timelines	☐	none	
References	☐	none	

Informational Text Feature Search

Instructions: Check the features that you found in your text. List the page number for the page you found it on and write its purpose.

Book Title: _____

Author: _____

Feature	☑	Page #	Purpose
Table of contents	☐		
Headings	☐		
Bolded words	☐		
Glossary	☐		
Index	☐		
Sidebars	☐		
Fact box	☐		
Captions	☐		
Photographs	☐		
Diagrams	☐		
Tables	☐		
Graphs	☐		
Maps	☐		
Flowcharts	☐		
Webs	☐		
Timelines	☐		
References	☐		

PART TWO

Building Background
Strategies

Strategy 5

Anticipation Guide

GRADE LEVELS: K–12

| Getting Started |
| **Building Background** |
| Vocabulary |
| Reading Closely |
| Comprehension |
| Discussion |
| Writing |

Building Background Strategies

CCSS Anchor Standards: Reading

➤ **CCSS.ELA-Literacy.CCRA.R.1** Read closely to determine what the text says explicitly and to make logical inferences from it; cite specific textual evidence when writing or speaking to support conclusions drawn from the text.

➤ **CCSS.ELA-Literacy.CCRA.R.2** Determine central ideas or themes of a text and analyze their development; summarize the key supporting details and ideas.

➤ **CCSS.ELA-Literacy.CCRA.R.3** Analyze how and why individuals, events, or ideas develop and interact over the course of a text.

What Is It?

Anticipation Guides (called *prediction guides* by Herber, 1978) are a prereading strategy that can be used with informational texts such as newspaper articles or textbooks at a variety of levels. Before they read, students respond to carefully worded statements that focus their attention on the topic to be learned. They then read the text in an effort to confirm or deny the statements provided. In addition, they identify evidence to support their position regarding the truth of the statement.

What Is Its Purpose?

Anticipation Guides help students activate their prior knowledge and arouse their curiosity about the topic at hand. Students then read to confirm or disconfirm their reactions to the statements presented before they read. After they read, they have the opportunity to go back and change their responses based on what they have learned from their reading and provide evidence for their responses.

Anticipation Guides can be used with any content, but are especially useful with science-related content. Many students have misconceptions about science-related information; Anticipation Guides can help students confront and later reflect on their misconceptions. Anticipation Guides can also be used with material from any content area, including English, social studies, health, or mathematics.

What Do I Do?

Anticipation Guides require preparation on the part of the teacher. Here are suggested steps in creating and using Anticipation Guides:

1. Analyze the text to identify key ideas and information. Select ideas from the text that help students reflect on what they know about the topic and are interesting, controversial, or thought provoking.

2. Create eight to 10 written statements that students will label true or false.

3. Briefly introduce the topic of the text. Before they read have students identify statements as true or false in pairs. Give students time to discuss their responses to the statements as a large group. They can record their responses in the Before Reading column. When using Anticipation Guides with younger students, teachers can read the items aloud and let them do "thumbs up/thumbs down" as a group response to each statement.

4. After reading, students can work in pairs or individually to record as true or false in the After Reading column based on their new information. Students should cite textual evidence for all of their responses based on the reading. Review the guide with the whole class, asking students to identify whether and how they have changed their responses based on their new information. Be sure to have them provide evidence for their answers.

Example

High school history teacher Dale Newton wanted to prepare his students for the study of the Industrial Revolution in Britain as part of a 10th-grade world history class. Prior to reading the chapter in the textbook, Dale had his students work in pairs to complete the Anticipation Guide designed to activate their prior knowledge and arouse their curiosity about the topic. Before reading, students were required to answer "T" to the statements they thought were true and "F" to those they thought were false. After completing the guide in pairs, students shared their responses with the whole group, discussing their opinions about each statement and supporting their answers with evidence from their own background knowledge. Many students, for example, disagreed with the statement "The potato crop contributed to industrialization in England." After students read the textbook chapter, Dale asked them to review their guides and work with their partners to record their after-reading answers based on what they had learned. They also recorded evidence from the text that supported their responses. Students were surprised to learn that the humble potato provided a food source that led to increased population, which helped provide the workforce necessary for the Industrial Revolution. He then led the group in a discussion of their answers, how they had changed them, and what evidence they used to support their answers. A sample completed Anticipation Guide is provided on page 42.

Reference

Herber, H. (1978). Prediction as motivation and an aid to comprehension. In H. Herber, *Teaching reading in content areas* (2nd ed., pp. 173–189). Englewood Cliffs, NJ: Prentice Hall.

Your Turn!

Select a text from the Appendix at the back of this book or one of your own choosing. Create an Anticipation Guide for your students using the form on page 42 and have them work in pairs to complete it. They should record answers before and after they read and provide evidence for their answers.

Sample Anticipation Guide

Before Reading	Statement	After Reading	Text Evidence
T (F)	1. Industrialization is always good for workers because it creates jobs.	T (F)	Industrialization also caused loss of jobs, brutal working conditions, and child labor.
T (F)	2. The potato crop contributed to industrialization in England.	(T) F	The advent of the potato provided food, leading to population increases that fueled industrialization.
(T) F	3. England could not have industrialized without its many rivers.	(T) F	Rivers powered mills and provided transportation and water for industry.
(T) F	4. Large numbers of cities sprang up well before the Industrial Revolution.	T (F)	Industrialization brought people to cities to work in factories.
T (F)	5. Entrepreneurs had the capital needed to invest in machines.	T (F)	Expansion of credit gave entrepreneurs the money they needed.
(T) F	6. Inventions like the steam engine and cotton gin improved life for everyone in a society.	T (F)	They led to harsh factory conditions, pollution, and child labor.
T (F)	7. Economic cooperation is better than competition in a society.	T (F)	Competition can lower prices, creating more money for everyone.

Anticipation Guide for _____

Instructions: Circle "T" for the statements you agree with, and "F" for the ones you disagree with before you read. Then, after you have read the material, record your answers in the After Reading column based on your new information. Provide evidence from the text to justify all of your answers.

Before Reading	Statement	After Reading	Text Evidence
T F	1.	T F	
T F	2.	T F	
T F	3.	T F	
T F	4.	T F	
T F	5.	T F	
T F	6.	T F	
T F	7.	T F	

Strategy 6

KWHL

GRADE LEVELS: K–12

Getting Started
Building Background
Vocabulary
Reading Closely
Comprehension
Discussion
Writing

CCSS Anchor Standards: Reading

➤ **CCSS.ELA-Literacy.CCRA.R.1** Read closely to determine what the text says explicitly and to make logical inferences from it; cite specific textual evidence when writing or speaking to support conclusions drawn from the text.

➤ **CCSS.ELA-Literacy.CCRA.R.2** Determine central ideas or themes of a text and analyze their development; summarize the key supporting details and ideas.

➤ **CCSS.ELA-Literacy.CCRA.R.3** Analyze how and why individuals, events, or ideas develop and interact over the course of a text.

What Is It?

KWHL (Ogle, 1992) is an adaptation of the KWL strategy (Ogle, 1986). It helps students activate their prior knowledge about a topic and strategically locate information as they read. During the first step of KWHL students identify what they *know* (K) about a topic. They brainstorm a list of things they know related to the topic and record these in the first column of a chart. During the second step, students identify what they *want to know* (W) about the topic. They pose questions and record these questions in the second column of a chart. These questions later provide a purpose for their reading. For the third step, students list *how* (H) they could answer the questions. For example, students could mention using their textbooks, reference materials (dictionaries, Internet research, class charts, etc.), research methodologies (research, survey, etc.), and/or specific text features as ways to answer the questions.

After reading, students have the opportunity to identify what they have *learned* (L) about the topic. They record the answers to their questions in the third column of the KWHL Chart.

What Is Its Purpose?

KWHL Charts are designed to arouse curiosity about a text, activate prior knowledge, and engage students in identification of their own questions about a topic as well as available information sources. They also provide a record of what students have learned through their reading.

What Do I Do?

1. Select a book, newspaper, or magazine article appropriate to your students' abilities.

2. Prepare copies of a KWHL Worksheet or create a KWHL Chart on large chart paper or a transparency. The worksheet or chart should be divided into four columns, with the "K" column on the far left, the "W" and "H" columns in the middle, and the "L" column on the right.

3. Activate students' prior knowledge about the topic of the text by asking them to brainstorm what they know about the topic. Have them record this information under the "K," or "What I Know," column.

4. Involve students in generating questions they want to answer as they read. Have them record these questions under the "W," or "What I Want to Know," column of the chart.

5. Have students list ways they can answer the questions in the "H," or "How I Will Find Out," column.

6. Involve students in reading or listening to you read a text aloud. Instruct them to read or listen to find the answers to the questions they posed. Then have them record their answers to the questions in the "L," or "What I Learned," column.

Example

Sixth-grade health teacher Dina Fabian created a KWHL lesson prior to beginning a unit on medicines and drugs. She was particularly interested in having her students learn about identifying appropriate sources for locating information, since she wanted students to create multimedia presentations as part of the culminating activity for this unit, and KWHL provided a good opportunity for engaging students in this effort. She distributed copies of a KWHL Chart to every student. Before she introduced the first text in the unit, she asked students to work in pairs to brainstorm what they already knew about medicines and prescription drugs, which was the first of several topics she would cover within the unit. She recorded each team's response in the far left "K," or "What I Know," column of the chart (see sample chart on the facing page). Students identified information about the costs and dangers of drugs, illegal drug use, and more. Students then teamed once again to discuss what they *want to know*. Dina listed these questions in the middle column, or "W" ("What I Want to Know") portion of the chart. Students were interested in learning about the drug problem in the United States, regulation of drugs, dangers of drugs, and their costs. At this point, Dina asked the students to think about how they might locate the answers to their questions, and she recorded these responses in the "H" ("How I Will Find Out") column. Students identified a variety of possible sources for information, including online resources, the *Merck Manual*, and interviews with doctors and pharmacists. She then introduced the first text of the unit, entitled "Smart about Medicine," an article she obtained from ReadWorks (*www.readworks.org*) that provided guidelines for safe uses of medicines and drugs. She directed students to read the text and look for the answers to at least some of the questions they posed. After reading the text, students worked in pairs once again to brainstorm answers to the questions posed earlier. They were not able to answer all of the questions with information obtained in the article, but were able to answer some of them. They then completed the "L," or "What I Learned," column of the chart (see example on the facing page), citing answers to the questions based on evidence provided in the text. Following this activity, students worked in teams to answer the questions that had not been answered. They consulted the sources identified in the "H" column, using the Internet, interviewing pharmacists and physicians, and consulting the *Merck Manual* (2015) to locate answers to their questions. In this way, Dina introduced them to the many uses of sources for getting information related to their unit of study.

References

Magic, J. (n.d.). Smart about medicine. Retrieved July 22, 2015, from *www.readworks.org*.

Merck manual: Consumer version. Retrieved July 22, 2015, from *www.merckmanuals.com/home*.

Ogle, D. (1986). K-W-L: A teaching model that develops active reading of expository text. *The Reading Teacher, 39*, 563–570.

Ogle, D. (1992). KWL in action: Secondary teachers find applications that work. In E. K. Dishner, T. W. Bean, J. E. Readence, & D. W. Moore (Eds.), *Reading in the content areas: Improving classroom instruction* (3rd ed., pp. 270–282). Dubuque, IA: Kendall Hunt.

Sample KWHL Chart

K (What I Know)	W (What I Want to Know)	H (How I Will Find Out)	L (What I Learned)
Drugs and medicines are prescribed for medical problems	How well does the government regulate medicines and drugs?	Internet Government documents	
Medicines can be dangerous	Why are medicines dangerous?	Interview a pharmacist or doctor	They can affect different people in different ways. They can damage the kidneys and liver. Expired medicines may not work. Taking someone else's drugs can hurt you.
Drugs are expensive	Why are the costs of medicines so high?	Internet search Interview a pharmacist	
Illegal drugs are a problem in the United States and Mexico	Why do people overdose on medicines?	Internet search	Sometimes people think that taking more of a medicine will help them get well faster.
Methamphetamine is a popular recreational drug	What are some solutions to the drug problem in the United States?	Newspapers Magazines	
Lots of kids die from drug overdoses	Are drugs like heroin and cocaine ever prescribed for illnesses?	Check the Merck Manual online	

Building Background Strategies

Your Turn!

Select a text from the Appendix in the back of the book, or one of your own choosing, or a magazine or newspaper article. Involve your students in completing the KWHL Chart on the facing page by identifying the "K," "W," and "H" columns before they read, and the "L" column after they read.

KWHL Chart for _____

Instructions: Before you read, record what you KNOW about the topic in the first column, what you WANT to know in the second, and HOW you can find out in the third column. After you read, record what you LEARNED in the last column.

K (What I Know)	W (What I Want to Know)	H (How I Will Find Out)	L (What I Learned)

Strategy 7

KLEW

GRADE LEVELS: K–12

Getting Started
Building Background
Vocabulary
Reading Closely
Comprehension
Discussion
Writing

CCSS Anchor Standards: Reading

> **CCSS.ELA-Literacy.CCRA.R.1** Read closely to determine what the text says explicitly and to make logical inferences from it; cite specific textual evidence when writing or speaking to support conclusions drawn from the text.

> **CCSS.ELA-Literacy.CCRA.R.3** Analyze how and why individuals, events, or ideas develop and interact over the course of a text.

> **CCSS.ELA-Literacy.CCRA.R.8** Delineate and evaluate the argument and specific claims in a text, including the validity of the reasoning as well as the relevance and sufficiency of the evidence.

What Is It?

KLEW (Hershberger, Zambal-Saul, & Starr, 2006) is an adaptation of the KWL strategy (Ogle, 1986). It helps students map ideas over time that activate their prior knowledge about a topic, create claims about their learning, provide evidence to support their claims, and identify new questions about their learning. It is especially suited to the study of science because of its emphasis on providing proof and engaging in a cycle of inquiry, but it can be used in any content area. During the first step of KLEW, students identify what they *know* (K) about a topic. They brainstorm a list of things they know related to the topic and record these in the first column of a chart. After reading, students have the opportunity to identify what they have *learned* (L) about the topic. These facts are stated as claims. During the third step, students *record evidence* (E) for their claims. In this way, students are required to think critically about the claims they made earlier. For the last step, students pose and record questions about what they *still want to know* or *wonderings* (W) in the fourth column of a chart. These questions later provide a purpose for additional reading about the topic.

What Is Its Purpose?

KLEW Charts are designed to provide an ongoing record of student learning about a topic. They also provide a record of learning processes in which students have engaged through their readings on a topic. They allow students to document what they know about a topic, what they have learned, what evidence they have for their learning, and what they still want to know. The process demonstrates to students that learning is not literal and linear, but that it requires critical thinking and is an ongoing effort.

What Do I Do?

1. Select a book, newspaper, or magazine article appropriate to your students' abilities. For younger children, this could involve text read-alouds. The KLEW chart is also applicable to learning based on multiple readings from a variety of texts related to the same topic.

2. Prepare copies of a KLEW Chart (see page 54) or create a KLEW Chart on large chart paper. The KLEW chart is divided into four columns, with the "K" column on the far left, the "L" and "E" columns in the middle, and the "W" column on the right.

3. Activate students' prior knowledge about the topic of the text by asking them to brainstorm what they know about the topic. Have them record this information under the "K," or "What I Know," column.

4. Involve students in identifying what they learned (L) as they read. Model how to state these learnings as claims. Have students record these questions under the "L," or "What I Learned" column of the chart.

5. Have students record textual evidence (E) for each of the claims they made.

6. Following this, students can work with partners or as a class to identify additional questions or wonderings (W) that they still have. Then have them record their answers to the questions in the last column.

Example

Second-grade teacher Melanie Carter created a KLEW lesson for the book *Boy, Were We Wrong about Dinosaurs!* (Kudlinski, 2008). She distributed copies of the KLEW Chart to students. Because this text was rather challenging for her students, Melanie planned to read some sections aloud and have students partner-read some sections. She created a large version of the chart on page 53 so that it could be completed as a class.

Before students began to read or listen, she asked them to work in pairs to brainstorm what they already knew about dinosaurs. Students eagerly shared what they knew, and she recorded their ideas in the "K," or "What I Know," column of the chart (see sample on the facing page). Students then read and/or listened to the text. Melanie chunked the text into four-page segments and helped students work again with partners to create jot lists of what they had learned (L). Following this, Melanie modeled for students how to write these learnings as claims. Using the example "Dinosaurs had bones that held up their tails," she showed students how to create a claim that could be confirmed or denied using evidence. After framing these learnings as claims, Melanie recorded this example and others in the "L" column of the KLEW chart. Students then worked with partners to identify evidence for each claim. In the previous example, students noted that the text said that many fossil footprints have been found with no tail drag marks, and some fossils show that dinosaur tailbones had tendons inside to hold them straight. Melanie recorded this evidence and other evidence for each of the student claims. She reminded students, however, that evidence about dinosaurs changes over time, and this evidence may be refuted as scientists make new discoveries. Finally, students identified additional questions or wonderings that they continued to have about the information provided in the book. One student wondered how what we know about dinosaurs might change in the next 20 years. They recorded these in the "W" column of the chart.

References

Hershberger, K., Zambal-Saul, C., & Starr, M. L. (2006). Evidence helps the KWL get a KLEW. *Science and Children, 45*(5), 50.
Kudlinski, K. V. (2008). *Boy, were we wrong about dinosaurs!* New York: Puffin. (P)
Ogle, D. (1986). K-W-L: A teaching model that develops active reading of expository text. *The Reading Teacher, 39*, 563–570.

Your Turn!

Select a text from the suggested list in the Appendix, one of your own choosing, or a magazine or newspaper article. Involve your students in completing the KLEW Chart on the facing page by completing the "K" column before they read and the "L," "E," "W" columns after they read.

Sample KLEW Chart

K (What I Know)	L (What I Learned)	E (What Evidence Do I Have for My Learning?)	W (What Additional Questions or Wonderings Do I Have?)
They had long tails.	They held up their tails.	Fossils show that they had tendons in their tailbones and didn't drag their tails.	How will what we know about dinosaurs change in the next 20 years?
They were gray and green.	They had patterned skin.	If they were gray they would have been too easy to see. Their patterns hid them in the grasses.	What evidence is there that some dinosaurs are still alive?
They were huge with big heads and tails.	They were both large and small.	Some were as small as a pigeon, some were huge.	Have scientists decided if dinosaurs are cold or warm blooded or something else?
They died out from heat and disease.	They died out from a comet or asteroid that killed them.	Scientists have found fossil dust from outer space, suggesting the comet or asteroid killed them.	What did dinosaurs have on their skin? Scales? Feathers? Or what?

Building Background Strategies

KLEW Chart for _____

Instructions: Before you read, complete the first column by writing down what you KNOW about the topic. After reading, write down what you LEARNED in the second column. Provide EVIDENCE for what you learned in the third column. In the fourth column, write down additional questions or WONDERINGS you have about the topic.

K (What I Know)	L (What I Learned)	E (What Evidence Do I Have for My Learning?)	W (What Additional Questions or Wonderings Do I Have?)

Strategy 8

Table of Contents Prediction

GRADE LEVELS: K–12

Getting Started
Building Background
Vocabulary
Reading Closely
Comprehension
Discussion
Writing

Building Background Strategies

CCSS Anchor Standards: Reading

➤ **CCSS.ELA-Literacy.CCRA.R.2** Determine central ideas or themes of a text and analyze their development; summarize the key supporting details and ideas.

➤ **CCSS.ELA-Literacy.CCRA.R.3** Analyze how and why individuals, events, or ideas develop and interact over the course of a text.

➤ **CCSS.ELA-Literacy.CCRA.R.5** Analyze the structure of texts, including how specific sentences, paragraphs, and larger portions of the text (e.g., a section, chapter, scene, or stanza) relate to each other and the whole.

What Is It?

Table of Contents Prediction is a strategy uniquely suited to informational texts and can be used at all grade levels. It involves having students make predictions about informational text content by creating a table of contents for the text based on their predictions. By reading the title and examining the cover of a book, students can begin to think about the content found within. In addition to identifying possible topics, creating a table of contents for the text requires students to consider how the text might be organized. They can then read the text and compare the author's way of organizing the text with the way they predicted he or she might arrange the ideas.

What Is Its Purpose?

The purpose of Table of Contents Prediction is to help students activate their prior knowledge about a topic and make predictions about text content. This strategy pushes students to speculate about the topics and main ideas that will be addressed in an informational text. It helps them consider how ideas will be developed over the course of the text, and also engages students in examining text organization, since they must not only identify content, but also consider how it is structured in the table of contents.

What Do I Do?

1. Have students locate a table of contents in a text. Review with students what a table of contents is and how it helps the reader understand the topic to be studied, the way ideas are developed, the organization of the information provided in the text, and how it helps the reader locate information.

2. Provide students with a variety of informational trade book titles that have tables of contents or give them the title of a textbook chapter or website.

3. Instruct students not to open the books. Ask them to consider the title and examine the cover of the book, if available.

4. Pair students with a partner. Provide them with the Table of Contents Prediction handout.

5. Ask students what they think the table of contents might include. Instruct them to also think about how the information in the table of contents will be organized. Have them record their table of contents on the handout.

6. Ask students to share the table of contents they have created with a partner or with the whole class.

7. Have students open their books to compare their table of contents with the one the author used. Emphasize that there is no one way to organize information; the author could use many different ways.

8. Ask students to read the book and discuss why they think the author chose to organize the text the way he did.

Example

Marilyn Cates teaches second graders who are learning about informational texts. While her students have developed skills in making predictions about narrative texts, she is interested in helping them learn to predict content found in informational texts.

Marilyn began the Table of Contents Prediction lesson by reviewing with students the form and purposes of a table of contents. She had students turn to the table of contents in their social studies text. She showed them the titles of each section of the table of contents and its page number and location. She helped her students see that the title of the section in the table of contents matched the chapter title found on the page indicated. Marilyn used the book *The Life Cycle of an Earthworm* (Kalman, 2004) to model the Table of Contents Prediction strategy with her students. She demonstrated that the table of contents indicates how the text is organized. Students could clearly see that the text is arranged chronologically. Students then read the book in pairs and discussed why the author chose to arrange the text this way.

After this introduction, Marilyn handed out a number of easy-to-read informational trade books from the National Geographic Society that contained tables of contents. She instructed students not to open the books. She modeled for students how to examine the cover and title and then created a sample table of contents for one of the books on the Table of Contents Prediction handout. She then had the whole group create a table of contents for a different book. They then read the book and discussed why the author picked the organizational pattern he did.

At this point Marilyn arranged students in pairs and let each pair select a book. The students created a table of contents for their texts and recorded them on the form (see below). Marilyn next invited students to share their books and tables of contents with peers and with the class. One pair of students' table of contents is shown below for the book *Time for Kids: Our World* (Walsh, n.d.).

Sample Table of Contents Prediction

Title of Book: Time for Kids: Our World   **Author:** Kenneth Walsh

Chapter 1: Water and Our World

Chapter 2: Air and Our World

Chapter 3: Plants and Our World

Chapter 4: Deserts and Our World

Finally, Marilyn told students to open their books and look at the table of contents. Students discussed with their peers how their tables of contents were similar to or different from the ones in the text. Marilyn reminded students that authors arrange information in many different ways, and that there is no one way to organize information in an informational text. They read their books and discussed with a peer the reason for the author's choice of organizational pattern. She asked students to think about how they might organize the information in a book they would write themselves, and identify different tables of contents that might work for that writing experience.

References

Kalman, B. (2004). *The life cycle of an earthworm*. New York: Crabtree. (I)
Walsh, K. (n.d.). *Time for kids: Our world*. New York: Time. (I)

Your Turn!

Introduce your students to Table of Contents Prediction using a textbook or trade book from the list in the Appendix in the back of this book or one of your own choosing. Have them complete the Table of Contents Prediction form provided on the facing page.

Table of Contents Prediction

Instructions: Look over the front and back covers of your book without opening it. What topics do you think the book will cover? What do you think the titles of the chapters will be? What order will they be in? Record your answers below.

Title of Book: _____ **Author:** _____

Chapter 1: _____

Chapter 2: _____

Chapter 3: _____

Chapter 4: _____

Chapter 5: _____

Chapter 6: _____

You may add more chapters below if needed.

Strategy 9

IEPC

GRADE LEVELS: 4–12

Getting Started
Building Background
Vocabulary
Reading Closely
Comprehension
Discussion
Writing

CCSS Anchor Standards: Reading

> **CCSS.ELA-Literacy.CCRA.R.6** Assess how point of view or purpose shapes the content and style of a text.

> **CCSS.ELA-Literacy.CCRA.R.8** Delineate and evaluate the argument and specific claims in a text, including the validity of the reasoning as well as the relevance and sufficiency of the evidence.

> **CCSS.ELA-Literacy.CCRA.R.9** Analyze how two or more texts address similar themes or topics in order to build knowledge or to compare the approaches the authors take.

What Is It?

The IEPC (Imagine, Elaborate, Predict, and Confirm) strategy (Wood, 2002) requires students to visualize (Imagine) and verbalize (Elaborate), which are important skills for reading comprehension. In addition, the IEPC strategy encourages students to make predictions (Predict) and to refer to the text to check or to modify these predictions (Confirm). In this way, students are also working on their critical thinking skills. This strategy is especially helpful for supplementing texts that are not supported by pictures. (As students enter the upper grades, more and more of their readings are text intensive.)

The IEPC strategy also works as an anticipatory activity since students are introduced to a topic, apply their prior knowledge, and then asked to learn more about the topic.

What Is Its Purpose?

According to Lenihan (2003), many students, particularly English language learners and struggling readers, have difficulty creating mental images of a text, especially if the text is a chapter book or has no pictorial support; as a result, these students also have trouble comprehending the content. The IEPC strategy encourages students to use visual imagery and prediction skills in order to enhance their text comprehension.

What Do I Do?

The procedures for the IEPC strategy are as follows (Wood, 2002):

1. Select a text related to the topic of study. Then, select a specific passage that contains content appropriate for developing imagery and that introduces the topic to be studied.

2. Distribute the IEPC chart or have students fold a piece of paper horizontally into four columns labeled accordingly.

3. Point out the "Imagine" column: Set a purpose for reading and tell the students to imagine a scene as you read the passage out loud. Have students close their eyes and encourage them to use their senses by thinking about the tastes, smells, sights, and feelings associated with the topic.

4. Ask students to record their images in either words or pictures in the "Imagine" column. If they draw their images, ask students to label them as well.

5. Have students share their images with a partner or with a group.

6. Point out the "Elaborate" column: Have students consider their classmates' initial responses. Ask them to think of additional details associated with the scene they originally visualized. The following questions can be used to prompt their responses:

- What did you learn from talking to your classmates?

- What had you forgotten that you remembered when talking to your classmates?

- What textual connections can you make? (For example, have the students make a text-to-self, text-to-text, or text-to-world connection.)

7. Ask students to record their elaborations in the "Elaborate" column.

8. Point out the "Predict" column: Have students use the information they wrote in the previous two columns to make predictions about the content found in the rest of the text. Ask the following guiding questions:

- What do you think the rest of the book will be about?

- What do you think will happen next?

9. Ask students to record their predictions in the "Predict" column.

10. Have students read the rest of the text independently or read the text aloud to the class.

11. Point out the "Confirm" column: During and after reading, encourage students to refer to their predictions. Ask the following questions:

- Were you able to confirm your predictions? Cite evidence from the text.

- Did you have to modify your predictions based on what you learned from the text? If so, how and why?

12. Ask students to record their confirmations and modifications in the "Confirm" column.

Example

Franny Prall teaches 12th-grade U.S. Government. During the last few weeks of school, she wanted to address the topic of social activism. As her students were heading off to college, she wanted them to feel a sense of political and personal agency. She had them study contemporary figures who have made a significant difference in shaping national policies such as Barack Obama, the first African American president of the United States; Aung Sang Suu Kyi, the leader of Burma's struggle for democracy; Vaclav Havel, the first president of the Czech Republic; and Nelson Mandela, the South African civil rights leader.

In addition to these famous world leaders, Franny wanted to demonstrate how an "average" person could make a difference. For this reason, she chose to introduce her students to Greg Mortenson, an American mountain climber turned humanitarian who builds schools in Central Asia. As her text, she used *Three Cups of Tea: One Man's Journey to Change the World . . . One Child at a Time* (Thomson, Mortenson, & Relin, 2007).

Franny distributed an IEPC Chart and read an excerpt from the book describing how Greg Mortenson's daughter felt about her father being away all the time to build schools for children in disenfranchised countries and how she dealt with the perils he faced that included death threats. She set the purpose for reading by telling students that she wanted them to pay attention to how global tensions can affect individual families. Franny asked her students to visualize and imagine how the little girl must have felt. She then had them discuss their imaginings and record their elaborations in the "I" and "E" columns of the chart, respectively. Next, she asked students to predict (P) what they thought the rest of the book would be about.

For homework, she had them read various sections of the book. In class the next day, they completed the "Confirm" (C) section of the chart. She followed up with a whole-class discussion of the text.

She followed up student reading of the text with an online article from *USA Today* entitled "Greg Mortenson's 'Tea' Brews Up a Controversy" (Minzesheimer, 2011), which detailed the controversy created when it was revealed that Mortenson fabricated key events in the book and used money donated to his charity for personal gain. She asked students to evaluate the evidence against Mortenson provided in the article and to consider how it affected their response to the book and its claims. The IEPC strategy and the article served as a springboard for a writing task Franny assigned in which students took a position regarding Mortenson's credibility as a writer and fund-raiser and provided evidence for their position, based on both the *USA Today* article and additional online sources (see Strategy 39).

References

Lenihan, G. (2003). Reading with adolescents: Constructing meaning together. *Journal of Adolescent and Adult Literacy, 47*(1), 8–12.

Minzesheimer, B. (2011). Greg Mortenson's "Tea" brews up a controversy. Retrieved July 21, 2015, from *http://usatoday30.usatoday.com/life/books/news/2011-04-19-mortenson19_ST_N.htm.*

Thomson, S., Mortenson, G., & Relin, D. O. (2007). *Three cups of tea: One man's journey to change the world . . . one child at a time.* New York: Penguin. (YA)

Wood, K. (2002). Aiding comprehension with the imagine, elaborate, predict, and former (IEPC) strategy. *Middle School Journal, 33*(3), 47–54.

Your Turn!

Select an informational trade book from the Appendix at the back of this book or one of your own choosing. Carefully identify a text with a good introductory passage that will evoke imagery and anticipation. (It would be helpful for the students to use a text about which they have some prior knowledge of the topic.) Then have them complete the IEPC chart.

IEPC Chart

Instructions: Record your mental images under the "I" column on the IEPC Chart. Then record your elaborations (E) and predictions (P) under the second and third columns. And last, refer to the text to confirm and/or modify (C) your thinking.

I (Imagine)	E Elaborate	P Predict	C Confirm

PART THREE

Vocabulary
Strategies

Word Map

GRADE LEVELS: 2–12

| Getting Started |
| Building Background |
| **Vocabulary** |
| Reading Closely |
| Comprehension |
| Discussion |
| Writing |

CCSS Anchor Standards: Reading

➤ **CCSS.ELA-Literacy.CCRA.R.4** Interpret words and phrases as they are used in a text, including determining technical, connotative, and figurative meanings, and analyze how specific word choices shape meaning or tone.

What Is It?

Word Maps (Schwartz & Raphael, 1985) provide a way for students to organize conceptual information as they seek to not only identify, but also understand a word. This particular map illustrates the class or category to which the concept belongs, the attributes or characteristics of the concept, and examples of the concept. Word Maps can be used for students in grades 2 and up, and are equally effective as a pre- or postreading activity.

What Is Its Purpose?

Word Maps are useful for introducing students to vocabulary they are likely to encounter while reading or for helping them to reflect on word meanings after they have completed their reading. They engage students in thinking deeply about words and give them the opportunity to record their thoughts on a visual organizer. In this way, students increase their understanding of the academic vocabulary found in various content areas.

What Do I Do?

1. To create a Word Map, the teacher or students first write the name of the concept being addressed in the center of the map.

2. They then answer the question "What is it?" by thinking of a word or phrase that best indicates the answer to this question.

3. After that, students need to identify and list three examples of the concept ("What are some examples?") in the appropriate boxes.

4. Then, students identify attributes or properties of the concept ("What is it like?"). More advanced students might be encouraged to list metaphors and similes for the word.

Example

Third-grade teacher Alan Brugman's students were studying civil rights during African American History Month. They studied the life and work of Martin Luther King, Jr., Rosa Parks, and other civil rights leaders. As part of that study, Alan read the book *Teammates* (Golenbock, 1992) aloud to his class. *Teammates* is the story of the friendship between Jackie Robinson, the first black man to play major league baseball, and his teammate, Pee Wee Reese, a white man from the South.

Prior to reading, Alan presented his students with the Word Map focusing on the word *discrimination* (see example on the facing page). He explained the term to his students and distributed copies of the Word Map to each child. He helped the students fill in the box containing the question "What is it?" with the answer "prejudice" or "being mean to others who are different in some way" after explaining the term to the students. He asked them to think about the word *discrimination* as he read the book aloud. After he read the book, he asked students to think of other words that tell what discrimination is like. Students gave the answers "mean," "unfair," and "making fun" as examples. Finally, he asked the students to work with a partner to list three examples of discrimination as described in the book. An example of their completed Word Map is on the facing page.

References

Golenbock, P. (1992). *Teammates*. San Diego, CA: Harcourt Brace Jovanovich. (I)

Schwartz, R. M., & Raphael, T. (1985). Concept of definition: A key to improving students' vocabulary. *The Reading Teacher, 39*, 198–205.

Vocabulary Strategies

Sample Word Map

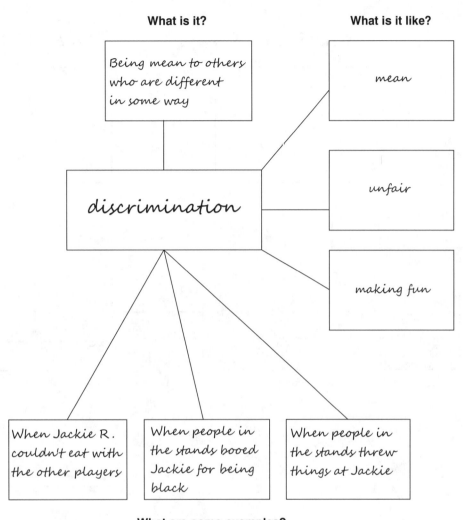

What is it?

Being mean to others who are different in some way

What is it like?

mean

unfair

making fun

discrimination

When Jackie R. couldn't eat with the other players

When people in the stands booed Jackie for being black

When people in the stands threw things at Jackie

What are some examples?

Your Turn!

Select a text from the Appendix at the back of this book or one of your own choosing. Write a word for a critical concept found in the book in the middle of the Word Map. Before and/or after students read the text, have them fill in the boxes on the Word Map, answering the questions "What is it?", "What is it like?", and "What are some examples?"

Word Map

Instructions: Put the word you are studying in the box in the middle. Then complete each of the other boxes by providing examples of what the word is, what it is like, and examples of the word.

What is it?   **What is it like?**

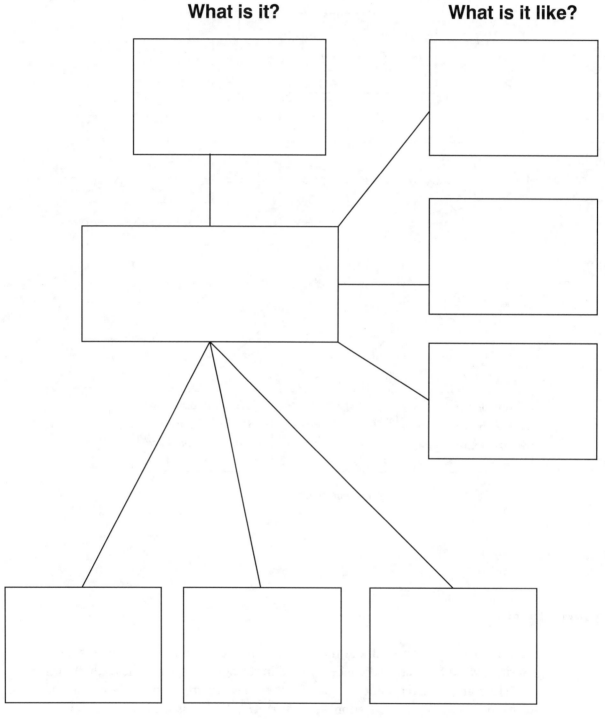

What are some examples?

Strategy 11

SLAP

GRADE LEVELS: 2–12

Getting Started
Building Background
Vocabulary
Reading Closely
Comprehension
Discussion
Writing

CCSS Anchor Standards: Reading

➤ **CCSS.ELA-Literacy.CCRA.R.4** Interpret words and phrases as they are used in a text, including determining technical, connotative, and figurative meanings, and analyze how specific word choices shape meaning or tone.

What Is It?

SLAP (Katz & Carlisle, 2009) is an acronym for a strategy designed to help students determine word meanings using context clues. The letters stand for the following concepts: S, Say the unknown word; L, Look for clues to the word's meaning; A, Ask yourself what the word might mean; and P, Put the word in the sentence in place of the unfamiliar word and ask yourself whether it makes sense.

What Is Its Purpose?

The purpose of SLAP is to give students a specific strategy or structure for approaching words whose meanings may be unclear or unknown to them. It requires students to do more than just decode an unknown word; it requires them to attempt to determine the word's meaning based on the context provided by the text itself. Because vocabulary skills are essential to developing reading comprehension (Beck, Perfetti, & McKeown, 1982), students need specific strategies for figuring out new words.

Using an acronym like SLAP helps students regulate their own learning by promoting the ability to independently identify vocabulary using context clues. They need to be explicitly taught each step and be given opportunities to practice the strategy. Nagy and Herman (1987) state, "Because the bulk of children's vocabulary growth occurs incidentally . . . the single most important goal of vocabulary instruction should be to increase the amount of incidental word learning by students" (p. 26). By teaching the SLAP strategy, teachers help students think through how to tackle challenging vocabulary by using the context of the text.

What Do I Do?

1. Select an appropriate informational text. Trade books, textbooks, newspaper articles, or websites would work well.

2. Select several key sentences that contain words that your students will not know. Be sure that the sentences are contextually rich; in other words, the sentences must contain clues to the meaning of the unknown word.

3. Select one of the sentences and write it on the board, underlining the unknown word. Model for students the four steps in the process. Thinking Aloud (see Strategy 20) would work well here. The four steps of SLAP are as follows:

- S—Say the word.

- L—Look for context clues.

- A—Ask yourself what the word might mean and think of another word that has the same meaning (synonym).

- P—Put the synonym in place of the word in the text. Does it still make sense? If so, then you understand the meaning of the word. If not, repeat the last two steps.

4. After you have modeled, engage students in guided practice.

For the first step, students will repeat the challenging vocabulary word. They may need help with pronunciation. In this case, say the word for them and have students repeat after you. In the second step, students study the sentence context. Direct them to focus on the words that they do know. Have them use prior knowledge to fill in their gaps. Have them look for words or phrases that are similar in meaning to the unknown word. In the third step, students think of synonyms. They may need an explicit definition of synonym. Ask a question like "What other words could be used here?" In the fourth step, students replace the challenging word with a synonym chosen during the third step. They ask themselves, "Does the word make sense?" If it does, then they probably understand the word. If not, then they need to repeat the last two steps until they identify a word that makes sense.

Example

Ninth-grade social science teacher Emily Carter's students were involved in a unit study of immigration past and present. Many of her students were English language learners whose families had emigrated from Mexico to the United States, which created an important connection to this topic for these students. In addition to studying aspects of immigration that were familiar to her students, she wanted them to understand the role of forced immigration and its connection to slavery in colonial America. To that end, she located an informational article on ReadWorks (*www.readwords.org*) titled "African Immigration to Colonial America" (Berlin, n.d.). She knew that this article would pose a challenge for her students, largely because of the many difficult vocabulary terms it contained. She carefully reviewed the article for challenging terms and identified those most central to understanding the passage. She decided that she would preteach the vocabulary by demonstrating the SLAP strategy and then having students practice it with a partner. Ultimately she wanted students to use the strategy on their own.

Emily began the lesson by reviewing the steps in the SLAP strategy by using a poster. She explained each step, then briefly explained the contents of the article and the term *Middle Passage*. She explained that they would use the SLAP strategy to explore some key terms from the passage.

She wrote the following sentence on the board, underlining the term *dehumanized*:

> But the Middle Passage also represents the will to survive,
> the determination of black people not to be <u>dehumanized</u> by
> dehumanizing circumstances.

She referred students to the poster as she modeled use of the strategy. She said:

"OK. The first step in SLAP is to **say the word**, which is *dehumanized*. I see forms of it twice in this sentence, so it must be important. I'm not sure of its meaning, but I'll use the SLAP strategy to try to figure it out. I'll write it in the first column on the SLAP Chart. [See page 74.] The next step in the strategy is to **look for context clues,** or the other words in the sentence. It talks about the will to survive and determination not to be dehumanized. So it must mean something that is bad and requires determination to get over. I'll record these as notes in the L column. Let's try the third step now. It says that I should **ask myself what it means** and if I can think of a synonym. I can see the word *human* in the word, and the prefix *de*. I know that *demerit* is not getting merit, so maybe *dehumanized* has something to do with being treated in a way that is not human. A synonym for that might be *degraded*. I'll write that in the third column, which is the A column. The last step says to try to **put the synonym in the sentence** and see if it makes sense, so I'll try *degraded* in place of *dehuman-*

Sample SLAP Chart

S (Say the word and write it here.)	L (Look for context clues. List them here.)	A (Ask myself what it means and write it here.)	P (Put the synonym in the sentence and write it here. Does it make sense? If not, start over with steps 3 and 4.)
dehumanized	Something bad that requires determination to overcome	degraded	But the Middle Passage also represents the will to survive, the determination of black people not to be *degraded* by dehumanizing circumstances.

ized. I'll write that in the P column of the chart. That seems to make sense in the sentence, so I'll continue to read."

Following this modeling, Emily gave students context-rich sentences from the passage containing words like *commodity, trajectory,* and *acculturated.* Students worked with partners to complete the SLAP Chart on page 76 for each term. After completing this activity, students had a foundation for understanding these key terms, and Emily engaged students in a shared reading of the text that would build on this foundation.

References

Beck, I. L., Perfetti, C. A., & McKeown, M. G. (1982). The effects of long-term vocabulary instruction on lexical access and reading comprehension. *Journal of Educational Psychology, 74,* 506–521.

Berlin, I. (n.d.) African immigration to colonial America [abridged]. Retrieved June 5, 2015, from *www.readworks.org/passages/african-immigration-colonial-america-abridged.*

Katz, L. A., & Carlisle, J. F. (2009). Teaching students with reading difficulties to be close

Vocabulary Strategies

readers: A feasibility study. *Language, Speech and Hearing Services in Schools, 40,* 325–340.

Nagy, W., & Herman, P. (1987). Breadth and depth of vocabulary knowledge: Implications for acquisition and instruction. In M. McKeown & M. Curtiss (Eds.), *The nature of vocabulary acquisition* (pp. 19–35). Hillsdale, NJ: Erlbaum.

Your Turn!

Select an informational text from the Appendix at the back of this book or one of your choosing. Identify challenging terms from the text and present them in the sentences in which they appear in the text. Use the reproducible on page 76 to have students use the SLAP strategy to determine the meanings of these words.

SLAP Chart

Instructions: Follow the instructions found in each column and record your answers in each column.

S (Say the word and write it here.)	L (Look for context clues. List them here.)	A (Ask yourself what the word might mean and think of a synonym. Write it here.)	P (Put the synonym in the sentence in place of the unknown word and write it here. Does it make sense? If not, start over with steps 3 and 4.)

Root Wheels

GRADE LEVELS: 1–12

Getting Started
Building Background
Vocabulary
Reading Closely
Comprehension
Discussion
Writing

CCSS Anchor Standards: Reading

➤ **CCSS.ELA-Literacy.CCRA.R.4** Interpret words and phrases as they are used in a text, including determining technical, connotative, and figurative meanings, and analyze how specific word choices shape meaning or tone.

What Is It?

Root Wheels provide a way for students to develop knowledge of roots, prefixes, and suffixes using a visual representation of a circle. Students record a root, prefix, or suffix and its meaning in the middle of the inner circle. In the outer circle, which is divided into four or more parts, students can write words containing the selected root, prefix, or suffix, along with a picture of the word and a sentence containing the word. Students may also wish to record Spanish cognates, for example, which can help them remember the target word's meaning.

What Is Its Purpose?

The purpose of Root Wheels is to introduce students to vocabulary they are likely to encounter while reading and help them analyze word parts to facilitate understanding. More than 90% of words students encounter are based on Greek and Latin prefixes, roots, and suffixes. Learning the meanings of these prefixes, roots, and suffixes will help students unlock new words they encounter in every content area, including English language arts, science, mathematics, social science, and health. Root wheels engage students in thinking deeply about words and give them the opportunity to record their thoughts on a visual organizer that can be displayed in the classroom or kept in a vocabulary notebook. In this way, students increase their understanding of the academic vocabulary found in various content areas.

What Do I Do?

1. To create a Root Wheel, the teacher or students first write the root, prefix, or suffix being studied, as well as its meaning, in the center of the inner circle.

2. They then identify additional words containing the root, prefix, or suffix and record them in the sections of the outer circle.

3. After that, students can define, draw pictures, and create sentences using the words found in each outer circle.

Example

Eighth-grade science teacher Lisa Erwin was interested in having her students read an article entitled "Electromagnetic Radiation" from ReadWorks (*www.readworks.org*) as part of their study of light. Despite her eagerness to focus on the content of the article, she knew that students would have difficulty with the passage if they did not get teacher support in understanding a number of key terms, which included *electromagnetic, infrared, ultraviolet,* and the more familiar *microwave.* These terms represented technical terms that students needed to understand in order to successfully read the article. Furthermore, they represented words containing roots, prefixes, and suffixes. Understanding these word parts would prepare students for future encounters with other related scientific terms.

Lisa decided to preteach these terms since most of them were unfamiliar to her students. She created a sample Root Wheel on chart paper so that she could model for her students how to complete it. Using the term *electromagnetic,* she noted that the base or root word is *magnet,* but that the prefix is *electro.* She wrote the prefix *electro* in the center and explained to students that it refers to electricity (see example on the facing page). Following this, she asked students to think of additional words that use this prefix. They identified the following words: *electrolyte, electrocardiogram,* and *electrocute.* She also showed students how to locate word examples for different prefixes, roots, and suffixes on WordFind (*www.wordfind.com*). Lisa recorded each term on the outer circle (see example on the facing page). She had students work with a partner to create definitions for these terms; they were permitted to look up word meanings they did not know and were encouraged to write the defi-

Sample Root Wheel

Electrocute—to kill or injure from electric shock.

You can be *electrocuted* by lightning.

Electrolyte—a mineral in the body that carries an electric charge.

Your body needs *electrolytes* to be healthy.

Electro—electricity

Electronics—devices using electricity.

During a power loss, we can't charge our own *electronics*.

Electrocardiogram—a test to measure heart's electrical activity.

They gave me an *electrocardiogram* to check my heart function.

nitions in their own words. In addition, she had students write sentences containing each term. Students might also draw pictures to remind them of each word.

References

Electromagnetic radiation. Retrieved July 5, 2015, from *www.readworks.org/passages/electromagnetic-radiation*.

WordFind. Retrieved July 5, 2015, from *www.wordfind.com*.

Your Turn!

Select an informational text from the Appendix at the back of this book or one of your own choosing. Identify key words that contain roots, prefixes, and suffixes. Have students record the focus prefix, root, or suffix in the center and define it and add several words containing the focus prefix, root, or suffix in the outer circle. They can add definitions, pictures, and sentences for each of these words as well.

Vocabulary Strategies

Root Wheel

Instructions: Put the root, prefix, or suffix you are studying in the inner circle. Then list other words containing the root, prefix, and suffix in the outer circle. Add a definition, a sentence, and an illustration for each one.

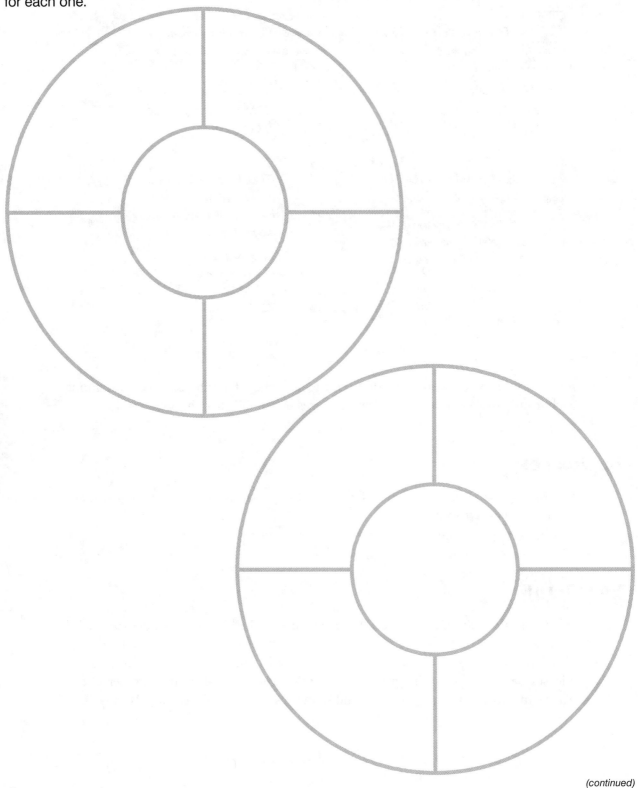

(continued)

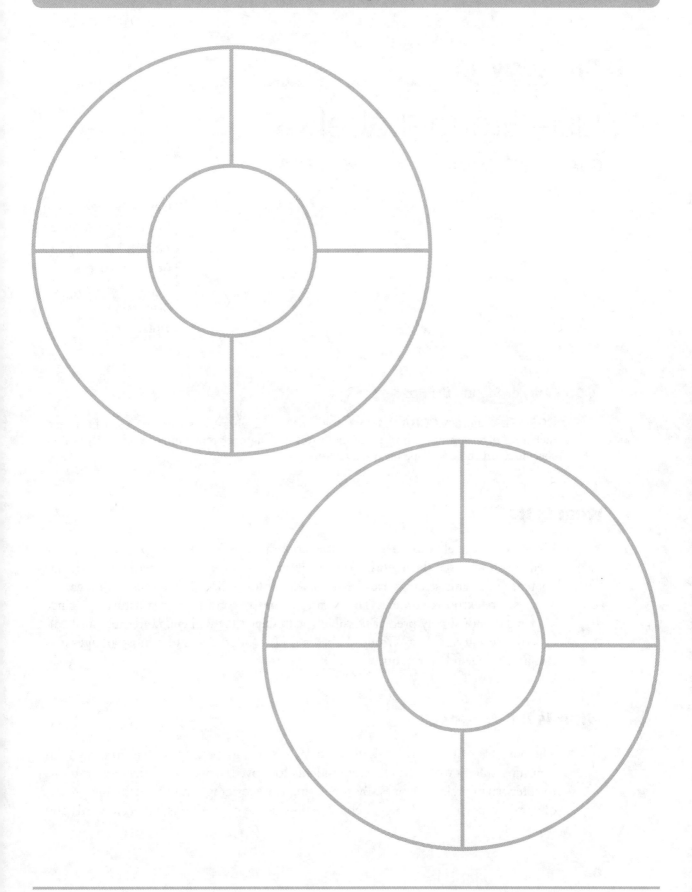

Strategy 13

List–Group–Label

GRADE LEVELS: 2–12

Getting Started
Building Background
Vocabulary
Reading Closely
Comprehension
Discussion
Writing

CCSS Anchor Standards: Reading

➤ **CCSS.ELA-Literacy.CCRA.R.4** Interpret words and phrases as they are used in a text, including determining technical, connotative, and figurative meanings, and analyze how specific word choices shape meaning or tone.

What Is It?

List–Group–Label (Taba, 1967) is a form of brainstorming that helps students make predictions about and categorize the vocabulary they will encounter in a particular content area. This strategy can be used with informational trade books, magazine articles, or textbook content. This strategy goes beyond basic brainstorming since students do not simply predict possible vocabulary they will encounter, but also categorize those terms. List–Group–Label is useful for students of almost all ages and can involve them before, during, and after reading.

What Is Its Purpose?

The purpose of List–Group–Label is to help students predict content and see relationships among words. It requires students to move beyond memorizing definitions to categorizing related words. By predicting, categorizing, and then labeling groups of words, students develop greater awareness of the connections between words and concepts.

Vocabulary Strategies

82

What Do I Do?

1. Select an appropriate informational text. Trade books or textbooks work best for this activity.

2. Before they read, ask students to *list* words they know related to the topic addressed in the reading material. They can complete this step individually, in pairs, or in small groups. These words should be recorded on a chart (see page 84).

3. Ask students to *group* or cluster related words into categories. These word groupings should be recorded on the chart.

4. After completing this step, students identify words that can serve as *labels* for each category.

5. At this point, students read the material. During their reading, students should jot down new words that they have learned about the topic.

6. After reading, students should add these new terms to those identified before their reading, placing them in the appropriate category. They may wish to record these words on their chart using different colored ink from the words they generated before reading.

Example

Mary Chaney, a sixth-grade history teacher, used the book *Tales Mummies Tell* (Lauber, 2003) to introduce a unit on ancient Egypt. In order to activate students' prior knowledge before reading the book, she asked them to brainstorm a list of words related to the topic of mummies that they thought might appear in the book. The students' list appears below:

Egypt
pyramids
ancient times
wrapped in cloth
organs removed
preserved
coffins
pharaohs
buried with food and jewels

After they listed these ideas, students grouped them into categories, which they then labeled. Their categories and labels are listed on page 84.

Where mummies were buried	Who they were	How mummies were buried	When mummies were buried
Egypt	pharaohs	wrapped in cloth	ancient times
pyramids		coffins	
		buried with food and jewels	
		preserved	
		organs removed	

Following their reading, students added more information to each category and also chose to add a new category titled "Studying Mummies." The **underlined** words indicate ideas that were added to the original categories (see below).

Where mummies were buried	Who they were	How mummies were buried	When mummies were buried	Studying mummies
Egypt	pharaohs	wrapped in cloth	ancient times	archaeologists
pyramids	queens	coffins		illnesses like arthritis
Valley of the Sun	animals	buried with food and jewels		CT scans
		preserved		religion and afterlife
		amulets		
		sarcophagus		
		embalmed		
		resin		

References

Lauber, P. (2003). *Tales mummies tell*. New York: Scholastic. (M)

Taba, H. (1967). *Teacher's handbook to elementary social studies: An inductive approach.* Reading, MA: Addison-Wesley.

Your Turn!

Select a text from the Appendix at the back of this book or one of your own choosing. Involve students in completing the List–Group–Label strategy. Have them begin by brainstorming terms about the topic. Then they can group and label their words by categories. After reading, they can add more words and categories to their chart. Students can record their answers on the chart included on page 86.

Vocabulary Strategies

List–Group–Label Chart

Instructions: Follow the instructions for each step in the strategy.

Before you read, LIST 10 words related to the topic of your book.

1. _____   6. _____

2. _____   7. _____

3. _____   8. _____

4. _____   9. _____

5. _____   10. _____

Now, GROUP all the words that have something in common in one column. Then make up a name for the category. This is a LABEL. Write it in the square at the top of the column. Then do the same for each of the remaining columns.

After you read the book, add new words that you have learned to each column.

Strategy 14

Word Sort

GRADE LEVELS: 2–12

| Getting Started |
| Building Background |
| **Vocabulary** |
| Reading Closely |
| Comprehension |
| Discussion |
| Writing |

CCSS Anchor Standards: Reading

➤ **CCSS.ELA-Literacy.CCRA.R.4** Interpret words and phrases as they are used in a text, including determining technical, connotative, and figurative meanings, and analyze how specific word choices shape meaning or tone.

What Is It?

Word Sorts (Gillet & Kita, 1979) are a way to help students understand the content-related vocabulary found in a text. Word Sorts help students discover relationships among words or phrases and categorize words or phrases based on those relationships. Word Sorts differ from List–Group–Label (Strategy 13). With List–Group–Label, students themselves generate words related to a topic. With Word Sorts, teachers identify key words about a topic in advance and involve students in arranging them logically. There are two types of Word Sorts—open sorts and closed sorts. Open sorts require students to determine their own categories for like words that have been grouped together. No two students will generate exactly the same categories in an open Word Sort. With closed sorts, the teacher provides students with the categories ahead of time and the students sort the words with these categories in mind. Closed sorts are typically easier for students because the categories have been provided for them. Word Sorts can be used as a prereading activity to activate students' prior knowledge about the vocabulary in a text. They can also be used as a postreading activity to assess student understanding of what has been read.

What Is Its Purpose?

Like List–Group–Label, the purpose of a Word Sort is to help students see relationships between words found in informational texts. By sorting words that the teacher has identified, students gain familiarity with the new vocabulary in the text. Through the process of categorizing words, students will have greater retention of word meanings than if they just try to remember words in isolation.

What Do I Do?

1. Select a content-related text. Identify 15–20 critical terms related to the topic at hand.

2. Select terms that have relationships to one another so that they can be categorized. Using the reproducible provided on page 91, write the words on 3" × 5" cards, or print them on the computer on business card–size printer sheets. Create enough sets of cards so that each pair of students will have a set. If you are doing a closed sort, write the category names in all capital letters on the appropriate number of cards.

3. Introduce the Word Sort activity before or after students read.

4. Give each pair of students a set of cards. Read the words to the students, asking them about the meanings of words that are new to them. Be sure that the words are arranged in alphabetical order or scrambled (not in categories) when you give them to the students.

5. If students are completing a closed sort, list the categories they will be using on the board. If students are doing an open sort, tell them to group words that have relationships to one another and label those words with a category name card.

6. Circulate around the room to check on students' progress. Then ask students to explain how they categorized the words and why.

Example

Seventh-grade science teacher Carol Newman was teaching a unit on endangered species. To make this issue more relevant to the students in her San Diego, California, School, she decided to use Caroline Arnold's (2000) *On the Brink of Extinction: The California Condor*. This book describes how the efforts of the San Diego Zoo led to the reintroduction of the California condor into the wild after its near extinction. This book could serve as an introduction to the students' visit to the San

Diego Zoo, where they would have the opportunity to see the condors and learn about scientists' efforts to save them.

Carol introduced the book by engaging students in a discussion of what they already know about endangered species. She then assigned students to read the book and discuss it in small groups over the next 2 weeks. After students completed their reading, she had them form pairs to complete this open Word Sort. She explained the Word Sort strategy, and gave each pair of students a set of word cards containing the words listed below.

vultures	boxes	6 oz.	DDT	shooting
cliffs	caves	57 days	15,000 feet	urbanization
crop	scavengers	mice	poison	social
pip	10-foot wingspan	primaries	55 mph	monogamous

Students then sorted their words into groups and identified the category terms at the top of each column.

Characteristics	Breeding areas	Causes of extinction	Flight	Chicks
vultures	caves	DDT	55 mph	57 days
10-foot wingspan	cliffs	poison	15,000 feet	pip
social	boxes	shooting	primaries	6 oz.
scavengers		urbanization		crop
monogamous				mice

After completing the sort, students explained and compared their word categorizations and provided rationales for the categories they developed.

References

Arnold, C. (2000). *On the brink of extinction: The California condor (Houghton Mifflin Soar to Success)*. Boston: Houghton Mifflin. (I, M)

Gillet, J., & Kita, M. (1979). Words, kids, and categories. *The Reading Teacher, 32,* 538–542.

Your Turn!

Select a text from the Appendix at the back of this book or one of your own choosing. Create a list of words related to the book that can be categorized. Have students list these terms on the sheet on the facing page. If you prefer, you may put the words on cards. Then pair students and have them sort the words and identify categories for each cluster. Have students discuss their sorts and provide a rationale for how they grouped the words.

Vocabulary Strategies

Word Sort

Instructions: Follow the instructions for each section.

1. List the words to be sorted here.

2. Cluster similar words. List related words in each column. Write the category name in the top box of each column.

Semantic Feature Analysis

GRADE LEVELS: 3–12

Getting Started
Building Background
Vocabulary
Reading Closely
Comprehension
Discussion
Writing

CCSS Anchor Standards: Reading

➤ **CCSS.ELA-Literacy CCRA.R.4** Interpret words and phrases as they are used in a text, including determining technical, connotative, and figurative meanings, and analyze how specific word choices shape meaning or tone.

What Is It?

Semantic Feature Analysis (Anders & Bos, 1986) is an activity where students identify important features or characteristics of a concept on a matrix and analyze similarities and differences among those concepts. Semantic Feature Analysis can be used as a prereading activity to activate what students know about words. Students can then reexamine their matrix after reading to clarify and amend their initial responses on the matrix. It can also be used as a postreading comprehension check to determine whether students understand how particular concepts are alike and different.

What Is Its Purpose?

Semantic Feature Analysis helps students visually compare and contrast concepts through the use of a matrix. It helps students to draw conclusions based on the information that is represented.

What Do I Do?

1. The teacher must first identify a category of concepts for the topic being taught. For example, the category might be transportation.

2. The teacher must then identify several terms within the category. Using the example of transportation, the teacher might identify terms like *bicycle* or *car*. Then he or she would identify features they share, such as tires or seats.

3. The terms (*bicycle, car*) are listed in the left-hand column and the shared features are listed across the top (*see example for snakes below*).

4. Students then identify whether the example exhibits the features by marking a "+" or "−" in the appropriate box.

5. Following this, students discuss what they have learned about the terms and their similarities and differences.

Example

Fifth-grade teacher Amy Peale's students were involved in a study of reptiles. As part of that study the students read *Amazing Snakes (Eyewitness Juniors)* (Parsons, 1990). After they completed their reading, Amy presented the students with a Semantic Feature Analysis matrix about snakes on the document camera. In the left-hand column, she listed the various types of snakes mentioned in the book, including pythons, cobras, rattlesnakes, milk snakes, and vine snakes. Across the top, she listed characteristics of snakes, including "poisonous," "squeezes to kill," "can eat people," and "lays eggs."

Students worked in teams to consider whether each snake listed in the left column possessed the features listed across the top of the page. They checked back in the book to determine the characteristics that each snake possessed. The student discussed their answers while Amy filled in the matrix with pluses and minuses (see page 94). Following this, she asked students to draw conclusions about which snakes were most alike and which were most different.

References

Anders, P., & Bos, C. (1986). Semantic feature analysis: An interactive strategy for vocabulary development and text comprehension. *Journal of Reading, 20*(7), 610–616.

Parsons, A. (1990). *Amazing snakes (Eyewitness juniors)*. New York: Dorling Kindersley. (I)

Vocabulary Strategies

Sample Semantic Feature Analysis Matrix

Type of snake	Poisonous	Squeezes to kill	Can eat people	Lays eggs
python	−	+	+	+
cobra	+	−	−	+
rattlesnake	+	−	−	−
milk snake	−	−	−	+
vine snake	+	−	−	+

Your Turn!

Select a text from the Appendix at the end of this book, one of your own choosing, or a newspaper or magazine article mentioning people or concepts that can be compared based on their attributes. Introduce the Semantic Feature Analysis Matrix on the facing page by giving students the terms that go in the left column and the attributes to be listed across the top. Tell students to think about these concepts and their attributes as they read. When students are finished, they can complete the matrix in pairs. Following this they should discuss the chart and what they have learned about the terms.

Semantic Feature Analysis Matrix

Instructions: Look at the words in the first column. Then look at the characteristics of each word in the first row. Rate each attribute with a plus (+) if it is accurate and with a minus (−) if it is not.

PART FOUR

Reading
Closely
Strategies

Close Reading

GRADE LEVELS: 3–12

Getting Started
Building Background
Vocabulary
Reading Closely
Comprehension
Discussion
Writing

CCSS Anchor Standards: Reading

➤ **CCSS.ELA-Literacy.CCRA.R.1** Read closely to determine what the text says explicitly and to make logical inferences from it; cite specific textual evidence when writing or speaking to support conclusions drawn from the text.

➤ **CCSS.ELA-Literacy.CCRA.R.2** Determine central ideas or themes of a text and analyze their development; summarize the key supporting details and ideas.

➤ **CCSS.ELA-Literacy.CCRA.R.3** Analyze how and why individuals, events, or ideas develop and interact over the course of a text.

➤ **CCSS.ELA-Literacy.CCRA.R.5** Analyze the structure of texts, including how specific sentences, paragraphs, and larger portions of the text (e.g., a section, chapter, scene, or stanza) relate to each other and the whole.

➤ **CCSS.ELA-Literacy.CCRA.R.6** Assess how point of view or purpose shapes the content and style of a text.

➤ **CCSS.ELA-Literacy.CCRA.R.7** Integrate and evaluate content presented in diverse media and formats, including visually and quantitatively, as well as in words.

➤ **CCSS.ELA-Literacy.CCRA.R.8** Delineate and evaluate the argument and specific claims in a text, including the validity of the reasoning as well as the relevance and sufficiency of the evidence.

➤ **CCSS.ELA-Literacy.CCRA.R.9** Analyze how two or more texts address similar themes or topics in order to build knowledge or to compare the approaches the authors take.

➤ **CCSS.ELA-Literacy.CCRA.R.10** Read and comprehend complex literary and informational texts independently and proficiently.

What Is It?

Close Reading is a specific type of classroom reading that requires students to do multiple readings of a short, complex text in order to develop deep understanding of what the text says, how it works, and what it means (Kurland, n.d.). Close Reading is most appropriate for repeated reading and intense study of a brief, layered, complex informational text that students read themselves in grades 3–12 and may be read aloud to them in grades K–2. We explain how to do a Close Thinking lesson in grades K–2 on page 109. We typically recommend that students read a text three times, but more or fewer readings may be appropriate. A good Close Reading text is like a great poem or painting. Every time you reread a great poem or resee a great painting, you see something new. The same is true of a great text for Close Reading. Whether a scientific article, a complex diagram, or a primary source document, learners should deepen their understanding with each reading, discovering more and more about what the text says, how it works, and what it means.

During each reading, students answer and discuss text-dependent questions (see Strategy 19) focused on the text itself, rather than personal connections to the text. Teachers scaffold student understanding using graphic organizers, peer discussion, think-alouds, and other strategies designed to deepen student thinking.

First Reading

Teachers do not spend time building background for reading the text before the first reading, but may include that step later in the process. Text-dependent questions begin with literal questions ("What does the text say?") that are asked during the first reading and require students to focus on the general meaning of the text. A teacher might ask: "What was this text about?" Students may also annotate the text during this first reading (see Strategy 18). They discuss their responses with a partner and then share with the larger group.

Second Reading

During the second reading, text-dependent questions and discussions help students explore how the text works in terms of vocabulary, organization, and format. Text-dependent questions might include: "How was this text organized?" or "Why do you think the author wrote this text?" Once again, teachers engage students in discussions around the text, using appropriate scaffolds such as graphic organizers, modeling and think-alouds, and so on.

Third Reading

During the third reading students explore more deeply what the text means. They consider the arguments the author poses and formulate their own opinions and connections to other texts (for more on text-dependent questions, see Strategy 19).

Questions might include "Do you agree with the author's argument? Why or why not?" Teachers should continue to scaffold student learning appropriately. The third reading is often followed by a writing activity or project extension that demonstrates student learning.

A good Close Reading involves more than just teachers questioning students. During a Close Reading, teachers scaffold student understanding. They may think aloud about the text, provide visuals to support student learning, or have students complete graphic organizers such as those found in this text. Student talk also scaffolds learning during Close Reading. When doing Close Reading, your classroom should be alive with conversations where students talk to partners, tablemates, and to the larger group about their responses to questions. This verbal rehearsal supports students as they explore challenging texts by sharing with others and provides a foundation for later writing extensions in response to a text.

What Is Its Purpose?

The purpose of Close Reading is to engage students in deep study of a short informational text, focusing on meaning at the word, sentence, paragraph, and passage levels. It is designed to help students consider what the text says, how it works, and what it means. Close Reading lets students dig deeply into a text, gaining new information with each reading. Teacher modeling helps students internalize the strategy so that they can become close readers without teacher support.

What Do I Do?

1. Select a short, worthy complex text. The text exemplars in Appendix B of the CCSS and ReadWorks (*www.readworks.org*) or CommonLit (*www.commonlit.org*) are good sources for informational Close Reading texts.

2. Determine the standard that will provide the lesson focus and identify the lesson purpose.

3. Determine the areas of complexity (see Strategy 3) and potential problem areas for students.

4. Decide how you will chunk the text (break into sections) and how students will number the lines in the text.

5. Create text-dependent questions (see Strategy 19).

6. First reading. Plan the first reading based on your text complexity analysis. Explain the lesson purpose to your students. During this first reading you can ask text-dependent questions focused on **what the text says**, have students annotate the text (see Strategy 18), and/or have students discuss their responses with partners or tablemates. You need not build background before the first reading; let students "have a go" at the text first.

7. **Second reading.** Plan the second reading based on student responses to the questions you asked in the first reading. Now ask a text-dependent question or two that pushes students back to the text to expand their thinking about **how the text works.** They may continue to annotate in response to those questions and discuss their responses with partners. They might also complete a graphic organizer in response to these questions.

8. **Third reading.** The next reading should help students discover **what the text means** through inferencing and making intertextual connections. During this reading students will explore text-dependent questions that require critical thinking skills. Once again, students will discuss their responses with peers.

9. **Assessments.** At this point, students can complete writing assignments or multimedia projects that demonstrate their text understanding. You may also want to create a performance task like those found in Appendix B of the CCSS, since these are the types of items found on many state-adopted assessments. These serve as assessments for the lesson, allowing students to use what they have learned from the Close Reading.

Example

Greg Wilson, an eighth-grade social science teacher, had his students read many primary source documents as he began implementing the CCSS. He decided to create a Close Reading experience for his students by using General Winfield Scott's (1838) speech entitled *An Address to the Cherokee Nation.* In preparing for the lesson he noted that in terms of complexity, the text was primarily easy or at grade level, but he still had some concerns about how well his students would understand the archaic language of the speech and the condescending tone of the author toward the Cherokees. Greg focused attention on the CCSS reading standard for grade 8, which addressed the citing of textual evidence of explicit and inferred text meanings.

Greg began the lesson by reviewing the title of the text with his students. He explained that the purpose of the lesson would be for students to evaluate General Scott's attitude toward the Cherokees based on their reading of this text. He modeled for students how to number the lines in the text for easy reference.

First Reading (What the Text Says)

Greg first asked students to read the text silently to get the overall meaning. He asked, "If someone asked you what this text is about, what would you answer?" Following a brief discussion of this question, students used annotation, which they had practiced in the past, to circle words that they thought would be challenging (Strategy 18). They then shared these terms with a partner, and used the SLAP Strategy (Strategy 11) to determine the meanings. Students then shared their terms with the whole class and identified word meanings as a group.

Second Reading (How the Text Works)

For the second text reading, Greg decided to ask students an additional vocabulary question that had not been addressed during the first reading. He asked students, "What do you think Scott means when he refers to 'the error that you have committed' in paragraph one?" He then redirected students to consider relationships among the ideas in the text, asking them to consider other text-dependent questions: "What message is General Scott trying to convey to his listeners? What concerns did General Scott express about removing the Cherokees? What evidence do you have for your answers?" After students reread the text, they answered these questions and shared their responses with a partner.

Third Reading (What the Text Means)

For the third text reading, Greg directed students' attention to deeper text meanings by pointing out specific ideas in the text. He focused on the author's language and intent by using annotation and asking: "What words and phrases does Scott use to convince the Cherokees of his concern for their welfare? Highlight those terms in blue." Following this, students discussed those terms as a group. Greg then asked students: "What words and phrases does Scott use that may show his real feelings toward the Cherokees? Highlight these in yellow." Following this, students discussed their responses with their tablemates. He then asked students to consider Scott's tone toward the Cherokees. Students provided examples of this and reported to the group.

Assessment Writing Activity

Greg then asked students to complete a quick-write explaining how Scott's message was contradictory and provide evidence for their answers. As an extension activity, students might speculate on what the Cherokees' reaction to this speech might have been, giving evidence for their answers. In addition, they might make intertextual connections with texts they have already read that illustrate Andrew Jackson's views about the Cherokees.

References

CommonLit. Retrieved May 10, 2015, from *www.commonlit.org.*
Kurland, D. (n.d.). *Dan Kurland's www.criticalreading.com: Reading and writing ideas as well as words.* Retrieved July 10, 2015 from *www.criticalreading.com*

ReadWorks. Retrieved May 10, 2015, from *www.readworks.org.*

Scott, W. (1838). An address to the Cherokee nation. Retrieved May 30, 2015, from *http:// www.cherokee.org/aboutthenation/history/trailoftears/majorgeneralscottsultimatum. aspx.*

Your Turn!

Now it is your turn to create a Close Reading lesson. The form on the facing page provides a template where you can record your ideas about your lesson. You may want to review Assessing Text Complexity (Strategy 3) and Text-Dependent Questions (Strategy 19) as you complete this guide. First you will complete information about your lesson title, grade level, standards, and objectives. From there the form is divided into five sections:

- Step 1: Choose a Text.

- Step 2: Determine Text Complexity.

- Step 3: Progression of Text-Dependent Questions.

- Step 4: Planning the Lesson.

- Step 5: Teacher Reflections.

Directions and pointers for thinking about each step are provided in *italics.*

Informational Text Close Reading Planning Guide

Instructions: Record your planning notes for your Close Reading lesson here.

Subject Area: _____   **Grade Level:** _____   **Topic/Lesson Title:** _____

Common Core State Standard: _____

Content Objective: _____

Step 1: Choose a Text. *The text should be short, complex, and worthy of a Close Reading.*

Text title: _____

Author: _____

Pages: _____

Step 2: Determine Text Complexity. *Circle those areas of complexity that may be challenging for your students (see Strategy 3).*

Main Ideas and Details	Vocabulary	Point of View
Organization	Author's Purpose	Uses of Language
Visual Supports and Layout	Author's Tone and Style	Knowledge Demands
Relationship among Ideas	Theme	Inferences/Arguments

Step 3: Progression of Text-Dependent Questions. *Identify question categories and list text-dependent questions here. Be sure to focus on areas of text complexity. Be sure to ask students to provide evidence for their answers. You may want to use the categories and question stems provided on pages 127–128.*

What the text says (first reading)	
Category: _____	Text-dependent question: _____ _____ Evidence-based answer: _____ _____ p. ____

(continued)

Category:	Text-dependent question: _____
_____	_____
	Evidence-based answer: _____
	_____ p. ____

How the text works (second reading)

Category:	Text-dependent question: _____
_____	_____
	Evidence-based answer: _____
	_____ p. ____

Category:	Text-dependent question: _____
_____	_____
	Evidence-based answer: _____
	_____ p. ____

What the text means (third reading)

Category:	Text-dependent question: _____
_____	_____
	Evidence-based answer: _____
	_____ p. ____

Category:	Text-dependent question: _____
_____	_____
	Evidence-based answer: _____
	_____ p. ____

(continued)

Step 4: Planning the Lesson

- Establish the purpose. Let's read to find out . . . *complete this sentence.*

- Chunking. *Number the lines in the text in the following way.*

- First Reading Focus (What the Text Says): *Students should struggle with the text; limit teacher front-loading and background building. Engage students in getting the main idea of the passage and/or annotating key terms, difficult ideas, main ideas, etc., using highlighters. List text-dependent questions here and explain what students will annotate here in detail.*

  - *Text-Dependent Question(s)*

  - *Annotation Activities*

- First Student Chat: *Students engage in partner talk about their annotations and/or their responses to the first text-dependent questions.*

- Second Reading Focus (How the Text Works): *Students reread to dig more deeply into the text and answer more challenging text-dependent questions, such as how the text works, vocabulary, or text structure. Explain what you will do here in detail. Students might continue to complete a graphic organizer, complete annotations, and so on. You may use a graphic organizer here, model key learnings, have students annotate again, and so on. Explain in detail what you will do here.*

  - *Text-Dependent Question*

  - *Text-Dependent Question*

  - *Scaffolds (graphic organizers, think-alouds, etc.)*

(continued)

- Second Student Chat: *Students discuss with a partner their responses to the questions.*

- Third Reading (What the Text Means): *Students read again, going more deeply into the text and focusing on more challenging text-dependent questions such as inference or intertextual connections. Students read with the intent of completing a writing activity, a multimedia project, or extended discussion focused on synthesis of their learnings based on the lesson purpose, the standard, and the content objective. They should be able to take a stance, convey information, or detail an argument supported by the text.*

  - *Text-Dependent Question*

  - *Text-Dependent Question*

  - *Scaffolds (graphic organizers, think-alouds, etc.)*

- Third Student Chat: *Students continue to share/discuss what they learned during the third reading.*

- Assessment (Writing Activity, Project or Performance Task): *Students demonstrate their learning about the text through completion of a writing activity, poster, multimedia project, etc.*

Step 5: Teacher Reflections. *What went well about the lesson? What might you change next time? What will your next steps be for students who need additional support?*

Close Thinking

GRADE LEVELS: K–2

Getting Started

Building Background

Vocabulary

Reading Closely

Comprehension

Discussion

Writing

CCSS Anchor Standards: Reading

> **CCSS.ELA-Literacy.CCRA.R.1** Read closely to determine what the text says explicitly and to make logical inferences from it; cite specific textual evidence when writing or speaking to support conclusions drawn from the text.

> **CCSS.ELA-Literacy.CCRA.R.2** Determine central ideas or themes of a text and analyze their development; summarize the key supporting details and ideas.

> **CCSS.ELA-Literacy.CCRA.R.3** Analyze how and why individuals, events, or ideas develop and interact over the course of a text.

> **CCSS.ELA-Literacy.CCRA.R.4** Interpret words and phrases as they are used in a text, including determining technical, connotative, and figurative meanings, and analyze how specific word choices shape meaning or tone.

> **CCSS.ELA-Literacy.CCRA.R.5** Analyze the structure of texts, including how specific sentences, paragraphs, and larger portions of the text (e.g., a section, chapter, scene, or stanza) relate to each other and the whole.

> **CCSS.ELA-Literacy.CCRA.R.6** Assess how point of view or purpose shapes the content and style of a text.

> **CCSS.ELA-Literacy.CCRA.R.7** Integrate and evaluate content presented in diverse media and formats, including visually and quantitatively, as well as in words.

> **CCSS.ELA-Literacy.CCRA.R.8** Delineate and evaluate the argument and specific claims in a text, including the validity of the reasoning as well as the relevance and sufficiency of the evidence.

> **CCSS.ELA-Literacy.CCRA.R.9** Analyze how two or more texts address similar themes or topics in order to build knowledge or to compare the approaches the authors take.

> **CCSS.ELA-Literacy.CCRA.R.10** Read and comprehend complex literary and informational texts independently and proficiently.

What Is It?

Close Thinking (Lapp, Moss, Grant, & Johnson, 2015) is a specific type of classroom reading or listening experience modeled upon the Close Reading approach. It typically requires K–2 students to carefully listen to multiple teacher read-alouds of a short, complex text in order to develop deep understanding of what the text says, how it works, and what it means (Kurland, n.d.). If students are able to read, it may involve them reading the text with teacher support. We explain how to do a Close Reading lesson for grades 3–12 in Strategy 16. For grades K–2 we typically recommend that students listen closely to a text three times, but more or fewer listening experiences may be appropriate. A good Close Thinking text is like a great poem or painting. Every time you reread a great poem or resee a great painting, you see something new. The same is true of a great text for Close Thinking. Whether a science article from *Ranger Rick,* an informational trade book, or a short textbook excerpt, learners should deepen their text understanding with each listening experience, discovering more and more about what the text says, how it works, and what it means.

During each listening experience, students answer and discuss text-dependent questions (see Strategy 19) focused on the text itself, rather than personal connections to the text. Teachers scaffold student understanding using graphic organizers, peer discussions, think-alouds, and other strategies designed to deepen student thinking.

First Read-Aloud

Teachers do not usually spend time building background for reading the text before the first listening experience, but may include that step later in the process. Text-dependent questions begin with literal questions ("What does the text say?") that are asked during the first reading and require students to focus on the general meaning of the text. These questions could include: "What is the text about?" or "What would you tell a friend that you learned from this text?" Students may also annotate the text during this first reading (see Strategy 18). This annotation may involve finding and marking key words or phrases on the document camera or creating Post-it Notes to mark key places in the text. Students discuss their responses with a partner and share out to the larger group.

Second Read-Aloud

During the second read-aloud of the text, questions and discussions help students explore the question "How does the text work?" in terms of vocabulary, organization, and format. Text dependent questions might include: "What does _____ mean?", "How does the [selected punctuation] help you?", or "What did you notice about the format of this text?" Teachers engage students in discussions around the text, using scaffolds to support their learning.

Third Read-Aloud

During the third read-aloud students explore more deeply what the text means. They consider the question "What does the text mean?" as the teacher asks questions like "Look at the pictures of _____. Do they match what you think the author is saying? Why or why not? Provide text evidence." (For more on text-dependent questions, see Strategy 19.) The third reading is often followed by a writing activity, a project extension that demonstrates student learning, or a performance task like those found in Appendix B of the CCSS. These assessments are similar to those that will appear on state assessments.

A good Close Thinking lesson involves more than just teachers questioning students. During a Close Thinking lesson, teachers scaffold student understanding. They may think aloud about the text, provide visuals to support student learning, or have students complete graphic organizers. Student talk also scaffolds learning during Close Thinking. When doing Close Thinking, your classroom should be alive with conversations where students talk to partners, to tablemates, and to the larger group about their responses to questions. This verbal rehearsal supports students as they explore challenging texts by sharing with others and provides a foundation for later writing extensions in response to a text.

What Is Its Purpose?

The purpose of Close Thinking experiences with informational texts is to engage students in deep study of a short text, focusing on meaning at the word, sentence, paragraph, and passage levels. It is designed to help students consider what the text says, how it works, and what it means. Close Thinking lets students dig deeply into a text, gaining new information with each reading.

What Do I Do?

1. Select a short, worthy, complex text. The read-aloud text exemplars in Appendix B of the CCSS are good sources for informational Close Thinking texts.

2. Determine the standards that will provide the lesson focus and identify the lesson purpose.

3. Determine the areas of complexity (see Strategy 3) and potential problem areas for students.

4. Decide how you will chunk the text (i.e., break it into sections) and how students will number the lines in the text.

5. Create text-dependent questions (see Strategy 19).

6. First read-aloud. Plan the first read-aloud based on your text complexity analysis. Explain the lesson purpose to your students. During this first reading you can ask text-dependent questions focused on what the text says. Have students annotate the text (see Strategy 18), and/or have students discuss their responses with partners or tablemates. You need not build background before the first reading; let students "have a go" at the text first.

7. Second read-aloud. Plan the second read-aloud based on student responses to the questions you asked in the first reading. Now ask a text-dependent question or two that push students back to the text to expand their thinking about how the text works. They may continue to annotate in response to those questions and discuss their responses with partners. They might also complete a graphic organizer in response to these questions.

8. Third read-aloud. The next reading should help students discover the meaning of the text through inferencing and making intertextual connections. During this reading students will explore text-dependent questions that require critical thinking skills. Once again, students will discuss their responses with peers.

9. Assessments. At this point, students can complete writing assignments or multimedia projects that demonstrate their text understanding. You may also want to create a performance task like those found in Appendix B of the CCSS, since these are the types of items found on many state adopted assessments.

Example

Teacher Cathy Williams decided to do a close thinking lesson on the informational picture book *How a Seed Grows* (Jordan, 2000) with her first-grade students. She analyzed the text and found that most aspects of text complexity could be rated as easy or at grade level. The key ideas and details in the text were fairly easy to grasp, vocabulary was well supported with context clues and illustrations, and the text structure was predominantly sequential. Cathy pinpointed two possible areas of challenge: comprehending abstract ideas and inferring relationships among ideas. Her lesson purpose involved helping students identify and analyze the steps in the growth of a seed, a concept that was part of the science curriculum at her grade level. She focused her lesson on the standards for reading information in grade 1, which addressed asking and answering questions about key details and identifying and retelling key details of a text. In addition, she made contingency plans for using alternate texts in case her students needed additional supports.

First Read-Aloud (What the Text Says)

Cathy shared the book on the document camera and had students listen to the first three pages of the text and share with their partner questions they had about the content. She recorded these on a list in front of the room. She then read the next two pages, asking students: "What three things does a plant need in order to grow?" She modeled how to find evidence for the answer and noted it with a Post-it Note, demonstrating annotation in a way that met the needs of her young students. She continued reading the text a few pages at a time, asking students to identify questions they had about the text.

Second Read-Aloud (How the Text Works)

Cathy reread several pages that focused on the steps in the bean-to-plant process. She asked students to listen carefully to identify the four steps involved in this process. She called different students to the document camera to place Post-it Notes on the places in the text that described each one. Following this, she gave students pictures of each step in the process. Students glued these on their papers in the proper order and used sequence words (*first, second, third, last*) studied earlier to describe the process to a partner. As Cathy circulated around the room she checked for understanding by listening to students' descriptions of the process and recorded anecdotal notes about each student's retelling. She knew that students needed deep understanding of this concept and needed to be able to express their understanding through elaborated retellings if they were to demonstrate true understanding of this process. To scaffold student learning, Cathy engaged students in a creative dramatics lesson. She had students look again at their sequenced pictures of the steps in the process and modeled for students how to act out each step in the process. Then she helped the children describe to a partner what they dramatized during each step, using key sequencing words like *first, next, then,* and *finally.* She listened in on these conversations and noted that students were using more elaborated language in their retellings.

Third Read-Aloud (What the Text Means)

For the final text read-aloud Cathy asked students to consider progressively more challenging questions such as "Why do some seeds grow better than others? Provide evidence for your answer," and "How is the life cycle of a plant similar to your growing up?" By this time, students could address the knowledge demands of the text successfully and locate evidence and complete annotations with Post-it Notes in their own text copies.

Assessment/Writing Activity

For the lesson assessment, Cathy gave students a graphic organizer on which students drew pictures of the steps in the seed-to-plant process and recorded each step in writing. The graphic organizers were differentiated to address the different levels in the class. Some students completed sentence frames that said "First _____. Next _____," and so on, while others required that students simply fill in a word or two in each sentence. Through the many forms of scaffolding provided, including modeling, annotation, paired talk, retelling, visuals, creative dramatics, and sentence frames, Cathy's students successfully completed their first close thinking lesson and the accompanying assessment (Lapp, Moss, Johnson, & Grant, in press).

References

Jordan, H. J. (2000). *How a seed grows (Let's read and find out science 1).* New York: HarperCollins. (P)

Kurland, D. (n.d.). Dan Kurland's *www.criticalreading.com*: Reading and writing ideas as well as words. Retrieved June 10, 2015, from *www.criticalreading.com*.

Lapp, D., Moss, B., Grant, M., & Johnson, K. (2015). *A close look at close reading: Teaching students to analyze complex texts K–5.* Alexandria, VA: ASCD.

Lapp, D., Moss, B., Johnson, K., & Grant, M. (in press). *Turning the page on close reading: Differentiated scaffolds for close reading instruction.* Bloomington, IN: Solution Tree.

National Governors Association Center for Best Practices & Council of Chief State School Officers. (2010). *Common Core State Standards for the English language arts and literacy in history/social studies, science and technical subjects: Appendix B. Text exemplars and sample performance tasks.* Washington, DC: Authors.

Your Turn!

Select an informational text from the Appendix at the back of the book or of your own choosing. The form on the facing page provides a template where you can record your ideas about your lesson. You may want to review the Assessing Text Complexity (Strategy 3) and the Text-Dependent Questions (Strategy 19) as you complete this guide. Instructions and pointers for thinking about each step are provided in *italics*.

Informational Text Close Thinking Planning Guide

Instructions: Complete this form in preparation for a K–2 Close Thinking lesson.

Subject Area: _____ **Grade Level:** _____ **Topic/Lesson Title:** _____

Common Core State Standard: _____

Content Objective: _____

Step 1: Choose a Text. *The text should be short, complex, and worthy of a Close Thinking lesson.*

Text title: _____

Author: _____

Pages: _____

Step 2: Determine Text Complexity. *Circle those areas of complexity that may be challenging for your students (see Strategy 3).*

Main Ideas and Details	Vocabulary	Point of View
Organization	Author's Purpose	Uses of Language
Visual Supports and Layout	Author's Tone and Style	Knowledge Demands
Relationship among Ideas	Theme	Inferences/Arguments

Step 3: Progression of Text-Dependent Questions. *Identify question categories and list text-dependent questions here. Be sure to focus on areas of text complexity. Be sure to ask students to provide evidence for their answers. You may want to use the categories and question stems provided on pages 127–128*

What the text says (first reading)	
Category: _____	Text-dependent question: _____ _____ Evidence-based answer: _____ _____ p. _____

(continued)

Category: _____	Text-dependent question: _____ _____ Evidence-based answer: _____ _____ p. _____

How the text works (second reading)

Category: _____	Text-dependent question: _____ _____ Evidence-based answer: _____ _____ p. _____

Category: _____	Text-dependent question: _____ _____ Evidence-based answer: _____ _____ p. _____

What the text means (third reading)

Category: _____	Text-dependent question: _____ _____ Evidence-based answer: _____ _____ p. _____

Category: _____	Text-dependent question: _____ _____ Evidence-based answer: _____ _____ p. _____

(continued)

Step 4: Planning the Lesson

● Establish the purpose. Let's read to find out . . . *complete this sentence.*

● Chunking the text. Number the lines for this section.

● First Reading Focus (What the text says): *Students should struggle with the text; limit teacher front-loading and background building. Engage students in listening for the main idea of the passage and/or annotating key terms, difficult ideas, main ideas, etc., using highlighters. List text-dependent questions here and explain what students will annotate here in detail.*

    ● *Text-Dependent Question(s)*

    ● *Annotation Activities*

● First Student Chat: *Students engage in partner talk about their annotations and/or their responses to the first text-dependent questions.*

● Second Reading Focus (How the Text Works): *Students listen to dig more deeply into the text and answer more challenging text-dependent questions, such as how the text works, vocabulary, or text structure. Explain what you will do here in detail. Students might continue to complete a graphic organizer, complete annotations, and so on. Explain in detail what you will do here.*

    ● *Text-Dependent Question*

    ● *Text-Dependent Question*

    ● *Scaffolds (graphic organizers, think-alouds, etc.)*

(continued)

- Second Student Chat: *Students discuss with a partner their responses to the questions.*

- Third Reading (What the Text Means): *Students listen again, going more deeply into the text and focusing on more challenging text-dependent questions about inferences or arguments. Students listen with the intent of completing a writing activity, a multimedia project, or extended discussion focused on synthesis of their learnings based on the lesson purpose, the standard, and the content objective. They should be able to take a stance, convey information, or detail an argument supported by the text.*

    - *Text-Dependent Question*

    - *Text-Dependent Question*

    - *Scaffolds (graphic organizers, think-alouds, etc.)*

- Third Student Chat: *Students continue to share/discuss what they learned during the third reading.*

- Assessment (Writing Activity, Project or Performance Task): *Students demonstrate their learning about the text through completion of a writing activity, poster, multimedia project, etc.*

Step 5: Teacher Reflections. *What went well about the lesson? What might you change next time? What will your next steps be for students who need additional support?*

Strategy 18

Text Annotation

GRADE LEVELS: 2–12

Getting Started
Building Background
Vocabulary
Reading Closely
Comprehension
Discussion
Writing

CCSS Anchor Standards: Reading

> **CCSS.ELA-Literacy.CCRA.R.1** Read closely to determine what the text says explicitly and to make logical inferences from it; cite specific textual evidence when writing or speaking to support conclusions drawn from the text.

> **CCSS.ELA-Literacy.CCRA.R.2** Determine central ideas or themes of a text and analyze their development; summarize the key supporting details and ideas.

> **CCSS.ELA-Literacy.CCRA.R.3** Analyze how and why individuals, events, or ideas develop and interact over the course of a text.

> **CCSS.ELA-Literacy.CCRA.R.4** Interpret words and phrases as they are used in a text, including determining technical, connotative, and figurative meanings, and analyze how specific word choices shape meaning or tone.

> **CCSS.ELA-Literacy.CCRA.R.5** Analyze the structure of texts, including how specific sentences, paragraphs, and larger portions of the text (e.g., a section, chapter, scene, or stanza) relate to each other and the whole.

> **CCSS.ELA-Literacy.CCRA.R.6** Assess how point of view or purpose shapes the content and style of a text.

> **CCSS.ELA-Literacy.CCRA.R.7** Integrate and evaluate content presented in diverse media and formats, including visually and quantitatively, as well as in words.

> **CCSS.ELA-Literacy.CCRA.R.8** Delineate and evaluate the argument and specific claims in a text, including the validity of the reasoning as well as the relevance and sufficiency of the evidence.

> **CCSS.ELA-Literacy.CCRA.R.9** Analyze how two or more texts address similar themes or topics in order to build knowledge or to compare the approaches the authors take.

119

Reading Closely Strategies

What Is It?

Text Annotation is a strategy that facilitates close reading of texts and involves having students interact with a text by creating a record of their thoughts while they are reading. Teachers often have students annotate a text during their first and/or subsequent readings of a complex text during a Close Reading lesson, but annotation can be used as a strategy on its own. Sometimes referred to as reading with a pen, annotation typically involves using symbols, circling words and phrases, putting question marks next to new words, or using bullet points to note key ideas. It also includes marginalia, or recording notes about the text in the margins. Annotation can be used with any text, in any content area, at any grade level.

What Is Its Purpose?

The purpose of Text Annotation is to engage students in thinking deeply about a text by recording their thoughts on the text. Through this physical interaction with the text, students have a record of their thoughts that they can refer to after the reading is finished. They can share these ideas with partners or with the entire class.

What Do I Do?

Preplanning

1. Select an informational text for use during any reading experience.

2. Carefully read the text.

3. Identify the aspects of the text that are important to your lesson. For Close Reading, this means analyzing the text for complexity (see Strategy 3). Areas of focus can include any combination of the following:

- Difficult vocabulary

- Author's tone

- Text structures

- Main ideas

- Key details

- Text features (captions, footnotes, headings)

- Supporting evidence

- Student questions

- Author's message
- Claims and arguments (Lapp, Moss, Grant, & Johnson, 2015).

4. Determine what annotation symbols you will use and how students will annotate. Examples are provided on page 123. You may want to create a poster showing these.

Instruction

5. Explain and model the annotation process using the annotation system you have chosen. This may include both symbols and marginalia (on page 123).

6. Have students annotate their texts. Remind them to refer to the class poster that illustrates each symbol. Don't have them use more than a few symbols at first and gradually increase the number over time.

7. Engage students in paired and group discussions of their annotations.

Example

Fourth-grade teacher Kevin Garcia wanted his students to learn the skill of annotation. He felt that many of his students were "surface" readers; they would skim and scan to get main ideas, but really didn't dig deeply into texts. He thought that teaching them to annotate would give them a tool that would help them read more thoughtfully. His students were studying inventions, so he selected the description of the invention of the Slinky in *Toys! Amazing Stories Behind Some Great Inventions* (Wulffson, 2000) for a Close Reading and Annotation lesson. He decided that students would use annotation for their first reading of the text. Because his students had not annotated before, he knew it was essential that he model this practice.

Kevin began the lesson by explaining that annotation is a reading skill that can help students record their thinking about a text by writing on it. He then directed student attention to the poster below, which contained the annotation symbols. He

---

Annotation

(Circle) confusing words.

Write a ? mark next to confusing ideas.

Write a comment in the margin telling why it is confusing to you.

Underline the main ideas. Write a note in the margin telling how you know it is the main idea.

Draw an → to show connections between ideas.

did not want students to have to remember too many symbols for this first experience with annotation. Notice that the chart shows symbols as well as ways for students to use marginalia.

Kevin reviewed the symbols on the annotation chart and shared the text on the document camera. He explained that this text excerpt focuses on how Richard James invented the Slinky toy. He directed students' attention to the first two paragraphs of the text. In these paragraphs the author explains that Richard James had been hired to create a stabilizing device that would keep ship navigational instruments level. Kevin thought aloud as he thought aloud (see Strategy 20) and read the text aloud:

"OK. As I am reading this sentence, I see the word *stabilizing*. I will circle this word with my pencil because I'm not sure what it means. Later in this paragraph I see the word *counterbalance*, and I don't know what it means, so I will circle it as well. The text goes on to say that 'Richard's job was to come up with something that would counterbalance the instruments so that they would be level at all times.' I will place a question mark next to this sentence because I am not clear on what it means. I will write a note in the margin that says 'confusing' because why do instruments need to be level?' I think that maybe this has something to do with the stabilizing device mentioned earlier, so I will draw an arrow between this sentence and the one mentioning that."

Following this modeling, Kevin gave students the opportunity to practice this new skill. Students annotated the remainder of the text, using at least two of the symbols and marginalia suggested on the poster. Following this, students discussed their annotations with a partner, then shared out with the larger group. During this time, Kevin elicited student feedback about unknown terms, confusing ideas, and so on. This feedback helped him scaffold student understanding during subsequent text readings.

References

Lapp, D., Moss, B., Grant, M., & Johnson, K. (2015). *A close look at close reading: Teaching students to analyze complex texts K–5*. Alexandria, VA: ASCD.
Wulffson, T. (2000). *Toys! Amazing stories behind some great inventions*. New York: Holt. (I)

Your Turn!

The Text Annotation Planning Guide on the facing page will help you plan an informational text annotation lesson with your students. The annotation symbols and marginalia ideas can be distributed to your students and they can check off the ones you want them to use. For younger students you may only teach the first four symbols, while for older students you may use more. The marginalia examples may be combined with symbols, as in the example above.

Text Annotation Planning Guide

Instructions: Complete the Annotation Planning Guide below. You may want to copy the Annotation Symbols for Student Use so that each student can refer to it.

Text Title: _____

Lesson Standard: _____

Lesson Objective: _____

1. What annotation symbols will I teach students?

2. What will students write in the margins?

3. How will I explain/model annotation using these symbols and marginalia?

4. What will students discuss after completing their annotations?

Annotation Symbols for Student Use

- (Circle) confusing words.

- Write a *?* mark next to confusing ideas.

- Underline the main ideas.

- Draw an → to show connections between ideas.

- Write EX next to an example the author gives.

- Draw a star ★ next to words, ideas, or concepts you have learned in other classes.

- Number key ideas 1, 2, 3.

Marginalia

- *Write a comment* in the margin about an idea you found interesting.

- Paraphrase key parts of the text into your own words. Write this in the margin.

- Explain why you think a specific idea is the main idea.

- Draw a picture or diagram in the margin that helps you understand something you read.

- Explain in the margin why you thought a word or idea was confusing.

Text-Dependent Questions

GRADE LEVELS: K–12

Getting Started
Building Background
Vocabulary
Reading Closely
Comprehension
Discussion
Writing

CCSS Anchor Standards: Reading

> **CCSS.ELA-Literacy.CCRA.R.1** Read closely to determine what the text says explicitly and to make logical inferences from it; cite specific textual evidence when writing or speaking to support conclusions drawn from the text.

> **CCSS.ELA-Literacy.CCRA.R.2** Determine central ideas or themes of a text and analyze their development; summarize the key supporting details and ideas.

> **CCSS.ELA-Literacy.CCRA.R.3** Analyze how and why individuals, events, or ideas develop and interact over the course of a text.

> **CCSS.ELA-Literacy.CCRA.R.4** Interpret words and phrases as they are used in a text, including determining technical, connotative, and figurative meanings, and analyze how specific word choices shape meaning or tone.

> **CCSS.ELA-Literacy.CCRA.R.5** Analyze the structure of texts, including how specific sentences, paragraphs, and larger portions of the text (e.g., a section, chapter, scene, or stanza) relate to each other and the whole.

> **CCSS.ELA-Literacy.CCRA.R.6** Assess how point of view or purpose shapes the content and style of a text.

> **CCSS.ELA-Literacy.CCRA.R.7** Integrate and evaluate content presented in diverse media and formats, including visually and quantitatively, as well as in words.

> **CCSS.ELA-Literacy.CCRA.R.8** Delineate and evaluate the argument and specific claims in a text, including the validity of the reasoning as well as the relevance and sufficiency of the evidence.

➤ **CCSS.ELA-Literacy.CCRA.R.9** Analyze how two or more texts address similar themes or topics in order to build knowledge or to compare the approaches the authors take.

➤ **CCSS.ELA-Literacy.CCRA.R.10** Read and comprehend complex literary and informational texts independently and proficiently.

What Is It?

Text-dependent questions (TDQs) are questions that can only be answered by reading the text. When answering these questions, students should always provide evidence for their answers. TDQs are the heart of the Close Reading and Close Thinking strategies (see Strategies 16 and 17), and the success of these lessons will depend in large part on the quality of these questions. However, teachers can use TDQs during shared or guided reading experiences as well. When used with the multiple readings associated with Close Reading, TDQs for the first text reading should be literal, focusing on general understanding (what the text said) with questions like "What was this passage about?" or "What was the main idea of the text?" TDQs for the second text reading should focus on how the text works, or the text organization, or vocabulary, and author's purpose. Questions could include "How would you describe the organization of this text?" or "Why do you think the author wrote this text?" TDQs for the third reading should focus on deeper text meanings that answer the question "What does the text mean?" Sample questions might include: "Do you agree with the author's argument? Why or why not? Provide text evidence to support your answer."

As these examples illustrate, TDQs should be sequenced carefully and move from literal to inferential and evaluative comprehension.

What Is Its Purpose?

The purpose of asking TDQs with informational texts is to engage students in answering questions that promote comprehension of text that moves them from literal to inferential and evaluative text understanding. Because informational texts focus on individuals, events, ideas, and information, these questions will usually not involve discussion of characters, plot, setting, and other aspects of literary texts.

How Do I Do It?

1. Select a text that students will read. If used with Close Reading, the text should be a short, complex one. Identify areas of text complexity, and determine your lesson standards and objectives. Identify your assessments and plan your questions to prepare students to succeed on that assessment.

2. Be sure that the questions you create require that students read and identify evidence from the text. TDQs usually do not include text-to-self questions like the nonexample below.

Good example: What details did you learn about starfish from this text?

Nonexample: Have you ever seen a starfish?

3. Fisher and Frey (2015) identify six possible categories for TDQs that are illustrated in the figure below. Review the visual below, and identify questions that address each area of the text indicated on the chart, keeping in mind areas of complexity and your standards and objectives. As you construct these questions, think about their progression from basic literal comprehension (what the text says), to how the text works, to what the text means. The question samples on the facing page are just a starting point; your questions should not be generic like these examples, but

A Model for the Progression of Text-Dependent Questions

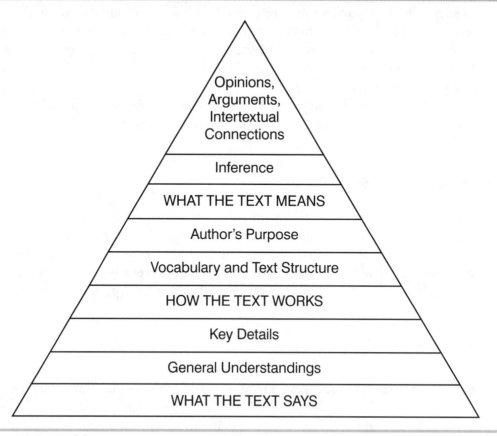

Reading Closely Strategies

should be specific to your text. You may also want to create more than one question for each category.

Questions That Address What the Text Says

- Question 1 should address **general understanding**. Questions might include:
  - What is this text mainly about?
  - How would you summarize this text?
  - What is the big idea of this text?

- Question 2 should address **main ideas/key details** about the content. Sentence stems might include:
  - What main ideas did the author want you to learn about _____?
  - What are three key details you learned about _____?
  - What are key events and details in this text?

Questions That Address How the Text Works

- Question 3 should address **text vocabulary**, **text structure**, and/or **visual supports**.
  - What words did the author use to describe _____ and why?
  - What does the word _____ in paragraph _____ mean? Why did the author choose to use this word?
  - What did you notice about how this text is organized? (see Strategy 26 for informational text structures)
  - How has the idea of _____ changed throughout the text?
  - What does the chart on page _____ mean?

- Question 4 should address the **author's purpose** for writing the text.
  - What was the author's intent in writing this text?
  - Why does the author _____?
  - Why was it important that the author discuss _____?
  - Why does the author's tone shift within this text?

Questions That Address What the Text Means

- Question 5 should address **inferences** readers make from the text.
  - Look at the text visuals (photos, maps, graphs, charts). Do they match what you think the author is telling you? Why or why not? Provide text evidence to support your answer.

- What can you infer about _____ from reading this text? What text evidence led you to this inference?
- What conclusions can you draw about _____ from reading this text?

- Question 6 should address **opinions, arguments,** and **intertextual connections.**

  - What argument does the author make in this text? What evidence does he use to support it?
  - In your opinion, what is the author's position on _____?
  - What is the author's strongest argument for _____?
  - How was the presentation of information about _____ in text one similar to or different from its presentation in text two?
  - What connections can you see between these two texts on this topic?
  - What conclusions can you draw about _____ after reading these (two or three) texts?

Example

We met teacher Svetlana Cvetkovic in our discussion of Text Complexity in Strategy 3. In that lesson we learned about how Svetlana analyzed her informational text, "Once Upon a Woodpecker," for text complexity in preparation for a Close Reading lesson with her third graders. The purpose of her lesson was to develop student understanding about animal adaptations. In her analysis she noted that the text was at grade level or below for the most part, but that students might have trouble inferring the author's point of view.

Svetlana knew that an important part of her planning for a Close Reading was the development of appropriate TDQs carefully sequenced to scaffold student learning. To complete this task, she read the text several times and carefully considered how each question would build student understanding about animal adaptations. Her TDQs are listed on the facing page.

References

Fisher, D., & Frey, N. (2015). *Common Core English language arts in a PLC at Work, grades 3–5.* Bloomington, IN: Solution Tree.

Hackett, J. K. (2011). Once upon a woodpecker. *Ranger Rick Magazine.* Reprinted in *Science: A closer look: Grade 3.* Macmillan/McGraw-Hill, pp. 170–171.

Sample Text-Dependent Questions Template

Question category	TDQ	Text evidence	Page #
	**TDQs: What the Text Says**		
1. General Understanding	What did you learn about woodpeckers from this text?	They have unique adaptations that include strong neck muscles, unique toes, a strong beak, and an extra-long barbed tongue.	170–171
2. Key Details	What is unique about the adaptation of a woodpecker's tongue?	It is long and barbed, which lets it get insects from inside a tree.	171
	**TDQs: How the Text Works**		
3. Vocabulary or Text Structure	What are shock absorbers? Why do you think the author compares the woodpecker's neck muscles with shock absorbers?	The strong neck muscles absorb the shock to the woodpecker's neck from all its hammering.	170
4. Author's Purpose	What is the author's attitude about woodpeckers?	He says they have amazing adaptations (p. 170) and are well adapted (p. 171).	170 and 171
	**TDQs: What the Text Means**		
5. Inferences	Based on what you have read, what habitat is the woodpecker best adapted for?	The text describes woodpeckers in a habitat with trees containing insects, suggesting a forest or another habitat containing trees.	170–171
6. Opinions, Arguments, Intertextual Connections	The author writes that bugs cannot hide from the well-adapted woodpecker. Is there sufficient evidence from the text to support the idea that woodpeckers are well adapted to survive in their environment?	The text provides much evidence of woodpecker adaptations including neck muscles, unique toes, a strong beak, and an extra-long barbed tongue.	170–171

Your Turn!

Now it is your turn to create TDQs for an informational text. Before you do this, be sure you read over your text a few times and complete the text complexity rubric (Strategy 3). As you complete the Text-Dependent Questions Template you will also want to identify the text evidence that provides the answers to the questions and the page numbers where that evidence appears. You may want to create multiple questions for each category.

Text-Dependent Questions Template

Instructions: Complete this template by identifying categories and text-dependent questions here (see pp. 127–128). Cite evidence for the answers.

Question category	TDQ	Text evidence	Page #
TDQs : What the Text Says			
TDQs: How the Text Works			
TDQs: What the Text Means			

Thinking Aloud

GRADE LEVELS: K–12

Getting Started
Building Background
Vocabulary
Reading Closely
Comprehension
Discussion
Writing

CCSS Anchor Standards: Reading

> **CCSS.ELA-Literacy.R.1** Read closely to determine what the text says explicitly and to make logical inferences from it; cite specific textual evidence when writing or speaking to support conclusions drawn from the text.

> **CCSS.ELA-Literacy.R.5** Analyze the structure of texts, including how specific sentences, paragraphs, and larger portions of the text relate to each other and the whole.

What Is It?

Thinking Aloud (Baumann, Jones, & Seifert-Kessell, 1993) is a way for teachers to make their thinking visible to students. By Thinking Aloud, teachers can help students hear what goes on in the mind of a skilled reader. When a teacher models Thinking Aloud for her students, students develop understanding of the kind of mental work good readers engage in as they read. Thinking Aloud demonstrates to students that reading is an active process that requires reader engagement. Thinking Aloud also helps students see how teachers can solve problems as they read, such as determining word meanings from context or figuring out sections of the text that may require extra effort. Thinking Aloud is especially appropriate for helping students to read complex texts closely. It allows teachers to demonstrate for students what Close Reading involves and provides them with the tools needed to think deeply about a complex text. Students should eventually practice Thinking Aloud themselves, so that they become proficient in using this strategy as they read increasingly complex texts.

What Do I Do?

1. Select a complex text somewhat above the reading level of most students. This can be a book, newspaper, or magazine article. For younger children, this could involve read-aloud texts.

2. Identify a section of the text you can use as a think-aloud. Consider what you want students to be able to do as a result of your Thinking Aloud.

3. Prepare a script for your think-aloud, using the Think-Aloud Prompts provided on page 134. (There is a sample script on page 135.) During your think-aloud you will want students to be able to see the text you are using to model how to make predictions, make connections, reread to check for meaning, create mental pictures of what you are reading, recognize text structures, identify areas of confusion, and so forth. You will not want to focus on all of these skills at once, but rather select a few appropriate to the text and your students' needs.

4. Project the text on the document camera. Read the text aloud to the students, Thinking Aloud as you go. Refer to your script as needed. As they listen, students can complete the Think Aloud Listening Guide found on page 137.

5. Have students discuss the kind of thinking they heard you do and what they learned about effective readers from this demonstration. As students become more experienced with this activity, they can create their own think-alouds with complex texts.

Example

Fifth-grade teacher Albert Romero was teaching his students about reptiles in science class. Since students were also studying the comparison–contrast organizational pattern for informational text (see Strategy 26) he decided that he would complete a think-aloud for his students as part of their Close Reading of a text that compared alligators and crocodiles. He began the Close Reading lesson by having students first read the text to get its overall meaning. Because he identified the text structure as one that students might find challenging, he conducted a think-aloud about the text prior to having students read it a second time. Albert's students were well acquainted with this strategy, since he used it quite frequently.

He planned for this think-aloud by reviewing the list of Think-Aloud Prompts provided on page 134.

After reviewing the think-aloud prompts, Albert created the following script. The *italicized* sentences show what he would say as he thought aloud as he demonstrated the strategy.

After preparing this script, Albert projected the text onto the document cam-

Think-Aloud Prompts

Activating Prior Knowledge

- I know some things about . . .
- That reminds me of . . .
- That fits/doesn't fit with what I know about . . .
- I predict that . . .

Identifying Text Structure

- The title/headings/graphics tell me that . . .
- I think the text is organized by . . .
- This section talked about . . . so the next one will be about . . .
- I noticed the word . . ., so this may have the _____ structure.

Unlocking Vocabulary

- I'm not sure of this word, but I see a part I know, which is . . .
- I can use the sentence to figure out this new word . . .
- I think this word means . . . I'll keep reading and check my prediction.

Monitoring Comprehension

- That doesn't make sense because . . .
- I didn't understand that part, I'd better reread.
- I still don't get it; I'm going to try . . .
- I think this means that . . .
- I pictured this in my mind as . . .
- This reminds me of . . .

Generating Questions/Commenting on Text

- I wonder . . .
- I noticed that . . .
- It's interesting that . . .

Summarizing

- So far I've read that . . .
- I think that the main points of this are . . .
- This was mostly about . . .

Sample Think-Aloud Script: Alligators and Crocodiles

It is hard to tell the difference between an alligator and a crocodile at a glance. *After reading this first sentence, I predict that this paragraph is going to list some ways that alligators and crocodiles are not the same, because the first sentence uses the word different.* Alligators and crocodiles are large amphibious reptiles. *I wonder what amphibious means. I'll keep reading and maybe I can find out.* They both live in warm parts of the world. *Hmm . . . I see the word both, which tells how they are alike. I guess they are talking now about how they are the same, but at first they said it would be about how they are different. I guess that this text is organized to first talk about similarities in the two reptiles.* Both have sharp teeth and can snap off your arm in one bite. *I see the word both again, so I guess they are still talking about how they are the same. This reminds me of a show I saw on TV about an alligator that attacked a man.*

There are a few differences in alligators and crocodiles. *OK, now they are talking about differences, so that word gives me the idea that in this section they will talk about how they are not alike, since the other section told how they were alike. What are some of the differences? I'll keep reading to find out.* Alligators have wider snouts than crocodiles. Crocodiles have a long fourth tooth on the lower jaw. *I can picture this in my mind.* Alligators and crocodiles have different habitats. Crocodiles are found near swamps, lakes, and rivers in tropical areas like Asia and South America. Alligators are only found in freshwater locations like Florida and Texas. *Yes, I've heard about alligators being on golf courses in Florida.* These are some ways crocodiles and alligators are alike and different.

So to summarize, alligators and crocodiles are alike because they are reptiles, and live in warm parts of the world and have sharp teeth. They are different because alligators have wider snouts and crocodiles have a long tooth on the bottom and live in different habitats.

era (without the italicized sentences). He explained to students that he would be Thinking Aloud about the text. He reviewed with them a variety of think-aloud strategies from the Think-Aloud Prompts list, and explained that as they listened to his think-aloud, they needed to record examples of the strategies he used on their Think-Aloud Listening Guide (page 137). As he thought aloud, using the script as a reference when needed, students recorded what they heard him say under the appropriate category. In this way, students could not only hear how he thought about the text, but also consider different strategies that could be used during think-alouds. Albert then invited students to practice with a partner, using this text to create their own think-aloud experience. At this point students were ready for their next text reading, during which they would answer text-dependent questions about the text structure, since they now knew how to approach the text because of the scaffolding Albert provided for them.

Reference

Baumann, J. F., Jones, L. A., & Seifert-Kessell, N. (1993). Using think-alouds to enhance children's comprehension monitoring abilities. *The Reading Teacher, 47,* 184–193.

Your Turn!

Select a text from the suggested list in the Appendix, one of your own choosing, or a magazine or newspaper article. Create a script for your think-aloud. Then as you complete it, involve your students in completing the Think-Aloud Listening Guide as you think aloud from a text of your choice. In addition, students can create their own think-alouds as they become more comfortable with the strategy.

Think-Aloud Listening Guide

Instructions: Listen as your teacher thinks aloud about a text. Record your notes next to the strategy used.

Strategy	Notes about when the teacher used this strategy
Making a prediction or connection	
Identifying text structure	
Unlocking vocabulary	
Monitoring comprehension by asking a question	
Monitoring comprehension by rereading or clarifying something that was confusing	
Monitoring comprehension by creating pictures in the mind	
Commenting on the text	
Summarizing	

Strategy 21

Sticky Notes Bookmark

GRADE LEVELS: K–5

Getting Started
Building Background
Vocabulary
Reading Closely
Comprehension
Discussion
Writing

CCSS Anchor Standards: Reading

➤ **CCSS.ELA-Literacy.CCRA.R.1** Read closely to determine what the text says explicitly and to make logical inferences from it; cite specific textual evidence when writing or speaking to support conclusions drawn from the text.

➤ **CCSS.ELA-Literacy.CCRA.R.2** Determine central ideas or themes of a text and analyze their development; summarize the key supporting details and ideas.

➤ **CCSS.ELA-Literacy.CCRA.R.4** Interpret words and phrases as they are used in a text, including determining technical, connotative, and figurative meanings, and analyze how specific word choices shape meaning or tone.

➤ **CCSS.ELA-Literacy.CCRA.R.7** Integrate and evaluate content presented in diverse media and formats, including visually and quantitatively, as well as in words.

➤ **CCSS.ELA-Literacy.CCRA.R.10** Read and comprehend complex literary and informational texts independently and proficiently.

What Is It?

The Sticky Notes Bookmark strategy (adapted from McLaughlin & Allen, 2002) uses sticky notes for bookmarks and is a way for young students to become active readers. The strategy focuses young students on making meaning from text by locating and writing about four specific things in the text they are reading. Sticky Note Bookmark 1, denoted with an exclamation point (!), involves student identification of the most interesting part of the book. Bookmark 2, denoted with a "V," involves student identification of a vocabulary word the class needs to discuss. Bookmark 3, denoted with a question mark (?), involves identification of something the student found confusing. Bookmark 4, denoted with a graphic of a chart, involves identification of an illustration, map, chart, or graph that helped the reader comprehend the text. Sticky Note Bookmarks can be used during one of the readings during a Close Reading or a Close Thinking lesson. They represent a form of annotation ideal for young readers.

What Is Its Purpose?

The purpose of the Sticky Notes Bookmark strategy is to help students read with specific goals in mind. By reading to locate specific information, students maintain a clear focus and identify information that is important to their understanding of the text. This strategy helps students derive understanding from what they read and moves them beyond simply identifying words to the recognition that they need to construct meaning from what they read.

What Do I Do?

1. Give each student four sticky notes. Explain to students that they will be reading to locate specific information from their text. They might use Sticky Note Bookmarks as they read or listen to a text for the first time during a Close Reading lesson.

2. Demonstrate for students how to label each sticky note. The first bookmark will be labeled with an exclamation point (!) for the most interesting part of the text. The second should be labeled with a "V" for a vocabulary word the class needs to discuss. Bookmark 3 should have a question mark (?) to remind students to identify a confusing part of the text. Bookmark 4 will have a small chart, designed to remind students to look for an illustration, map, chart, or graph that helped them understand the text.

3. Place each labeled sticky note on the blackboard. Model for students how to bookmark their texts with sticky notes by reading an informational text and Thinking Aloud about how you identified and marked an interesting part, a new vocabulary term, a confusing part, and a visual that helped you understand the text. Model how to write responses related to each item (see page 142).

4. Provide each student with a copy of an informational text excerpt if you are doing Close Reading, or a longer informational text if you are not.

5. You will not frontload if you are doing a Close Reading (Strategy 16) or Close Thinking (Strategy 17). If not, you may want to involve students in prereading activities related to their texts. These can include KWHL (Strategy 6), Anticipation Guide (Strategy 5), or Table of Contents Prediction (Strategy 8).

6. Have students read or listen to you read the text, bookmarking the text as they go and writing notes on the sticky notes. If you are reading aloud, children can come up and bookmark the text on the document camera.

7. After students have finished, have them pair together to share each of their bookmarks or discuss the bookmarks they made on the document camera.

Example

First-grade teacher Marva Allegro wanted to involve her students in reading more informational texts during independent reading. She had purchased an array of easy-to-read informational texts at appropriate levels for her students including titles from Sundance Publishing and National Geographic School Publishing.

Marva began her lesson by reviewing with students how to select "just right" informational trade books for independent reading. Once each student had identified a book, she involved them in activating their prior knowledge about the topic of the text by predicting content from the table of contents (Strategy 8). Through this activity, students gained experience in thinking about the content of the text they had selected.

Following this activity, Marva distributed four sticky notes to each student. She modeled for students how to code each sticky note bookmark. She referred the students to a chart that would remind them what each code meant.

After students had prepared their bookmarks, Marva used the book *An Egg Is Quiet* (Aston, 2006) to model how to bookmark their texts with sticky notes. She thought aloud as she read the book to them, noting when she identified parts of the book that addressed each of the sticky notes and modeling how to place the sticky notes on the appropriate places.

After she had finished modeling this process, Marva gave students the opportunity to look over the books they had selected. Students worked independently to bookmark the specified sections of the text and write responses to the questions about each text. After this, students formed teams to share with a partner the places they had bookmarked.

References

Aston, D. H. (2006). *An egg is quiet.* New York: Chronicle Books. (P)
McLaughlin, M., & Allen, M. B. (2002). *Guided comprehension: A teaching model for grades 3–8.* Newark, DE: International Reading Association.

Your Turn!

Select an informational text from the Appendix at the back of this book, or let your students select their own text. You may use Close Reading (Strategy 16) or Close Thinking (Strategy 17). Use the sample sticky notes on page 142 to help students create their own Sticky Note Bookmarks. Model for students how to bookmark text, and then let them perform the task independently.

Sticky Note Bookmarks

Instructions: Follow the instructions for each bookmark found below.

!	**V**	**?**	**[grid with zigzag line]**
Bookmark 1	Bookmark 2	Bookmark 3	Bookmark 4
Write about an interesting part of the book.	Write a new vocabulary word.	Write about a confusing part of the book.	Mark a visual (map, graph, chart, etc.) that helped understanding.

PART FIVE

Comprehension
Strategies

Strategy 22

Study Guide

GRADE LEVELS: 3–12

Getting Started
Building Background
Vocabulary
Reading Closely
Comprehension
Discussion
Writing

CCSS Anchor Standards: Reading

➤ **CCSS.ELA-Literacy.CCRA.R.1** Read closely to determine what the text says explicitly and to make logical inferences from it; cite specific textual evidence when writing or speaking to support conclusions drawn from the text.

➤ **CCSS.ELA-Literacy.CCRA.R.2** Determine central ideas or themes of a text and analyze their development; summarize the key supporting details and ideas.

➤ **CCSS.ELA-Literacy.CCRA.R.3** Analyze how and why individuals, events, or ideas develop and interact over the course of a text.

➤ **CCSS.ELA-Literacy.CCRA.R.7** Integrate and evaluate content presented in diverse media and formats, including visually and quantitatively, as well as in words.

What Is It?

A Study Guide (Herber, 1978; Vacca & Vacca, 2013) provides a way for teachers to guide students through content-related text. It helps students to distinguish important information from unimportant information and focus on content the teacher considers critical. It allows the teacher to pose questions and provide students with guidance during a reading task. Furthermore, it requires students to provide evidence for their answers, which is an important area of emphasis for the CCSS.

What Is Its Purpose?

The purpose of a Study Guide is for the teacher to support student learning by providing questions for students to answer that guide them through the text. The questions help students identify important information that is crucial to their overall understanding of the content. In addition to answering the questions, students must provide evidence for their answers.

What Do I Do?

1. Select a piece of content-related text.

2. Identify the information in the text that you consider to be most crucial to student understanding.

3. Develop a series of questions designed to guide students through the text. Be sure to include questions that require critical thinking as well as factual information. Require students to provide evidence for their answers.

4. Ask students to complete the Study Guide as they read the assigned text.

5. Discuss the students' answers to the questions on the guide after they have completed it.

Example

Tenth-grade life science teacher Tim Goodspan's students were studying reptiles. He located an interesting article entitled "Beware: Don't Tread on Me: Spring Brings Serpents out of Hibernation" (Stetz, 2002) (*http://legacy.sandiegouniontribune. com/news/metro/20020422-9999_1m22snakes.html*) from the *San Diego Union Tribune* online about the dangers posed by rattlesnakes in the spring. Tim helped the students preview the article, showing them the headings and the large graphic that accompanied the article. He first introduced the text, asking students to reflect on the meaning of the title "Beware: Don't Tread on Me." To guide his students' reading of this informative article, he presented them with a Study Guide designed to focus their learning as they made their way through the text. Tim then distributed the Study Guide, asking students to complete it as they read the article (see sample on the facing page). The students completed the guide as they read, and after they finished their reading they formed pairs. Each pair of students compared their answers, checking for accuracy. Students later used the Study Guides again as they prepared for the chapter test.

Sample Study Guide

1. Why don't snakes want to bite humans? _They don't want to use their venom or injure their fangs._

Evidence: _A senior herpetologist at San Diego Zoo said that they prefer not to waste their venom on humans or hurt their fangs._

2. Why are snakes more active in the spring? _They quit hibernating._

Evidence: _The text says they wake up in the spring and start moving around._

3. How many people die each year from snakebites? _About 12 a year._

Evidence: _The text says about 8,000 people are bitten by venomous snakes, and about 12 die annually. The visual says fewer than 15 people die each year._

4. Compare the gopher snake and the rattlesnake. _Gopher snakes have round pupils and a round head but no rattles and are harmless. Rattlesnakes have broad, flat heads, facial pits, vertical pupils and rattles and are harmful._

Evidence: _The visual shows the heads of both a rattlesnake and a gopher snake._

5. Why is it important to get to the hospital quickly if you are bitten by a snake? _Because prompt treatment prevents the venom from harming the victim._

Evidence: _The text says that the venom can stop blood from clotting so you can bleed to death._

6. How can people prevent snakebites? _Don't touch them or poke them or pick them up._

Evidence: _The text says that most bites happen when people do things to the snakes that they should not._

7. What does "Don't tread on me" mean? _It means don't walk on them._

Evidence: _The text says it comes from an old flag with the words "Don't tread on me" and a picture of a rattlesnake._

8. In what ways have rattlesnakes had to adapt to humans? _They have had to change environments because we have encroached on their space._

Evidence: _The text says their habitats have shrunk because of development and that they survive in canyons that are near housing developments._

References

Herber, H. (1978). *Teaching reading in the content areas*. Englewood Cliffs, NJ: Prentice Hall.

Stetz, M. (2002, April 22). Beware: Don't tread on me. *San Diego Union Tribune*. Retrieved July 15, 2015, from *http://legacy.sandiegouniontribune.com/news/metro/20020422-9999_1m22snakes.html*.

Vacca, R., & Vacca, J. (2013). *Content area reading* (11th ed.). New York: Pearson.

Your Turn!

Select an informational text from the Appendix at the back of this book, or of your own choosing. For middle school and high school students, you may wish to use "Beware: Don't Tread on Me" (*http://legacy.sandiegouniontribune.com/news/metro/20020422-9999_1m22snakes.html*), which can be found online. You can fill in the Study Guide template with the questions suggested on page 147, or you may wish to create your own questions.

Study Guide for _____

Instructions: Locate the answers to the questions listed below. Provide evidence for your answers.

1. _____

_____

Evidence: _____

_____

2. _____

_____

Evidence: _____

_____

3. _____

_____

Evidence: _____

_____

4. _____

_____

Evidence: _____

_____

5. _____

_____

Evidence: _____

_____

6. _____

_____

Evidence: _____

_____

7. _____

_____

Evidence: _____

_____

8. _____

_____

Evidence: _____

_____

Strategy 23

Four-Box Comment Card

GRADE LEVELS: 3–12

| Getting Started |
| Building Background |
| Vocabulary |
| Reading Closely |
| **Comprehension** |
| Discussion |
| Writing |

CCSS Anchor Standards: Reading

➤ **CCSS.ELA-Literacy.CCRA.R.1** Read closely to determine what the text says explicitly and to make logical inferences from it; cite specific textual evidence when writing or speaking to support conclusions drawn from the text.

➤ **CCSS.ELA-Literacy.CCRA.R.2** Determine central ideas or themes of a text and analyze their development; summarize the key supporting details and ideas.

➤ **CCSS.ELA-Literacy.CCRA.R.10** Read and comprehend complex literary and informational texts independently and proficiently.

What Is It?

The Four-Box Comment Card (adapted from Vacca & Vacca, 2008) is a template for guiding comprehension of informational texts. The teacher provides four thinking prompts, one for each square. Each prompt requires students to think about the text in a slightly different way. For example, the prompts that appear in each of the boxes could ask students to include one comment, one surprise, one question, or one observation. This is the most popular format for this strategy, and it is shown in the example described on page 155. To better align with the CCSS, the teacher could require students to provide textual evidence for each of the four prompts.

After having students independently complete the Four-Box Comment Card, the teacher could use this strategy as a springboard to guide small-group discussions, which could further advance students' comprehension of the text. Small groups could convene to discuss a particular text, using this template as a guide. In small-group discussions, students have the opportunity to practice consensus-building skills in addition to other important discussion skills, such as turn taking, respectfully disagreeing, and so on. A recorder writes down the group's responses and a reporter shares the responses with the whole class. Instead of small groups, this template can also be used to solicit individual responses; in this way, this strategy can also be used as an assessment.

Furthermore, this strategy is easily adaptable to most grade and ability levels and all content areas. The prompts can be changed for various purposes and populations. For example, for secondary students, we suggest employing prompts that address critical literacy. Essential questions like the following from Morgan (1997) can help teachers elicit critical thinking from their students:

- Box 1: Who constructs the texts whose representations are dominant in a particular culture at a particular time?

- Box 2: How do readers become complicit with the persuasive ideologies of texts?

- Box 3: Whose interests are served by such representations and readings?

- Box 4: How can readers reconstruct inequitable texts and readings?

These particular Four-Box Comment Card prompts will require a whole-class discussion with teacher scaffolding in order to maximize effectiveness. The chart on page 152 clarifies Morgan's (1997) prompts in more detail. For teachers new to implementing critical literacy, we suggest applying these prompts to a visual advertisement and then moving on to informational texts. One of the samples on page 157 shows how we adapted these questions for the Four-Box Comment Card strategy. The samples give more examples of prompts to suit a variety of levels and purposes.

What Is Its Purpose?

The Four-Box Comment Card is an easy strategy to implement, requiring very little preparation, but when used correctly, this strategy will yield great results. As a result of this strategy, students learn how to critically think about a text and are exposed to multiple perspectives about it. By completing a Four-Box Comment Card, students are positioned to think about the text's message and/or methods; thus students deepen their comprehension. In addition, the strategy can be used to guide small-group discussions; as such, the purpose of the Four-Box Comment Card is to encourage students to take a position on a text, aligning with the tenets of the CCSS and critical literacy. Critical literacy encourages readers to not passively accept the status quo, but to examine the underlying dynamics at play and to assume one of three stances toward the text:

Critical Literacy Prompts

Prompt	Explanation and suggested prompts
1. Who constructs the texts whose representations are dominant in a particular culture at a particular time?	Have students consider the author's perspective, the author's position, and the author's message. Have students consider funding sources, research institutions, and so on. *Suggested prompts:* Does the author present a dominant viewpoint that is accepted by the mainstream? If so, why? Who is the author and what is his/her political, cultural, and personal background and beliefs? How does the author's point of view present itself in the text? Explain your reasoning with evidence from the text.
2. How do readers become complicit with the persuasive ideologies of texts?	Have students consider their own positions or opinions in regard to the text's message(s). Have them think about how the author is persuading them as readers. Have them consider the author's methods such as rhetorical or literary devices. *Suggested prompts:* What are the messages the author wants his/her readers to accept? How is the author attempting to appeal to the readers? How effective is the author in conveying his/her message? Do you, as the reader, agree or disagree with the author? Explain your reasoning with evidence from the text.
3. Whose interests are served by such representations and readings?	Have students consider the targeted audiences. Have students consider who's benefiting from the author's message. *Suggested prompts:* Who is the author trying to persuade and why? Who is the author serving? Whose interests are served by this text? How so? Explain your reasoning with evidence from the text.
4. How can readers reconstruct inequitable texts and readings?	Have students reconsider whether they agree with the message and how they would change the meaning or desired outcomes of this text to fit their own system of beliefs. This prompt asks students to think about personal agency and social action. *Suggested prompts:* If you were the author of this text, what would you delete? What new information and/or perspectives would you add? How could you make the text more balanced? How would you change the desired outcome or meaning of this text? Explain your reasoning with evidence from the text.

- Stance 1: This is the dominant stance, in which the reader accepts the message.
- Stance 2: This is the negotiated stance, in which the reader disputes a particular claim but accepts the overall message.
- Stance 3: This is the oppositional stance, in which the reader rejects the message (Apple, 1992).

Through the Four-Box Comment Card, students are introduced to multiple perspectives and are encouraged to not passively rely on authoritative interpretations. Most important, students are asked to think critically and to express and explain their opinions.

What Do I Do?

1. Select an informational text that is slightly controversial and/or has potential for dissenting viewpoints. For example, a text about tree frogs would not be effective; however, a text about the effects of deforestation on the habitats of tree frogs would be.

2. Select which prompts you would like to use and display these prompts so that all students can refer to them. Read the prompts to students and make sure they understand them. Consider the levels of your students, their prior knowledge, and the text you are using. Some samples provided in this section can be employed for all texts; some, like the critical literacy prompts, require particular texts. We suggest completing the Four-Box Comment Card yourself before disseminating to your students.

3. Have students read the text prior to implementing this strategy. (You can have students independently read the text for homework, or you can read the text aloud.)

4. Have students fold a piece of paper vertically and then horizontally to create four boxes. Have students copy the prompts into each box.

5. Have students independently respond to each prompt. Remind them to explain their thinking with evidence from the text.

6. Give students the opportunity to discuss their thinking in small groups of four to six members. Have each group select a reporter and a recorder. (You could also have each group select other roles: timekeeper, facilitator, and so on.)

7. Give each group 10–15 minutes to discuss the prompts. Recorders can keep notes on key points of the discussions. (You might want to establish norms for the discussion prior to this.)

8. Have each group reach a consensus about each prompt. Recorders can summarize the group's position on each prompt.

9. Have the reporter from each group share with the whole class. (*Optional:* Reporters can project their group's Four-Box Comment Card so that everyone can follow along.)

10. *Optional:* Record students' responses on a master Four-Box Comment Card template and compile the results to create a class opinion. This would further build students' skills of negotiating opinions and arriving at a consensus.

Example

Eleventh-grade American history teacher Felix Fortmann complains of having too many texts that need to be read in a short amount of time. He acknowledges that he does not have enough time in the school year to carefully go over all the texts that he requires his students to read. (Most of the texts are informational.) As a result, he uses the Four-Box Comment Card as a way to provide his students with an opportunity to deconstruct the text in a limited time.

During a unit on World War II that focused on Executive Order 9066 (Roosevelt, 1942), which required Japanese Americans to be interned, he assigned his students to read Ellen Levine's (1995) *A Fence Away from Freedom*, which consists of oral histories of Japanese American interns combined with Levine's commentaries and historical analyses. Felix wanted the students to understand more fully the personal experiences of Japanese Americans during the war in order to build personal connections. The essential question for the unit was "How does war affect people?" Prior to this reading assignment, Felix reviewed primary source documents such as Executive Order 9066 and Roosevelt's "Day of Infamy" speech in response to the attack on Pearl Harbor that marked the official entrance of the United States into World War II. He assigned the Levine book for homework.

When the students came into class the next day, Felix knew that he only had about 20 minutes to devote to this text. The Four-Box Comment Card strategy provided a creative way of allowing the students to have critical discussions where their voices were heard while maximizing class time.

Felix counted off his students and placed them into five groups. He had index cards with roles labeled on them. The students chose a card and were assigned to one of the following roles:

1. The recorder, who would be responsible for writing the group's answers to the prompts.

2. The reporter, who would be responsible for sharing the group's thoughts with the whole class.

3. The timekeeper, who would be responsible for managing time.

4. The facilitator, who would be responsible for asking the prompts and keeping everyone on track.

5. The fact checker, who would be responsible for referring to the text to find or confirm details.

6. The mediator, who would be responsible for making sure group members are respectful.

Then, Felix projected a blank copy of the Four-Box Comment Card and had the recorder write down the prompts (see sample below for his prompts and for sample student responses). He set a timer for 10 minutes and walked around as groups discussed their prompts and came to a consensus for each prompt, which the recorder was to write down and the reporter was to share with the whole class. Felix monitored and interjected as needed. A sample of one group's Four-Box Comment Card is provided below.

Optional: Have students provide textual evidence for each of their responses.

After 8 minutes, Felix called on the timekeepers to move their groups along. After 10 minutes, he gave each group's reporter 2 minutes to present to the entire group, projecting their Four-Box Comment Card. (The timekeeper is responsible for signaling to reporters when their 2 minutes are up.)

After all the groups shared, Felix gave each student another opportunity to voice his or her opinion via a 5-minute quick-write. His prompts were: (1) What is

Sample Four-Box Comment Card

One comment:	One surprise:
All these stories are so sad! They clearly show how racist Americans were even before Pearl Harbor, which was just an excuse.	Many Japanese Americans remained loyal to the United States, even volunteering for the all-Nisei 442nd Regimental Combat Team. (We wouldn't do that if we were forced to live in concentration camps for no reason.) Why weren't they angry and resentful?
One question:	**One observation:**
Why didn't Americans protest this? We want to know more about the Japanese Peruvians who were brought to the U.S. camps.	The U.S. government forced more than 110,000 Japanese Americans from their homes along the West Coast and made them live in "relocation camps," which are like the Nazi concentration camps. These camps were poorly constructed.

your opinion of the Japanese internment experience as a result of reading the text? and (2) How did the group discussions influence your opinion? Felix collected the quick writes and the templates and used them to assess student understanding of the material.

References

Apple, M. W. (1992). The text and cultural politics. *Educational Researcher, 21*(7), 4–11, 19.

Levine, E. (1995). *A fence away from freedom.* New York: Putnam Juvenile. (M)

Morgan, W. (1997). *Critical literacy in the classroom: The art of the possible.* New York: Routledge.

Roosevelt, F. (1942, February 19). *Executive order 9066.* Washington, DC: U.S. National Archives and Records Administration.

Vacca, R. T., & Vacca, J. L. (2008). *Content area reading: Literacy and learning across the curriculum* (9th ed.). Boston: Allyn & Bacon.

Your Turn!

Select an informational trade book from the Appendix at the back of this book or one of your own choosing. Make sure you use a text and topic with potential for a good discussion. Choose a Four-Box Comment Card from the samples provided on the facing page or create your own. When creating your own prompts, consider the level of your students and their prior knowledge in designing the four prompts.

Possible Templates for Four-Box Comment Cards

Instructions: Read the text. Then complete each box. Provide evidence from the text to support your thinking.

One comment:	One surprise:	I like . . .	I did not like . . .
Evidence from the text:	Evidence from the text:	Evidence from the text:	Evidence from the text:
One question:	One observation:	I wonder . . .	I would change . . .
Evidence from the text:	Evidence from the text:	Evidence from the text:	Evidence from the text:
1. Who is the author? How does his or her point of view show in the text? Evidence from the text:	2. What are the messages the author wants you to accept? Do you agree or disagree with the author? Evidence from the text:	I agree with: Evidence from the text:	I agree with reservations: Evidence from the text:
3. Whose interests are served by this text? Who benefits? How? Evidence from the text:	4. How would you change the desired outcome or meaning of this text? Evidence from the text:	I disagree with: Evidence from the text:	I need more information: OR I would like to further explore: Evidence from the text:

Strategy 24

I-Chart

GRADE LEVELS: 3–12

Getting Started
Building Background
Vocabulary
Reading Closely
Comprehension
Discussion
Writing

CCSS Anchor Standards: Reading

> **CCSS.ELA-Literacy.CCRA.R.1** Read closely to determine what the text says explicitly and to make logical inferences from it; cite specific textual evidence when writing or speaking to support conclusions drawn from the text.

> **CCSS.ELA-Literacy.CCRA.R.2** Determine central ideas or themes of a text and analyze their development; summarize the key supporting details and ideas.

> **CCSS.ELA-Literacy.CCRA.R.9** Analyze how two or more texts address similar themes or topics in order to build knowledge or to compare the approaches the authors take.

> **CCSS.ELA-Literacy.CCRA.R.10** Read and comprehend complex literary and informational texts independently and proficiently.

What Is It?

I-Charts, or Inquiry Charts (Hoffman, 1992), help students ascertain and organize information from multiple sources. The chart itself is a visual representation of data from various texts. The chart is based on inquiry, meaning that the I-Chart is designed around several questions that encourage students to think and investigate. As such, the key to this strategy is developing effective questions.

These questions should be text based; they should "elicit students' evidence-based reasoning skills" (Loh-Hagan & Bickel, 2014). Loh-Hagan and Bickel (2014) provide the following criteria for developing effective text-based questions:

Questions should:

- Be open ended
- Make students do the work
- Require students to look for textual evidence
- Push for higher-level thinking such as interpretation, analysis, synthesis, and evaluation

When first implementing this strategy, teachers should pose the questions as a model, but it is recommended that teachers allow students to generate their own questions as well. Doing so will help students become better researchers and critical thinkers.

What Is Its Purpose?

The purpose of I-Charts is to help students critically organize and analyze the information they obtain from texts. Students work within and across multiple texts. They are encouraged to closely read and annotate texts with inquiry questions in mind. They work on their ability to extract important details from texts and summarizing skills. They are given models of effective research questions and opportunities to practice generating these questions. In this way, they build on previous learning.

The chart can be used as a springboard for further discussion. It can also be used as notes for a written task. In addition to increasing students' comprehension of texts and deepening students' knowledge of a topic, the I-Chart is also an effective study skill strategy. Teachers can also use I-Charts as an evaluation tool for determining how much students have learned about a topic. In addition, teachers will be able to determine how well students comprehend texts.

What Do I Do?

1. Select a topic and develop a set of questions. Make sure the topic offers a little bit of controversy so that there are varied responses to the questions. Make sure the questions are interesting and robust. *Optional:* After giving several models and/or practice opportunities with this strategy, have students develop their own questions.

2. Select several texts related to the same topic for students to read. These text sets can include but are not limited to books, newspaper articles, media sources, blogs, or magazine articles and should address the topic from different perspectives. *Optional:* Have students select their own texts.

3. Provide students with a template of a blank I-Chart. This chart should have one column for each question, a row for students' prior knowledge relevant to the questions, additional rows equal to the number of sources used, and a final row for summarizing main ideas.

4. Have students use their prior knowledge to answer each question prior to reading the text set. Have them record their responses in the first row.

5. Have students read each text. Encourage them to annotate the text, making special notations of the answers to the I-Chart questions.

6. Have students summarize key ideas from each text by responding to the questions in the I-Chart. Then have them record responses in the relevant rows.

7. Have students summarize the key points of each column, analyzing consistencies and differences among the multiple data sources, and respond to each question based on their understanding of the multiple sources.

8. *Optional:* Facilitate a whole-class discussion in which students discuss competing ideas and reliability and validity of the different sources. Have students discuss the differences between what they knew and what they learned.

Example

Kathleen Brewer teaches 12th-grade government courses; the majority of her students are English learners. She has used the I-Chart strategy several times and found it to be successful with her students. She has modeled the strategy and given students several opportunities to practice the strategy. She has not, however, had the students generate their own questions. As students will be writing their senior research papers, Kathleen wants to prepare them to be better researchers. More specifically, she wants to help them develop effective research plans and thesis statements.

Kathleen spent one class period working on generating effective research questions. She showed examples, discussed the criteria of effective questions, and had students practice writing questions. She then had them review each other's work.

Kathleen designed a unit about women in politics. As a culminating project, she wanted her students to write a paper about a significant woman and how she shaped politics. She required students to use primary sources, which includes memoirs, autobiographies, and speeches. The project consisted of the following timeline: (1) Choose texts and create questions for I-Chart, (2) submit I-Chart, (3) generate a thesis statement, (4) write a four- to five-page research paper including citations, and (5) revise as necessary and submit a final copy. Students were allowed to work at their own pace. Kathleen checked their work at each stage before allowing them to move on to the next stage.

On the facing page is a student sample of the I-Chart. After students selected their topics, Kathleen directed them to select texts and generate questions. She did not want them to move on to reading and researching until she checked their

Sample I-Chart for "Women in Politics" Research Project

	Question 1: What is Malala's political agenda? What does she want others to do?	Question 2: How does Malala present her message?	Question 3: What are Malala's obstacles and how does she overcome them?	Notes:
Prior Knowledge	None	None	None	
Source 1: *Nobel Lecture (Malala Yousafzai, 2014)*	• She wants equal rights for women worldwide and world peace. • She wants children and world leaders to fight for these goals.	A speech	• She was shot. • Few rights for women in Pakistan • She speaks out.	Mentions other Nobel Prize winners like MLK
Source 2: *"Diary of a Pakistani Schoolgirl"* (Malala Yousafzai, BBC Blogs)	She wants the world to know what the Taliban are doing.	She kept a diary (blog) of the events that happened when the Taliban forbade girls from going to school.	She keeps on going to school in spite of the edict.	
Source 3: <u>I Am Malala: The Story of the Girl Who Stood Up for Education and Was Shot by the Taliban</u>, Chapter 1 (Malala Yousafzai & Christina Lamb, 2013)	She wants females to be empowered and wants the world to stand up against injustice.	She describes her life, her challenges, her culture, and the extremists in Pakistan in a book.	• She was shot. • The Taliban tried to prevent education for girls. • She spoke out for justice locally and globally.	Role of her parents in nurturing her dream
Summary	Her message is consistent across sources.	She uses a diary (blog), a speech, and a book to promote her beliefs.	She has faced terrible obstacles.	

I-Charts. She wanted to make sure her students were on the right track before proceeding to the next step.

After checking their I-Charts, Kathleen allowed her students to pursue their reading and research. By having students complete the I-Chart, students practiced generating questions and researching. The summarizing and analyzing across sources helped students develop a thesis statement. Kathleen told students that each column could possibly become notes for a section of their research paper. She encouraged them to keep neat and careful notes and to make sure that they cited their work. Kathleen thought the I-Chart was a great way to prepare them for college.

References

Hoffman, J. (1992). Critical reading/thinking across the curriculum: Using I-charts to support learning. *Language Arts, 69*(2), 121–127.

Loh-Hagan, V. & Bickel, D. (2014). Text-based questioning to support student attainment of the CCSS. *The California Reader, 48*(1), 20–28.

Yousafzai, M. (2009). Diary of a Pakistani schoolgirl. [BBC Blogs]. Retrieved January 15, 2016, from *http://news.bbc.co.uk/2/hi/south_asia/7834402.stm.*

Yousafzai, M. (2013, December). *Nobel Peace Prize 2014.* Speech presented at Nobel Peace Prize Ceremony, Oslo, Norway.

Yousafzai, M. & Lamb, C. (2015). *I am Malala: The girl who stood up for education and was shot by the Taliban.* New York: Little, Brown. (YA)

Your Turn!

Select an informational text from the Appendix in the back of this book or one of your own choosing. Make sure you design the strategy around interesting topics and questions. Involve your students in completing the I-Chart. Remember that you can add or subtract columns for more or fewer questions. Some other options are "Other Interesting Facts" and/or "New Questions."

I-Chart

Instructions: Write questions in the top row of each column. Answer the first row using your prior knowledge. Write title of sources in the left column. Read each source, answer the questions, and record what you learned in the box. Add notes in the last column. In the last row, summarize all your learning from your prior knowledge and sources. Record all responses in the boxes.

	Question 1	Question 2	Question 3	Notes
Prior Knowledge: How would I answer this question, given what I already know?				
Source 1: What did I learn from this first source?				

(continued)

Source 2: What did I learn from this second source?			
Source 3: What did I learn from this third source?			
Summary: What did I learn from all three sources?			

Strategy 25

CAATS

GRADE LEVELS: 4–12

Getting Started
Building Background
Vocabulary
Reading Closely
Comprehension
Discussion
Writing

CCSS Anchor Standards: Reading

➤ **CCSS.ELA-Literacy.CCRA.R.1** Read closely to determine what the text says explicitly and to make logical inferences from it; cite specific textual evidence when writing or speaking to support conclusions drawn from the text.

➤ **CCSS.ELA-Literacy.CCRA.R.6** Assess how point of view or purpose shapes the content and style of a text.

➤ **CCSS.ELA-Literacy.CCRA.R.7** Integrate and evaluate content presented in diverse media and formats, including visually and quantitatively, as well as in words.

➤ **CCSS.ELA-Literacy.CCRA.R.10** Read and comprehend complex literary and informational texts independently and proficiently.

What Is It?

CAATS is an acronym that stands for Creator, Assumptions, Audience/User, Time and Place, and Significance. This strategy encourages students to examine these elements of a text. It's founded upon media literacy principles, which emphasize ideological factors related to the relationships of texts, readers, and power (Kellner & Share, 2007). CAATS encourages students to examine the implicit and explicit messages of texts (including books, videos, photographs, etc.). Students are encouraged to investigate the contexts and values in which texts are created. Students are also encouraged to investigate the purposes for which texts are created.

An overview of the CAATS strategy is provided in the chart on page 166 (Loh-Hagan, 2014).

Overview of the CAATS Strategy

Creator	Who created this text? What do we know about the person(s) who created it? Why did the creator create this text? How did it influence his/her life at the time it was created?
Assumptions	What do you think you know about the context of this text? What assumptions does the creator make about his/her readers? What does the creator think about the content? What things were assumed during this time period? What were people's beliefs systems?
Audience/User	Who was the audience for this text when it was originally created? Whom does the text speak to today? How do readers respond to this text? What are readers supposed to do with this text?
Time and Place	When and where was this text created? What type of circumstances influenced the creation of this text?
Significance	Why is this text important? How has this text affected history, society, and politics?

What Is Its Purpose?

The purpose of the CAATS strategy is to critically analyze texts by examining contexts and implicit and explicit messages. According to Leu and Zawilinski (2007), such critical analysis during reading is more relevant now than ever as new technologies have increased access to unfiltered information. The CAATS strategy provides students with a tool to both screen and evaluate content.

Teachers are encouraged to push students to investigate issues of power and privilege by deconstructing texts. The CCSS asks students to think not only about what they are learning, but also about how they are learning it. The CAATS strategy pushes students to think beyond the notion that texts are "fixed"—that they are straightforward and have one explicit meaning. The CAATS strategy empowers students to research the various contexts of texts by examining content and construction. Students need to situate texts in time and place. To that end, teachers must provide students with the historical, social, and political contexts pertinent to the text. Students will greatly benefit from studying texts from various and multiple perspectives and/or lenses (Appleman, 2010).

What Do I Do?

1. Select a text. The CAATS strategy can be used for many different texts, including advertisements, but the best texts for the CAATS strategy are primary source documents and photographs/art.

2. Have students read the text. Make sure students can comprehend its main ideas.

3. Review each element of the CAATS strategy. Consider projecting the overview of the CAATS strategy. Make sure students understand each task. *Optional:* Model the use of this strategy on several texts before letting students implement it independently.

4. Provide students with a copy of the CAATS strategy.

5. Have students investigate each element. Allow them to use the Internet and/or other data sources. Make sure students record their findings and provide evidence for their thinking. *Optional:* Have students work in pairs and/or small groups. Provide prompts as needed.

6. Tell students they may also record any questions or notes in the last column.

7. As a whole group, collect students' findings. Record responses on a master template.

8. Facilitate a whole-class discussion about their new understandings of the text given more knowledge about its contexts and construction.

Example

Monika Foster is teaching a seventh-grade humanities unit about the U.S. Constitution. Her students memorized the Preamble for a school play and read textbook entries about it. They're able to answer questions such as: "Who wrote it? When and where was it written? Why was it written?" However, Monika realized that her students didn't really grapple with the text's content. They couldn't answer higher-order thinking questions like: "What is the historical significance of the Constitution given the time period? How did the document reflect the social and political thinking of the time? How is the document relevant to me today?" Monika wanted her students to understand that the Constitution is a relevant document today; she felt her students saw the Constitution as a decontextualized and archaic text.

For homework, she required students to complete Annenberg Learner's module, "The Constitution: Fixed or Flexible?" (*www.learner.org/courses/democracyin-america/dia_2/index.html*). In this module, students studied the document as a "living" entity. They examined their own role in perpetuating the principles set forth in the Constitution.

In class, she had students read a news article titled, "Founding Fathers Framed Today's Budget Battles, In a Sense" (McClatchy Washington, 2013) from *www.newsela.com*. (This site is a wonderful resource that allows teachers to access current news articles at different lexile levels.) During two class periods, Monika required her students to use the CAATS strategy in order to understand the McClatchy Washington (2013) article more deeply. She wanted her students to know that they could also use this strategy on a current document, not just historical documents. She had students work in triads and reserved time in the library/media center. Students were given access to the Internet and references. She provided assistance and prompting as necessary. On page 169 is an excerpt from a student example of the CAATS strategy. Remember these are the students' rough notes—the point is for students to stop and think about documents and texts as they read.

As evidenced by this sample, the student may not have fully understood the text, but the student is learning that the text is more than just its words. Monika understands that having students walk away from a text with more questions than answers is not necessarily a bad thing. The CAATS strategy gives students a road-map for further inquiry.

During the third class period, Monika created charts for each of the elements. She asked students to share their findings and recorded their responses on each chart. She guided them to think about how the news article related to what they previously learned about the U.S. Constitution. Monika helped students go beyond "what is this document" to also examine "why this document" and "how this document." As such, students were better positioned to understand their own roles and responsibilities. As a result of the CAATS strategy, students learned that the Constitution is a product of its people and that it is perpetuated by the people.

For some students, this text was a challenge to read; historical documents such as the Constitution are written in archaic language. By studying the "story" or context of the texts, Monika helped students better understand them.

References

Annenberg Learner. Democracy in America: The Constitution: Fixed or flexible? Retrieved October 10, 2015, from *www.learner.org/courses/democracyinamerica/dia_2/index.html*.

Appleman, D. (2010). *Critical encounters in high school English: Teaching literary theory to adolescents* (2nd ed.). New York: Teachers College Press.

Kellner, D., & Share, J. (2007). Critical media literacy is not an option. *Learning Inquiry*, *1*(1), 59–69.

Leu, D. J., & Zawilinski, L. (2007). The new literacies of online reading comprehension. *The New England Reading Association Journal*, *43*(1), 1–7.

Loh-Hagan, V. (2014). How to teach historical documents. Annenberg Learner. Retrieved October 10, 2015, from *http://learnerlog.org/socialstudies/how-to-teach-historical-documents*.

McClatchy Washington. (2013). Founding fathers framed today's budget battles, in a sense. Retrieved October 10, 2015, from *https://newsela.com/articles/politics-debtlimit/id/1372*.

Your Turn!

Select an informational text from the suggested list in the Appendix at the back of this book or one of your own choosing. Make sure to provide students with access to the Internet and/or other means to collect information. Consider having students work in groups to complete their investigations using the CAATS strategy. Provide and adjust prompts as necessary to support your assigned text.

Sample CAATS Template

	Prompts	Answers	Evidence	Questions/Notes
Creator	Who created this text? Why did the creator create this text?	McClatchy Washington is listed as the creator. This is not a person. McClatchy is a company. Washington must refer to the specific office in D.C. The creator seems to want readers to understand the weird relationship between Congress and the President as set forth by Articles 1 and 2.	The creator is noted in the byline. According to their website, McClatchy is a company that is "a leading newspaper and Internet publisher." Wikipedia says it operates 30 daily newspapers in 15 states. The opening line of the article has evidence of tone and suggests the creator's agenda.	Why is the text attributed to a company rather than a person? This could mean that the company's reputation is more important than an individual. It also means a lot of people read the article because it circulated in many newspapers owned by the company.
Assumptions	What assumptions does the creator make about his/her readers?	The creator assumes readers know about the debt ceiling issues and about the issues between Congress and President Obama. The creator also assumes readers know about Articles 1 and 2 of the U.S. Constitution.	Throughout the article, the creator provides really brief explanations of things like the Articles.	Readers also might need a basic review of economic principles. The debt stuff was a little confusing.

	Prompts	Answers	Evidence	Questions/Notes
Audience/ User	Who was the audience for this text when it was originally created? Whom does the text speak to today?	In 2013, the audience is U.S. citizens. The article seems to be critical of President Obama. Today, the article speaks to the same audience— but it would be interesting to compare numbers after Obama's presidency.	See the last two sentences of the first section and the last three paragraphs of the article.	Ask Ms. Foster about the tone and intention of these lines.
Time and Place	When and where was this text created? What type of circumstances influenced the creation of this text?	October 6, 2013—This article was written around the time of an "Occupation of Washington" march.	The text provides the date of article in a byline. Also, the photo and caption provides some context of setting. The caption reads, "Many citizens are tired of all the political fighting and angry over the partial shutdown."	Research the government shutdown of 2013. This seems to be important context for understanding the politics of the text.
Significance	Why is this text important?	This text shows that U.S. citizens are still trying to interpret the Constitution years later.	Quotation to think about: "Congress passes legislation to spend, but it's the president who must ensure those bills get paid. Those two objectives don't neatly line up."	The first sentence seems to be critical of Congress but other sentences seem to be critical of President Obama. Ask class about this.

CAATS Template

Instructions: Read the assigned text. Investigate the following elements. Record responses on this chart. Provide evidence for your thinking.

	Prompts	Answers	Evidence	Questions/Notes
Creator	Who created this text? Why did the creator create this text?			
Assumptions	What assumptions does the creator make about his/her readers?			

(continued)

From 40 *Strategies for Guiding Readers through Informational Texts* by Barbara Moss and Virginia Loh-Hagan. Copyright © 2016 The Guilford Press. Permission to photocopy this form is granted to purchasers of this book for personal use or use with individual students (see copyright page for details). Purchasers can download additional copies of this material (see the box at the end of the table of contents).

Audience/ User	Who was the audience for this text when it was originally created? Whom does the text speak to today?		
Time and Place	When and where was this text created? What type of circumstances influenced the creation of this text?		
Significance	Why is this text important?		

Strategy 26

Text Structures

GRADE LEVELS: K–12

Getting Started
Building Background
Vocabulary
Reading Closely
Comprehension
Discussion
Writing

CCSS Anchor Standards: Reading

➤ **CCSS.ELA-Literacy.CCRA.R.1** Read closely to determine what the text says explicitly and to make logical inferences from it; cite specific textual evidence when writing or speaking to support conclusions drawn from the text.

➤ **CCSS.ELA-Literacy.CCRA.R.2** Determine central ideas or themes of a text and analyze their development; summarize the key supporting details and ideas.

➤ **CCSS.ELA-Literacy.CCRA.R.5** Analyze the structure of texts, including how specific sentences, paragraphs, and larger portions of the text (e.g., a section, chapter, scene, or stanza) relate to each other and the whole.

➤ **CCSS.ELA-Literacy.CCRA.R.10** Read and comprehend complex literary and informational texts independently and proficiently.

What Is It?

Graphic organizers are effective tools for helping students visually organize their thinking. Graphic organizers make abstract concepts more concrete. In teaching students to read informational texts, it is beneficial to use graphic organizers to teach text structures (Moss, 2008). Text structures or patterns of organization (Langan, 2014) refer to how information in a text is organized. Authors of informational texts organize their thinking in a certain way to present their content. Teaching students to recognize these text structures helps them find relevant information and helps them monitor their comprehension (Dymock, 2005).

173

The chart below gives an overview of the most common text structures found in informational texts.

What Is Its Purpose?

Graphic organizers help students identify and analyze text structures. They focus students not only on identifying text structures, but also on recording them in a

Overview of Common Text Structures in Informational Texts

Text Structure	Description
Description	This text structure consists of main ideas and supporting details. Essentially, a topic is identified in the main idea and described in supporting details. Authors give readers a mental picture of the topic.
Sequence/Order	This text structure is one of the most common of all informational text patterns and one of the easiest to teach. Authors often use sequential order to chronologically organize facts, events, or concepts. The sequence pattern is also used to provide directions for making or doing something. Signal words like *first, second, third, then, next, last, before, after,* and *finally* indicate the order of events. It is easy for readers to grasp this pattern because they are familiar with this structure as it appears in narrative.
Compare–Contrast	This text structure involves readers in the process of comparing and contrasting. Readers are looking for similarities and differences. In some cases, readers are also pushed to evaluate one concept versus another. Signal words like *alike, different from,* and *on the other hand* are often used to alert readers to this text structure.
Cause–Effect	The cause–effect text structure introduces a description of events and their causes. This structure focuses on the causal relationships between an event, idea, or concept, and the events, ideas, or concepts that follow. Words like *if, so, so that, because of, as a result of, since, in order to,* and *cause and effect* cue readers to the presence of this structure. Readers often encounter cause and effect in science and social studies.
Problem–Solution	The problem–solution text structure is common in content-area material. In this text structure, authors generally present a problem and then explain solutions as well as the effects of the solutions. This text structure is signaled by words like *because, cause, since, as a result, so,* and *so that.*

Overview of Graphic Organizers

Graphic Organizer	Purpose
Cluster Map	A Cluster Map helps students understand the text structure of description. Students place the main idea or topic in the center circle, then indicate supporting details or descriptions in the smaller circles connected to the center circle.
Series of Events Chart	A Series of Events Chart helps students reflect on a sequence of events or steps in a process by recording these events in order on a graphic organizer. Like a timeline, a Series of Events Chart helps students focus on the sequencing of a text.
Venn Diagram	A Venn Diagram focuses student thinking on the comparison and contrast of ideas as a text structure. It provides a visual representation of information provided in a comparison–contrast text. A Venn Diagram is a visual composed of two overlapping circles, often used in the study of mathematics. It illustrates similarities and differences between concepts, ideas, events, or people. Differences are listed on each of the circles; similarities are indicated on the overlapping area of the two circles.
Cause–Effect Map	A Cause–Effect Map encourages students to analyze texts for causes and effects. Students identify causes in one box and then draw arrows to other boxes that indicate effects. In this way, students can see causal relationships.
Problem–Solution Outline	A Problem–Solution Outline is a visual organizer that focuses attention on passages that present a problem and a potential solution or solutions. Students complete the template and record information. This outline helps students focus on and record the nature of the problem and why it was a problem. It then requires students to consider attempted solutions to the problem, outcomes, and the end result.

way that helps them see the structure in action. The ability to comprehend different text structures is important; those students who can identify text structures are more able to comprehend informational texts than those who cannot. In addition, students can write paragraphs using these graphic organizers as a writing tool (Strategy 35). As such, this strategy helps students with both reading comprehension and writing.

The chart above gives an overview of the purpose of graphic organizers that are designed to help students understand text structures.

What Do I Do?

1. When explicitly teaching text structures, focus on one at a time. (The idea is to have students be able to independently recognize text structures.)

2. Select an informational text that reflects a specific text structure. (Keep in mind that some texts may have more than one text structure, but most texts have a dominant text structure.)

3. Discuss the specific text structure. For example, if you are focusing on sequencing, define it and explain how we use sequencing in everyday life—when we get up in the morning, we follow a particular sequence as we get ready to face the day. Make sure students understand what the text structure is.

4. Project the text. Read the text aloud, thinking aloud as you point out signal words and other clues that indicate text structure.

5. Present students with the graphic organizer and show them how to complete the chart.

6. Present students with a new text. Ask students to read the text carefully to note the text structure. Have them mark signal words.

7. After they have closely read the text, ask students to work in small groups to complete the graphic organizer.

Example

Joy Rawlins is a fifth-grade teacher who is teaching a unit on mitosis. Using a section of the science textbook that outlined this process, she created a lesson plan to make students aware of the sequence of events that occurs during mitosis. She began the lesson by asking students to consider how cell division might occur. She recorded their responses on the board. She then showed students an example of a sequentially organized paragraph using signal words like *first*, *second*, *then*, *after*, and so on. She encouraged students to look for these signal words to guide them through the passage in the textbook detailing the stages in the process of mitosis. At this point she distributed copies of a Series of Events Chart. Students read the passage silently and recorded key events in order on the chart (see the facing page).

Following completion of the Series of Events Chart, Joy divided her class into small groups of four. She had each team compare answers and then share their answers with the entire group. Finally, students wrote about the questions they still had about the process in their learning logs.

Sample Series of Events Chart

Initiating Event

Stage 1—Interphase

Chromosomes are dispersed in the nucleus and appear as thin threads or filaments, called chromatin.

↓

Event 2

Stage 2—Prophase

The two chromatids stay attached to each other in the centromere, but each contracts into the nucleolus. The nuclear envelope breaks down and disappears, and the spindle begins to develop.

↓

Event 3

Stage 3—Metaphase

Chromosomes congregate at the equatorial plane. Chromatids are attached to the spindle fibers at the centromeres.

↓

Event 4

Stage 4—Anaphase

Two chromatids of each chromosome separate and move to opposite poles.

↓

Event 5

Stage 5—Telophase

New nuclear envelopes form around the two groups of daughter chromosomes, new nuclei appear, and spindle fibers disappear. Cytokinesis finally separates the nuclei into two new individual daughter cells.

From Moss (2008). Copyright © 2008 Taylor & Francis Group. Reprinted by permission.

References

Dymock, S. (2005). Teaching expository text structure awareness. *The Reading Teacher, 59*(2), 171–181.

Langan, J. (2014). *Ten steps to improving college reading* (6th ed.). West Berlin, NJ: Townsend Press.

Moss, B. (2008). Facts that matter: Teaching students to read informational text. In D. Lapp, J. Flood, & N. Farnan (Eds.), *Content area reading and learning: Instructional strategies* (pp. 209–236). New York: Erlbaum.

Your Turn!

Identify a section from a textbook, a trade book, or a newspaper article that is clearly organized in one of the following text structures: Description, Sequence/Order, Compare–Contrast, Cause–Effect, or Problem–Solution. Introduce the text structure and associated signal words to your students. Direct them to closely read the text, then let them work in pairs to complete the chart.

Cluster Map

Instructions: Think about the text structure of description. Record the main idea in the center circle. Record the supporting details or descriptions in the smaller circles.

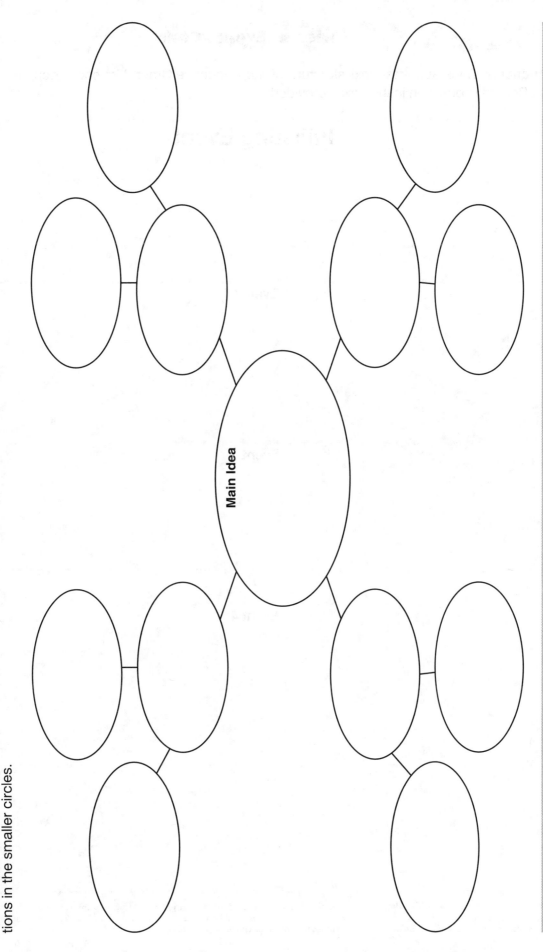

Main Idea

Series of Events Chart

Instructions: Think about the text structure of the Sequence/Order. List each event in the correct order. Record information in the boxes provided.

Initiating Event

Event 2

Event 3

Event 4

Event 5

Venn Diagram

Instructions: Think about the structure of Compare–Contrast. Label each circle with the name of one of the topics. Record the similarities and differences between the two topics you studied. List the similarities where the circles overlap (in the middle) and list the differences in the outer circles.

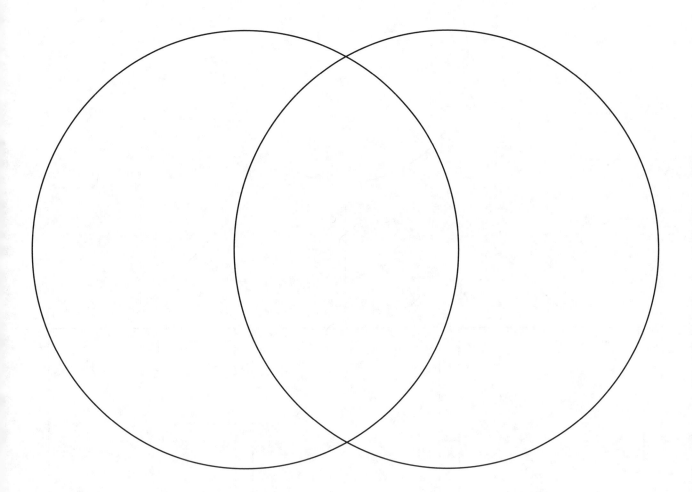

Instructions: Think about the text structure of Cause–Effect. Record the cause in the circle, then record the effects of that cause in the boxes beneath the circle.

Cause

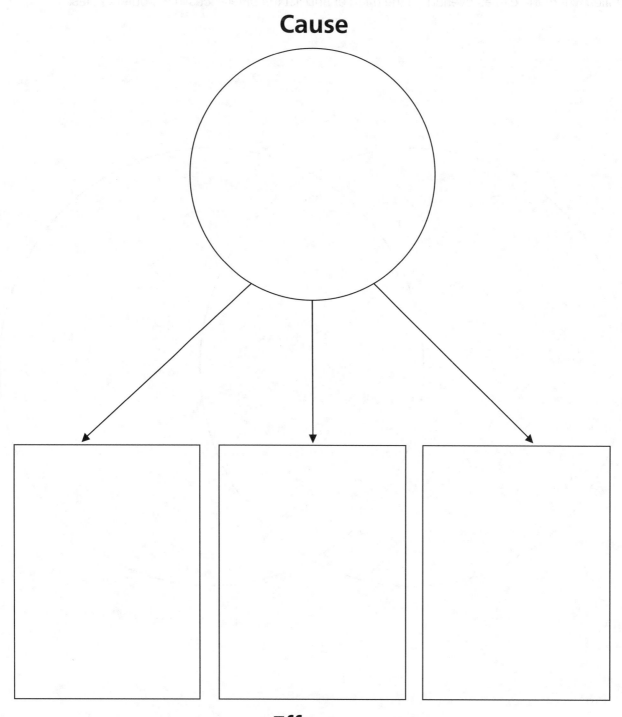

Effects

Problem–Solution Outline

Instructions: Think about the text structure of Problem–Solution. Record information about the problem, solution, outcome, and end result in the boxes below.

Problem
Who has the problem?
What was the problem?
Why was it a problem?

Solution	Outcome

End Result

Strategy 27

Interactive Notebooks

GRADE LEVELS: 3–12

Getting Started
Building Background
Vocabulary
Reading Closely
Comprehension
Discussion
Writing

> **CCSS.ELA-Literacy.CCRA.R.1** Read closely to determine what the text says explicitly and to make logical inferences from it; cite specific textual evidence when writing or speaking to support conclusions drawn from the text.

> **CCSS.ELA-Literacy.CCRA.R.2** Determine central ideas or themes of a text and analyze their development; summarize the key supporting details and ideas.

> **CCSS.ELA-Literacy.CCRA.R.4** Interpret words and phrases as they are used in a text, including determining technical, connotative, and figurative meanings, and analyze how specific word choices shape meaning or tone.

> **CCSS.ELA-Literacy.CCRA.R.10** Read and comprehend complex literary and informational texts independently and proficiently.

What Is It?

Interactive Notebooks are notebooks in which students record information about content-related material. This information can include Cornell notes, questions, drawings, webs, charts, and so on. Students can paste graphic organizers or other learning tools into their notebooks. There are many different formats for Interactive Notebooks. Some teachers have students paste graphic organizers on the left side of the page and write reflections about their learning on the right side, for example. Interactive Notebooks usually do not involve formal writing experiences, but emphasize using writing as a reflective task designed to facilitate information retrieval. Some teachers have students create tables of contents, authors' pages, unit title pages, and more for their Interactive Notebooks. Interactive Notebooks can be useful in any content area; teachers in many schools have students maintain Interactive Notebooks in every subject.

What Is Its Purpose?

Interactive Notebooks allow students to record information using a variety of formats including diagrams, drawings, illustrations, or texts. This strategy provides the student with a record of his or her learning over time, which becomes a portfolio of work that can be accessed throughout the school year. The Interactive Notebook can and should be used when students are reviewing for tests or quizzes. Teachers usually grade the Interactive Notebook periodically using a rubric so that they can monitor the completeness and quality of the work contained therein.

What Do I Do?

1. To involve students in using Interactive Notebooks, teachers should require them to purchase three-ring binders, spiral-bound notebooks, or bound composition books to be designated as their Interactive Notebooks. (We recommend having separate Interactive Notebooks for each subject area, topic, or unit of study.)

2. Select content-area materials appropriate to the students' abilities and the content being studied.

3. Model the various types of Interactive Notebook activities that students can use to respond to text. These experiences can occur before, during, or after reading. Students' Interactive Notebooks can also include completed templates of strategies described in this book. Students can also include illustrations to remember key pieces of information.

4. Assign Interactive Notebook activities. These activities can be completed in small groups. Direct students to review their Interactive Notebook entries in preparation for tests, group presentations, or other classroom-related activities.

Example

Sixth-grade science teacher Christian Meszaros was teaching his students a unit related to weather. He encouraged students to begin by reading their textbook chapter on weather and then required them to read a variety of other texts, including trade books, magazine articles, and Internet resources on the topic. They would later compile this information into an I-Chart (see Strategy 24) in teams. In order to make students accountable for their initial reading of these texts, he required that they record notes about their learning in their Interactive Notebooks. They had the opportunity to record this information by including key terms and definitions; written notes, such as drawings, flow charts, diagrams, and webs; and their thoughts about their learning. The example below illustrates one student's response to reading Patricia Lauber's (2001) *Hurricanes: Earth's Mightiest Storms*.

Sample Interactive Notebook

Topic: _Hurricanes_

New Vocabulary That I Learned:

Word	Definition	Picture/Sentence
anemometer	Measures wind speed	The <u>anemometer</u> clocked wind speeds at 80 mph.
eye	Low pressure center of the hurricane	The <u>eye</u> of the hurricane can be 10–20 miles wide.

Ideas That I Need to Remember:

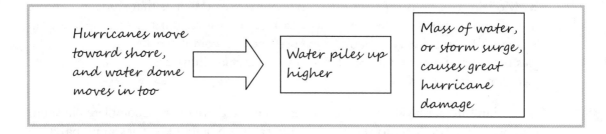

Thoughts about What I Learned:

I knew that hurricanes cause enormous damage.

I was surprised that they start in tropical waters and that they are the earth's biggest storms.

Reference

Lauber, P. (2001). *Hurricanes: Earth's mightiest storms*. New York: Houghton Mifflin. (M)

Your Turn!

Using an informational text, involve students in recording information in their Interactive Notebooks (template appears on page 188). First, show students samples of some of the different ways they can record information in their logs, such as diagrams, quick-writes, comic strips, storyboards, and/or graphic organizers. Then give them the opportunity to record information on the template. Finally, they should record a reflection about their learning as well.

Interactive Notebook

Instructions: Record the topic at the top of the page, and record the new vocabulary words, definitions, and a picture or sentence. After that, record ideas that you need to remember using a drawing, a comic strip, graphic organizer, text notes, or another form of your choice. Finally, write your thoughts about what you have learned.

Topic: _____

New Vocabulary That I Learned

Word	Definition	Picture/Sentence

Ideas That I Need to Remember

Record important information from the text here. You can use webs, quick-writes, or pictures to help you remember the information.

Thoughts about What I Learned

Record your reflection here.

PART SIX

Discussion
Strategies

Strategy 28

Discussion Web

GRADE LEVELS: 3–12

Getting Started
Building Background
Vocabulary
Reading Closely
Comprehension
Discussion
Writing

Discussion Strategies

CCSS Anchor Standards: Speaking and Listening

➤ **CCSS.ELA-Literacy.CCRA.SL.1** Prepare for and participate effectively in a range of conversations and collaborations with diverse partners, building on others' ideas and expressing their own clearly and persuasively.

➤ **CCSS.ELA-Literacy.CCRA.SL.2** Integrate and evaluate information presented in diverse media and formats, including visually, quantitatively, and orally.

➤ **CCSS.ELA-Literacy.CCRA.SL.4** Present information, findings, and supporting evidence such that listeners can follow the line of reasoning and the organization, development, and style are appropriate to task, purpose, and audience.

What Is It?

Discussion Webs (Alvermann, 1991) are graphic aids that help students think critically about what they have read. This organizer presents students with a central question to consider, along with spaces where readers can fill in supporting evidence in the "Yes" column, indicating agreement with the key question, or in the "No" column, indicating disagreement with the key question.

What Is Its Purpose?

Discussion Webs encourage students to consider different points of view about an issue, helping them to reflect on the fact that there are multiple ways to view a particular idea. This ability to take multiple perspectives in relationship to an idea is an important expectation of the CCSS. The Discussion Web directs students to not only support their own opinion about an issue, but also provide support for the opposing point of view. In this way, the Discussion Web helps to keep discussions focused and ensures that students support their viewpoints with relevant information.

What Do I Do?

1. Have students read an informational text.

2. Introduce the central question, writing it on the Discussion Web. Explain the format of the web, which includes two columns, one on the right side of the question and one on the left. The left-hand column is the "Yes" column where students record their reasons for agreeing with the central question. The right-hand column is the "No" column. This is where students record their reasons for disagreeing with the central question.

3. Put students in pairs to review the text, using sticky notes to identify three reasons they agree with the central question and three reasons they disagree. Be sure that they provide evidence to support their reasons.

4. Have students record these reasons in each of the two support columns on the web.

5. Have students combine partners to create groups of four. Each of the four students should present at least one reason and evidence in support of the question and one reason and one piece of evidence in opposition to the question to the rest of the group. This ensures that each student participates. The group of four compares their Discussion Webs and reaches a group conclusion. Dissenters may develop a minority report.

6. Each group presents its single best conclusion to the class and any dissenting opinions. Finally, the teacher opens up the discussion to the entire class.

Example

Eleventh-grade English teacher Ethan Chu was interested in helping his students develop critical literacy skills by engaging them in reflecting on their use of online literacy both in and out of class. He introduced the students to an online article from *The New York Times* entitled "Literacy Debate: Online RU Really Reading?" *(www. nytimes.com/2008/07/27/books/27reading.html)*. This persuasive essay examines the nature of online reading and raises a number of interesting questions about whether online reading is equivalent to more traditional forms of reading and contributes to the development of reading abilities. Prior to reading, Ethan involved students in a brief discussion of how they use reading as they engage with electronic texts. He explained that the article explores both sides of the debate around the question of whether online reading is as valuable as other forms of reading. Ethan then filled in the center of the Discussion Web with the question "Does online reading contribute to the development of reading skills students need for success in the 21st century?" He asked students to think about this question as they read the article.

Ethan projected the Discussion Web strategy, showing students how the web organizer asks them to consider a central question and list reasons and provide evidence for responding affirmatively or negatively to the question. He explained that they should be able to identify and record at least three reasons for answering "yes" to the central question and three reasons for answering "no." In other words, they were supposed to consider both sides of the issue. He instructed students to use sticky notes to write down examples for and against the central question within the article.

After reading the article, Ethan had students complete their webs in teams. A sample completed organizer is found below. After this, each group reported to the larger group on the reasons they listed on both sides of the web. A lively discussion ensued, with students arguing for their positions. Finally, students reached a consensus about their thoughts on online reading.

Sample Discussion Web

YES	Does online reading contribute to the development of reading skills students need for success in the 21st century?	NO
Online reading is motivating to many students and causes them to read more. Online reading develops new kinds of reading skills that will be necessary in the 21st century. Online graphics help students who don't read well to understand text better.		Online reading is fragmented and does not require the concentration required to read a book or other difficult text. Most online reading involves instant messaging or games, not reading that requires real thinking. There is no evidence that online reading improves reading achievement.

References

Alvermann, D. (1991). The discussion web: A graphic aid to learning across the curriculum. *The Reading Teacher, 45,* 92–99.

Rich, M. (2008, July 27). Literacy debate: Online RU really reading? *The New York Times.* Retrieved November 10, 2015, from *www.nytimes.com/2008/07/27/books/27reading. html.*

Your Turn!

Select an informational text that addresses a controversial topic or issue about which students may have strong opinions. Using the Discussion Web on the facing page, introduce and explain the question you want students to think about as they read. (*Optional:* You can encourage students to generate their own questions.) Write this question in the center box. Then have students form groups to discuss and record their opinions about the two sides of the question or issue. Have students record at least three reasons for their opinions on the two sides of the web. They should be prepared to provide evidence for their reasons. Then discuss their responses as a group.

Discussion Strategies

Discussion Web about _____

Instructions: Write the discussion question in the center box. Record at least three reasons for "yes" responses in the left column. Record at least three reasons for "no" responses in the right column. Be prepared to provide evidence for your answers.

YES	QUESTION	NO

Strategy 29

4–3–2–1 Discussion Guide

GRADE LEVELS: 2–12

Getting Started

Building Background

Vocabulary

Reading Closely

Comprehension

Discussion

Writing

CCSS Anchor Standards: Speaking and Listening

➤ **CCSS.ELA-Literacy.CCRA.SL.1** Prepare for and participate effectively in a range of conversations and collaborations with diverse partners, building on others' ideas and expressing their own clearly and persuasively.

➤ **CCSS.ELA-Literacy.CCRA.SL.4** Present information, findings, and supporting evidence such that listeners can follow the line of reasoning and the organization, development, and style are appropriate to task, purpose, and audience.

➤ **CCSS.ELA-Literacy.CCRA.SL.6** Adapt speech to a variety of contexts and communicative tasks, demonstrating command of formal English when indicated or appropriate.

What Is It?

The 4–3–2–1 Discussion Guide is adapted from the 3–2–1 Discussion Guide described on Reading Quest (*www.readingquest.org*). The strategy requires students to summarize, clarify, and analyze content. It serves as a discussion guide for collaborative group work.

To complete the guide, students read a text and then identify and record four new learnings, three comments/opinions, two questions, and one further exploration. New Learnings refer to things that students have learned as a result of reading the text. Comments/Opinions require students to think about how they feel about the new learnings and/or the text; they should consider how the text positions them and how they feel about the intended message. The Questions section asks students to state their misunderstandings or needs for clarification. Last, the Further Exploration section requires students to answer the questions: "So what? What does this text mean? How does it relate to society at large?"

The chart below provides some guiding questions and sample language prompts for the four main components of this strategy.

What Is Its Purpose?

The purpose of the 4–3–2–1 Discussion Guide is to provide students with an opportunity to identify and reflect on key ideas from a text. Once students have established their initial thinking about the text, they can use this strategy as a springboard for further examination via discussions. Through such discussions, students are encouraged to reevaluate their initial perspectives and to seek answers to their questions.

Teachers can ascertain where student understandings are incomplete or missing and use student responses to plan instruction and/or discussion topics for the next

Guiding Questions and Sample Language Prompts for the 4–3–2–1 Discussion Guide

4 New Learnings	What new things did you learn from the text? What new facts did you learn? How did the text build on your prior knowledge? *Sample language prompts:* I learned _____. It was interesting how _____.
3 Comments/ Opinions	What did you think about _____? What did you think about the author's message? How did you feel when _____? What would you change? Did you agree or disagree with something mentioned in the text? Did something surprise you? What textual connections can you make? *Sample language prompts:* I think _____. I felt _____. I was surprised when _____. This reminded me of _____.
2 Questions	What do you want to know more about? What did you find confusing? *Sample language prompts:* Why did _____? What is _____? How _____?
1 Further Exploration	Is there anything that needs to be clarified or studied more? What other topics did this text make you think about? What's the next step? What does this text mean in the larger context? *Sample language prompts:* I want to learn more about _____. The author's next step should be _____. This text is significant to society because _____.

day. Because the instruction is focused on ideas that students generated themselves, the students will be more motivated and engaged to learn about the topic.

What Do I Do?

1. Select an informational text that addresses the topic of study. Have all students read the text. (Read aloud text or assign as homework/independent reading.)

2. Have students complete the 4–3–2–1 Discussion Guide independently. Assure students that there are no wrong answers. This step allows students to capture their initial thoughts about the text. Tell students they can change their thinking during the group discussions.

3. Set norms for discussion. Norms could include but are not limited to the following: Take turns sharing ideas. Respectfully disagree. Be open to changing perspectives.

4. Have students discuss their responses in small groups. Have each group complete the 4–3–2–1 Discussion Guide. Assign a recorder to write down the group's responses. (*Optional:* Assign other roles. Other possible roles include a facilitator to ask the questions and guide the discussion, a timekeeper to manage the time, and a reporter to share aloud to the whole group.)

5. Facilitate a whole-group discussion. Record student responses on a projected master template of the 4-3-2-1 Discussion Guide.

6. Collect the templates and use the information to guide future instruction and future discussions.

Example

Buddy Gray's 10th-grade English students just finished reading John Steinbeck's (1939) *The Grapes of Wrath*. Based on their responses in class discussions, he learned that his students did not know very much about the Dust Bowl, so he wanted to contextualize Steinbeck's book by having the students read some informational texts about the subject. He felt that they needed to understand the historical context of the novel in order to fully comprehend it, so for homework, he had them read Jerry Stanley's (1993) *Children of the Dust Bowl: The True Story of the School at Weedpatch Camp*.

Buddy distributed the 4–3–2–1 Discussion Guide and had each student complete it independently. Then he had students work in small groups to discuss their thinking and complete the guide as a group. He walked around the room and listened in as the students discussed. Next, as a whole class, he had them complete a Venn Diagram (see Strategy 26), comparing and contrasting Steinbeck's and Stanley's depictions of the Dust Bowl. A sample of a 4–3–2–1 Discussion Guide completed by one group is provided below.

In reading the students' responses, Buddy discovered they were making personal connections between past (Dust Bowl, Great Depression, migration) and current events (economic downturn, border issues). For example, several groups recorded in the Comments/Opinions section how much the Great Depression reminded them of the recession because "people were losing their homes and jobs." Other students wrote about migration and immigration; they recorded responses such as "The Okies moving out West for a better life reminded me of my family immigrating to America. Both groups had to deal with hardships and prejudices." Students were clearly connecting their current lived experiences to the texts. As a result, Buddy modified his lesson for that week to include discussions about these topics in addition to an explicit lesson comparing and contrasting past and present national policies on the economy and immigration. He wanted to use what the students were already interested in and to expand their knowledge.

References

Reading Quest: Making sense of social studies. Retrieved from *www.readingquest.org*.
Stanley, J. (1993). *Children of the dust bowl: The true story of the school at Weedpatch Camp*. New York: Crown Books for Young Readers. (M)
Steinbeck, J. (1939). *The grapes of wrath*. New York: Penguin Classics. (fiction, YA)

Sample 4–3–2–1 Discussion Guide

4 New Learnings	I learned about the prejudice against the Okies.
	It was interesting to learn how Leo Hart believed in the Okie children and built a school for them.
3 Comments/ Opinions	I felt disappointed to learn how cruel the Californians were to the Okies.
	This reminded me of how the Great Depression was like our recession because people are losing their homes and jobs.
2 Questions	How did the Okies survive in California? Did things ever get better for them?
1 Further Exploration	I would like to study more about the Dust Bowl and why it happened.
	This text is significant to society because it documents how people can not just survive, but prevail in spite of terrible adversity.

Your Turn!

Select a text pertinent to your topic of study from the Appendix at the back of this book, or one of your own choosing. Project a blank template and model via a think-aloud each of the four steps of the 4–3–2–1 Discussion Guide. Then choose another text on the same topic and have students work in small groups to complete the guide. This strategy can be adapted in many different ways, such as having students write down four new vocabulary words, three differences between ideas, two similarities, and one question they still have.

4–3–2–1 Discussion Guide

Instructions: Record the topic and text. Record your responses in each of the boxes.

Topic: _____

Text: _____

4 New Learnings	1. 2. 3. 4.
3 Comments/ Opinions	1. 2. 3.
2 Questions	1. 2.
1 Further Exploration	1.

Strategy 30

Intra-Act

GRADE LEVELS: 4–12

Getting Started
Building Background
Vocabulary
Reading Closely
Comprehension
Discussion
Writing

CCSS Anchor Standards: Speaking and Listening

> **CCSS.ELA-Literacy.CCRA.SL.1** Prepare for and participate effectively in a range of conversations and collaborations with diverse partners, building on others' ideas and expressing their own clearly and persuasively.

> **CCSS.ELA-Literacy.CCRA.SL.3** Evaluate a speaker's point of view, reasoning, and use of evidence and rhetoric.

> **CCSS.ELA-Literacy.CCRA.SL.4** Present information, findings, and supporting evidence such that listeners can follow the line of reasoning and the organization, development, and style are appropriate to task, purpose, and audience.

> **CCSS.ELA-Literacy.CCRA.SL.6** Adapt speech to a variety of contexts and communicative tasks, demonstrating command of formal English when indicated or appropriate.

What Is It?

The Intra-Act strategy encourages students to place value on what they have read; as such, students are empowered to form evidence-based opinions (Hoffman, 1979). Intra-Act is a reflective postreading strategy. Aligned with the CCSS, Intra-Act supports critical reading skills in that students think about what they read, form opinions, and develop a solid line of reasoning. Hoffman (1979), the creator of the name "Intra-Act," said, "the inferred intra-personal dialogue is an exercise in intellectual self-actualization" (p. 605).

Hoffman used the four phases of value clarification as described by Casteel and

Stahl (1973): comprehension, relating, valuation, and reflection. First, students read the text and form small discussion groups to work on understanding what they just read; this is the comprehension stage. Second, students discuss their opinions and ideas; this is the relating stage. Third, students develop their opinions by applying personal values and feelings to the content; this is the valuation stage. Fourth, students discuss and challenge the ideas within their discussion groups; this stage is the reflection stage.

What Is Its Purpose?

The purpose of the Intra-Act strategy is to help students learn how their opinions may change and also how to change the opinions of others by presenting solid arguments. Intra-Act allows students to express their values and feelings in response to text and in response to others. The strategy empowers students to articulate their opinions in front of others. Another purpose of this strategy is to help students be sensitive and open to the ideas of others.

The key to this strategy is the small-group discussions, in which students increase their knowledge by working and learning together. They are given an opportunity to discuss, challenge, and support ideas. The Intra-Act strategy requires students to place value on content; this helps students understand and internalize what they have read. In addition, it helps students build argumentation skills.

What Do I Do?

1. Select a text that lends itself to controversy. Ideal texts prompt strong opinions from students.

2. Create opinion statements related to the topic of the text. These statements have to be points that can be agreed or disagreed with. Write these opinion statements in the left column of the template. (*Optional:* After modeling how to write opinion statements, you can have students generate their own opinion statements.)

3. Have students read the text. Encourage them to annotate.

4. Divide students into groups of four. Have students write their own names in the second column and the names of their group members at the top of the other columns.

5. Have students read each opinion statement and check "Yes" or "No," indicating whether they agree with the statements. Remind them to have reasons and evidence for their opinions.

6. Have students predict how each member of their teams would respond to the statements by marking the "Yes" or "No" boxes under their names. Remind students to have reasons to support their thinking. (This step pushes students to think about what they know about their classmates' belief systems based on previous discussions and/or interactions.)

7. Have students meet with their groups and share their responses. Have students mark correct and incorrect predictions and discuss their predictions.

8. Have students engage in a discussion about their reasons for supporting (or not supporting) specific statements. Allow students to share their reactions to the statements and to defend or question their own positions and those of others. Remind students to support their claims with evidence.

9. Reconvene students as a whole group. Reflect on the content and process. (*Optional:* Have students do a quick-write explaining how and why the discussion changed their thinking.)

Example

Jason Pupko is a seventh-grade social science teacher teaching a unit on immigration. His students are very familiar with Ellis Island, but they are not familiar with Angel Island, so Jason wanted his students to learn more about the latter.

The Angel Island Immigration Station is located on a remote island outside of San Francisco. Many Russian and Asian immigrants were processed at Angel Island at the turn of the 20th century. Prompted by "Yellow Peril," the Chinese Exclusion Act of 1882 prohibited Chinese laborers from immigrating to the United States; this was the only law to discriminate against a specific ethnic group. When city hall burned down during the San Francisco fire and earthquake of 1906, birth records were destroyed. As such, Chinese immigrants living in the United States claimed citizenship and also claimed to have children in China whom they could bring over to the United States. These Chinese immigrants sold "paper son slots" to Chinese people wanting to come to the United States. These paper sons had to pretend to be citizens. They had to pass intense interrogations at Angel Island and were often detained for long periods of time.

Jason assigned his students to read excerpts about the paper son system from Russell Freedman's (2014) *Angel Island: Gateway to Gold Mountain.* Freedman's book is considered to be a secondary source. So, in addition, Jason required his students to read a primary source titled "Immigration Inspector's Statement" (McKenzie, 1928). Next, Jason directed his students to complete the Intra-Act Template. First, he had them complete the form independently, then they discussed it in groups of four. The sample is on the facing page.

Last, he reconvened the students as a whole group and facilitated an inquiry-based discussion about the ethical, legal, and moral issues around the paper son

Sample Intra-Act Template

Think about It: Sometimes the paper son system is referred to as a "crime." Do you agree or disagree? Why or why not? What leads to the crime (causes)? What are the punishments (effects)? Consider the plight of paper sons. Do you think paper sons did the "right" thing? You must defend all your opinions with supporting evidence from the texts.

Opinion Statements	Name: _____	Name: _____	Name: _____	Name: _____
The paper son system is a crime, a crime that deserves proper punishment such as deportation.	Yes____ No____	Yes____ No____	Yes____ No____	Yes____ No____
The interrogations were a reasonable solution to the paper son issue.	Yes____ No____	Yes____ No____	Yes____ No____	Yes____ No____
Lee did the "right" thing in becoming a paper son.	Yes____ No____	Yes____ No____	Yes____ No____	Yes____ No____
The Chinese Exclusion Act was unfair and just cause for the paper son system.	Yes____ No____	Yes____ No____	Yes____ No____	Yes____ No____

system. After these discussions, Jason felt his students had a deep understanding of the topic. As a culminating task, he required his students to write a three- to four-page argument paper on the topic.

References

Casteel, J. D., & Stahl, R. J. (1973). *The social science observation record: Theoretical construct and pilot studies*. Gainesville, FL: P.K. Yonge Laboratory School.

Freedman, R. (2014). *Angel Island: Gateway to Gold Mountain*. New York: Clarion Books. (M, YA)

Hoffman, J. V. (1979). The intra-act procedure for critical reading. *Journal of Reading*, 22(7), 605–608.

McKenzie, R. D. (1928). Immigration inspector's statement. In *Oriental exclusion* (p. 50). Chicago: University of Chicago Press.

Your Turn!

Select an informational text from the Appendix at the back of this book or one of your own choosing. Work with students to complete the Intra-Act strategy. Because of the multiple steps, it would be beneficial to go over each step as a whole group. It would also be beneficial to model this strategy before having students implement it independently.

Intra-Act Template

Instructions: Write down the opinion statements. Write your name at the top of the first column. Then write the names of your team members in the rest of the columns. Read each opinion statement and check "Yes" or "No," indicating whether you agree with the statements. Predict how each member of your team will respond to the statements by marking the "Yes" or "No" boxes under their names. Be prepared to discuss your reasoning.

Opinion Statements	Name: _____	Name: _____	Name: _____	Name: _____
	Yes____ No____	Yes____ No____	Yes____ No____	Yes____ No____
	Yes____ No____	Yes____ No____	Yes____ No____	Yes____ No____
	Yes____ No____	Yes____ No____	Yes____ No____	Yes____ No____
	Yes____ No____	Yes____ No____	Yes____ No____	Yes____ No____

What changes and/or affirmations did you experience as a result of your discussion? Write your reflection in the space below.

Based on Hoffman (1979). From *40 Strategies for Guiding Readers through Informational Texts* by Barbara Moss and Virginia Loh-Hagan. Copyright © 2016 The Guilford Press. Permission to photocopy this form is granted to purchasers of this book for personal use or use with individual students (see copyright page for details). Purchasers can download additional copies of this material (see the box at the end of the table of contents).

Strategy 31

Talking Points

GRADE LEVELS: 3–12

Getting Started
Building Background
Vocabulary
Reading Closely
Comprehension
Discussion
Writing

CCSS Anchor Standards: Speaking and Listening

> **CCSS.ELA-Literacy.CCRA.SL.1** Prepare for and participate effectively in a range of conversations and collaborations with diverse partners, building on others' ideas and expressing their own clearly and persuasively.

> **CCSS.ELA-Literacy.CCRA.SL.4** Present information, findings, and supporting evidence such that listeners can follow the line of reasoning and the organization, development, and style are appropriate to task, purpose, and audience.

> **CCSS.ELA-Literacy.CCRA.SL.6** Adapt speech to a variety of contexts and communicative tasks, demonstrating command of formal English when indicated or appropriate.

What Is It?

The Talking Points strategy engages students in one of the most important study skills of all: note taking. Studies demonstrate that students who can effectively take notes perform better academically than students who cannot. Furthermore, giving students the opportunity to talk about their notes with partners helps to develop deeper understanding of the process of note taking as well as the pertinent content.

What Is Its Purpose?

The Talking Points strategy serves several purposes. First, it teaches students to take notes. Many students are expected to copy notes from PowerPoint presentations provided by their teachers. Research suggests that students need to be taught to take, not copy notes, if they are to succeed academically. It also suggests that students need to do more than just take notes; they need to reprocess the information by summarizing, discussing, and reflecting on its meaning. For this reason, the second purpose of the Talking Points strategy is to give students an opportunity to reprocess information through peer interaction. By talking about content in this way, students are more likely to remember the information and benefit from the peer support it provides. The third purpose of this strategy is student reflection. By reflecting on their note-taking skills and how they can improve them, students become increasingly aware of their abilities in this area and how they can develop greater skill over time.

What Do I Do?

1. Identify the source for student note taking. It is often helpful to start by having students take notes on a video that they can watch more than once, adding what they missed during the first viewing after they watch it a second time. Students also need to learn to take notes from print materials such as textbooks or articles. Finally, students must develop the ability to take notes from lectures if they are to succeed in college. This is probably the most challenging of all note-taking forms.

2. Share the note-taking topic with students and have them predict what they may learn from the video, text, lecture, and so on.

3. Teach students how to take notes. There are many different note-taking methods. One method is to teach students to use an outline format for notes, such as skeletal note taking described in the example on page 211. To do this form of note taking, teachers must first show students how to use bullet points, paraphrase, and condense ideas into as few words as possible. Teaching students to omit unimportant words (e.g., *and, the, of*) and abbreviate key terms is essential.

4. Model the note-taking process.

5. Give students opportunities to practice note taking frequently. Avoid having them copy notes.

6. Have students work collaboratively to review their notes with a partner. They can compare notes and identify missed points; create questions based on the video, text, or lecture; and summarize key points.

7. Students should individually record a content summary for each note-taking session. They should also reflect on how well they did as note takers and identify ways to improve their skills.

Example

Eighth-grade history teacher Diane Cranston wanted to prepare her students for taking notes on a lecture she prepared on the powers of the state and federal government. She provided each student with a copy of the Talking Points Template (see page 214).

- Step 1: Diane began the lesson by telling students that they would learn about the four powers of the state and federal government. She asked them to talk with a partner about what they expected to learn about this topic. They recorded their answers on the sample template shown on the facing page. Students then shared their answers. Student responses included *Presidential powers, states rights*, and *shared powers*.

- Step 2: Before beginning the lecture, Diane reviewed with students how to take bulleted outline notes like those on the template. She reminded them of the following note-taking guidelines:

  - Record key topics on the line provided.
  - Write each new note on a new, bulleted line.
  - Paraphrase.
  - Only write down important words.
  - Use abbreviations when possible.

  To scaffold student learning, Diane used skeletal notes. In other words, she completed portions of the outline to support students as they gained success in this skill, and left other portions blank for students to complete. The topics and bulleted notes she provided for students are **bolded** in the example on the facing page.

- Step 3: At this point, Diane delivered the first part of the lecture on express powers. She modeled how to take notes on this topic by recording the first topic and the first two bullet points on the template. She then had students add more bullets after talking to a partner.

- Step 4: Diane delivered the next part of the lecture on implied powers. Students recorded their notes on this topic with the help of a partner. She continued with the lecture and students completed their outlines independently.

- Step 5: Following this, students worked with partners to review their notes, create questions over the content, and identify key information (see Peer Collaboration page 212).

- Step 6: Students completed the On Your Own section of the Talking Points Template by writing a short text summary and reflecting on their note-taking skills.

Sample Talking Points Template

Before the Reading, Lecture, or Viewing

Today's Date/Topic: _May 15, 2015_   _Powers of the States and Federal Governments_

List something you expect to learn from the lecture.

I expect to learn about states' rights.

During the Reading, Lecture, or Viewing—Skeletal Outline

Overall Topic: _Powers of the States and Federal Government_

Topic 1: _Express Powers_
- Post office
- Coin money
- Declare war
- Maintain Army and Navy
- State militias

Topic 2: _Implied Powers_
- Regulating airlines
- Air Force and Marines
- Banking and commerce

Topic 3: _Concurrent Powers (shared with states)_
- Taxes
- Courts
- Schools

Topic 4: _Reserved Powers (belonging to the state)_
- State driving age
- State speed limits

Topic 5: _California Governor's Responsibilities_
- State of the State speech
- Submit budget
- Ensure laws enforced
- Maintain borders
- Interstate relationships

(continued)

Adapted in part from Alger and Moss (2012). Copyright © 2012 The Guilford Press. Adapted by permission.

After the Reading, Lecture, or Viewing

Peer Collaboration

Review your notes with a partner. Identify points that you might have missed and add them to your note-taking template.

Work with your partner to create three questions related to the lecture. Write them here.

1. *Identify four types of powers and explain each one.*

2. *Give examples of some implied powers.*

3. *What powers does the federal government have that the states don't?*

Discuss with your partner the key points you learned from today's lecture. List them below.

- *States have some powers that the federal government doesn't have.*
- *Some powers are shared.*
- *The governor of California has specific responsibilities.*

On Your Own

Write a 20-word-or-less summary of today's lecture.

There are four kinds of state and federal powers that include express, implied, concurrent, and reserve powers.

How effective was your note taking today? How might you improve your note-taking skills?

Pretty good. I need to remember to pay attention to the teacher when she points out key topics.

Reference

Alger, C., & Moss, B. (2012). If you want students to take notes instead of copying them—Teach them how. In D. Lapp & B. Moss (Eds.). *Exemplary instruction in the middle grades: Teaching that supports engagement and rigorous learning* (pp. 292–309). New York: Guilford Press.

Your Turn!

Select a video, text, or create a lecture on a topic of your choosing. Model the note-taking process. Then engage students in completing the note-taking portion of the Talking Points Template. Afterward, have students work in pairs to reprocess their notes. Finally, students can complete a short summary and reflection on their own.

Discussion Strategies

Talking Points Template

Instructions: Complete the template before, during, and after you view, read, or listen to a lecture.

Before the Reading, Lecture, or Viewing

Today's Date/Topic: _____   _____

List something you expect to learn from the lecture.

During the Reading, Lecture, or Viewing—Skeletal Outline

Overall Topic: _____

Topic 1: _____

- ●
- ●
- ●

Topic 2: _____

- ●
- ●
- ●

Topic 3: _____

- ●
- ●
- ●

Topic 4: _____

- ●
- ●
- ●

(continued)

After the Viewing, Reading, or Lecture

Peer Collaboration

Review your notes with a partner. Identify points that you might have missed and add them to your note-taking template.

Work with your partner to create three questions related to the lecture. Write them here.

1.

2.

3.

Discuss with your partner the key points you learned from today's lecture. List them below.

-

-

-

On Your Own

Write a 20-word-or-less summary of today's lecture.

How effective was your note taking today? How might you improve your note-taking skills?

Strategy 32

Three-Step Interview

GRADE LEVELS: K–12

Getting Started
Building Background
Vocabulary
Reading Closely
Comprehension
Discussion
Writing

CCSS Anchor Standards: Speaking and Listening

> **CCSS.ELA-Literacy.CCRA.SL.1** Prepare for and participate effectively in a range of conversations and collaborations with diverse partners, building on others' ideas and expressing their own clearly and persuasively.

> **CCSS.ELA-Literacy.CCRA.SL.3** Evaluate a speaker's point of view, reasoning, and use of evidence and rhetoric.

> **CCSS.ELA-Literacy.CCRA.SL.4** Present information, findings, and supporting evidence such that listeners can follow the line of reasoning and the organization, development, and style are appropriate to task, purpose, and audience.

> **CCSS.ELA-Literacy.CCRA.SL.6** Adapt speech to a variety of contexts and communicative tasks, demonstrating command of formal English when indicated or appropriate.

What Is It?

The Three-Step Interview strategy promotes student thinking and oral language development. This strategy is an adaptation of other strategies that promote collaborative talk practices (Kagan, 1989; Shea & Shanahan, 2011) in response to reading texts. By engaging in a Three-Step Interview, students work in small groups and take part in three separate interviews or discussions. As such, students have multiple opportunities to interact with both content and colleagues. Given these multiple exposures, students are more likely to comprehend and retain the information they learned from text. In addition, students learn valuable 21st-century communication skills such as generating questions, listening attentively, and arguing with evidence.

What Is Its Purpose?

The purposes of the Three-Step Interview are to give students several opportunities to share and apply different questioning strategies and to practice responding to questions. Over time, students can be introduced to higher levels of thinking to extend and enhance their questioning and thinking skills. In order to be able to generate effective questions, students must comprehend what they are reading. They need to know enough about the topic to ask robust questions. They also have to learn how to build on what their partners are telling them.

Teachers can consider the Three-Step Interview as a means to hold all students accountable for learning, as all students must engage in the activity. (In whole-group discussions, some students can choose to not participate. This is not the case for Three-Step Interviews.)

What Do I Do?

1. Select an informational text.

2. Divide the class into groups of four.

3. Label each member as A, B, C, or D. (*Optional:* Especially for young students, you might want to give students a sign or table card with their letters.)

4. Introduce your topic/issue, preferably in the form of a question.

5. Tell students that they will be discussing this topic/issue in three different interview sessions. Direct students to take turns generating and responding to questions. (*Optional:* Model how to conduct and participate in interviews via question-and-answer format.)

6. Provide students with 2–3 minutes for each interview. Implement the three steps:

- Step 1: Have Student A interview Student B. Have Student C interview Student D.

- Step 2: Have Student A interview Student C. Have Student B interview Student D.

- Step 3: Have all students in each group discuss the topic and attempt to reach a consensus.

7. Reconvene as a whole group. Facilitate an inquiry-based discussion about the topic/issue. Record students' responses on a chart.

8. *Optional:* Direct students to take notes while listening to their classmates.

Example

Jenn Beck is a second-grade teacher. In science, the students have been learning about animals and their habitats. As part of this unit, Jenn has read many texts with her students, shown them documentaries, and taken them on a field trip to the zoo. As a culminating activity, Jenn invited a scientist from the zoo to be a guest speaker. She wants her students to ask the scientist good questions. As such, she introduced the Three-Step Interview strategy to give them practice with interviewing techniques.

First, she had to explicitly teach interviewing, which means she had to teach her students how to ask questions. She read aloud Kathleen Krull's (2014) *A Zippy History of Zoos: What's New? The Zoo!* After she finished reading, she asked the students, "Pretend I'm the author of this book. What type of questions would you ask me?" She recorded their responses on chart paper.

- You included many people in your book like Pope Leo X, King of Ur, and Carl Hagenbeck. Who is your favorite zoo-keeper and why?

- You mentioned that Kublai Khan kept 10,000 white horses because he liked their milk. What does this mean? Can you milk a horse?

- According to your book, zoos have been helpful in saving endangered animals. How did this goal develop?

Jenn had her students note that questions begin with question words like *who, what, when, where, why,* or *how.* She made sure her students understood the differences between questions and answers. Next, she pointed out how good interviewers lead in with some information indicating that they know something about the topic. Then Jenn had her students discuss good interview questions versus bad interview questions. Her students learned that good interview questions are open ended, lead to interesting ideas, clarify what the speaker said, do not lead the speaker, and so forth.

Jenn also reviewed interview etiquette. She discussed the importance of waiting for responses, taking turns when talking, and responding to all parts of the question. She showed video clips of interviews and had the students critique the speakers.

Finally, Jenn encouraged her students to practice the Three-Step Interview. First, she modeled the strategy with a small group. She participated in the process while the rest of the class watched the small group. Then she divided her class into groups of four members and walked around the room to monitor their progress. She knew students would need to practice the strategy several times before they got the hang of it.

References

Kagan, S. (1989). The structural approach to cooperative learning. *Educational Leadership, 47*(4), 12–15.

Krull, K. (2014). *A zippy history of zoos: What's new? The zoo!* New York: Arthur A. Levine Books. (P)

Shea, L. M. & Shanahan, T. B. (2011). Talk strategies: How to promote oral language development through science. *Science and Children, 49*(3), 62–66.

Your Turn!

Select an informational text from the Appendix at the back of this book, or one of your own choosing. Before students try the Three-Step Interview strategy, have them practice asking the types of questions reporters ask and at what point in the interview they ask them. Tell students that interviewers usually record their notes so that they can refer back to them later. Depending on the age of your students, adjust the length of time for the interviews.

Discussion Strategies

Three-Step Interview Notes Template

Instructions: Write down the topic/issue. In the first row, collect your thoughts before engaging in your interview.

Topic/Issue: _____

What are your thoughts about the topic/issue?	What are some questions you have about the topic/issue?

Notes	
First Interview	
Second Interview	
Third Interview	

Strategy 33

3-Minute Pause

GRADE LEVELS: K–12

Getting Started
Building Background
Vocabulary
Reading Closely
Comprehension
Discussion
Writing

Discussion Strategies

CCSS Anchor Standards: Speaking and Listening

➤ **CCSS.ELA-Literacy.CCRA.SL.1** Prepare for and participate effectively in a range of conversations and collaborations with diverse partners, building on others' ideas and expressing their own clearly and persuasively.

➤ **CCSS.ELA-Literacy.CCRA.SL.3** Evaluate a speaker's point of view, reasoning, and use of evidence and rhetoric.

➤ **CCSS.ELA-Literacy.CCRA.SL.4** Present information, findings, and supporting evidence such that listeners can follow the line of reasoning and the organization, development, and style are appropriate to task, purpose, and audience.

➤ **CCSS.ELA-Literacy.CCRA.SL.6** Adapt speech to a variety of contexts and communicative tasks, demonstrating command of formal English when indicated or appropriate.

What Is It?

Because students are inundated with information, there is a good chance that they lack opportunities to reflect on and process that information. The 3-Minute Pause (Marzano et al., 1992; McTighe & Lyman, 1988) is a strategy that provides students with an opportunity for reflection that can enhance knowledge retention. At strategic points, teachers give students the chance to pause for 3 minutes, thereby providing an educational time-out. Students can use this time to reflect on concepts and ideas that have just been introduced to make connections to prior knowledge/ experience, and/or to seek clarification.

221

The 3-Minute Pause has many forms; the most popular is "Think–Pair–Share." The idea is to establish a pattern of regular breaks to allow students to process their learning. Without this reflection time, students may have incomplete knowledge of what is being taught, and so, teachers must often reteach. The 3-Minute Pause is efficient and immediately useful, requiring very little preparation; the teacher just has to deliberately implement it at crucial and relevant points during the text and/or instruction.

What Is Its Purpose?

The purpose of the 3-Minute Pause is to have students negotiate and construct their own meanings about a topic. In order to be critical consumers of information, students must be allowed time to reflect on and verbalize new learnings. The best way for students to learn about a topic is to manipulate it, even if this manipulation occurs inside one's head. Thinking involves the manipulation of ideas, and this strategy provides an excellent opportunity for this to happen.

What Do I Do?

1. Select an informational text. Project the text so that all students have access to it.

2. Read the text aloud or have students independently read sections of the text. Stop every so often and have students get into pairs or small groups for their 3-Minute Pauses. Use a timer to facilitate this and also to create a sense of urgency and efficiency.

3. First, ask the students to summarize the key points presented thus far. Give them 1 minute to complete this task.

4. Second, ask students to consider connections to themselves, to other texts, and/or to the world or society at large. Give them 1 minute to complete this task.

5. Third, ask the students to pose questions to each other. Give them 1 minute to complete this task. Here are some suggested prompts:

- Are there things that are still not clear to you?
- Are there any confusing parts?
- Are you having trouble making connections?
- Can you anticipate where we're headed?
- What do you think are the big ideas?

6. Move on to the next section of the text. Repeat each step.

Example

Seventh-grade world history teacher Gene Batchelder taught a unit on Confucianism in which the students had to analyze the influences of Confucianism and changes in Confucian thought during the Sung and Mongol periods. Gene is very familiar with the Think–Pair–Share strategy (a popular version of the 3-Minute Pause strategy) and used it all the time when he first started teaching. Although his students were given an opportunity to talk and process, they were not fully retaining the information. He discovered that in order for Think–Pair–Shares to be effective, the teacher must have a specific goal for student learning. Gene had neglected this aspect of the strategy; he was having his students talk in an unfocused, general way about the topic. Gene prefers the 3-Minute Pause strategy to Think–Pair–Share because it's more structured, and he changed his approach knowing that the success of this strategy depends on explicit instruction. As such, Gene introduced the strategy by telling his students what to discuss. In regard to this unit, he told his students, "I would like for you to Think–Pair–Share about how Confucius treated his students." A fan of Russell Freedman, he used the informational trade book *Confucius: The Golden Rule* (Freedman, 2002). Gene projected the text and read aloud significant excerpts. He would stop and have his students participate in a 3-Minute Pause. During these pauses, he displayed his expectations as shown below. He also incorporated sentence starters designed to help those students who had difficulty framing their responses.

Gene modified the 3-Minute Pause. The first 2 minutes involved an oral discussion between partners, and the last minute engaged students in an independent writing activity. Notice that Gene was very deliberate in what he wanted his students to do with a partner and what he wanted them to do independently. Gene established this strategy as a routine in his class; as such, his students were able to get a lot of

---

Rules for 3-Minute Pauses

First minute: With a partner, think about what you have just learned. Summarize what you have just learned about _____.

Prompt: I learned _____.

Second minute: With a partner, make a connection to yourself, to another text, or to society-at-large based upon what you have learned.

Prompt: This reminds me of _____.

Third minute: Independently, write your question(s) on a piece of paper. You will turn this in at the end of class.

Prompt: I want to know more about _____.

---

thinking done in 3 minutes. Gene used a timer and was very consistent about the time. After 3 minutes, he would continue reading the text.

At the end of the class session, Gene collected the questions from each student. He used that information to evaluate student learning and to help him plan the next class session.

References

Freedman, R. (2002). *Confucius: The golden rule.* New York: Arthur Levine Books. (M)

Marzano, R., Pickering, D., Arredondo, D., Blackburn, G., Brandt, R., & Moffett, C. (1992). *Dimensions of learning: Teacher's manual.* Alexandria, VA: ASCD.

McTighe, J., & Lyman, F. (1988). Cueing thinking in the classroom: The promise of theory-embedded tools. *Educational Leadership, 45*(7), 18–24.

Your Turn!

Select a text pertinent to your topic of study from the Appendix at the back of this book, or one of your own choosing. Use the 3-Minute Pause Planning Guide to help you decide where to pause to check for understanding during the lesson. This strategy can be modified in a variety of ways; the most important aspect of the strategy is to have students stop to think about what they are learning. An analogy to consider is the need to "save" when we are working on our computers; our students need a moment to "save" the information you present.

3-Minute Pause Planning Guide

Title of Text: _____   **Author:** _____

What key learnings do I want students to get from this text?	1.
	2.
	3.
3-Minute Pause #1	
Where will you pause in the text?	
What will students do?	
What prompt will you use for this pause?	

(continued)

3-Minute Pause #2

Where will you pause in the text?

What will students do?

What prompt will you use for this pause?

3-Minute Pause #3

Where will you pause in the text?

What will students do?

What prompt will you use for this pause?

PART SEVEN

Writing
Strategies

Strategy 34

Readers Theatre

GRADE LEVELS: 2–12

Getting Started
Building Background
Vocabulary
Reading Closely
Comprehension
Discussion
Writing

CCSS Anchor Standards: Writing

➤ **CCSS.ELA-Literacy.CCRA.W.2** Write informative/explanatory texts to examine and convey complex ideas and information clearly and accurately through the effective selection, organization, and analysis of content.

➤ **CCSS.ELA-Literacy.CCRA.W.4** Produce clear and coherent writing in which the development, organization, and style are appropriate to task, purpose, and audience.

➤ **CCSS.ELA-Literacy.CCRA.W.6** Use technology, including the Internet, to produce and publish writing and to interact and collaborate with others.

➤ **CCSS.ELA-Literacy.CCRA.W.9** Draw evidence from literary or informational texts to support analysis, reflection, and research.

What Is It?

The Readers Theatre strategy is the oral presentation of text by a group of readers. Readers Theatre does not typically include props, costumes, or memorization of lines, which makes it an ideal strategy to use with many students. Students must, however, read their parts fluently, with appropriate dramatic flair and proper intonation. Readers Theatre is often used with folktales or narrative texts, but can be easily adapted to informational texts. Young and Vardell (1993) offer guidelines to help teachers adapt informational texts to a Readers Theatre Script. We refer to these guidelines in the "What Do I Do?" section.

Readers Theatre can be enhanced in two ways. First, teachers can include a

Writing Strategies

229

technology component in which students actually film their presentations and/or use digital effects to enrich their presentation. Second, Readers Theatre scripts can be livened up by using voice in a process referred to as student-developed scriptwriting (Young & Rasinski, 2011; Miner, Follette, Rasinski, & Yildirum, 2014). Teachers are encouraged to give students a bigger role in developing scripts and to allow students to insert their own voice and commentaries. In adding voice, students demonstrate their deep knowledge of the content.

What Is Its Purpose?

The purpose of Readers Theatre is to give students the opportunity to engage in a dramatic presentation of a text as well as to develop reading fluency (Griffith & Rasinski, 2004; Young & Rasinski, 2009). Readers Theatre can help students visualize the action in a text in ways that simply reading a text cannot. It can provide a means for improving student comprehension in a motivating, engaging format. As such, Readers Theatre promotes interest in reading (Griffith & Rasinski, 2004; Young & Rasinski, 2009).

Informational books and biographies with dialogue are easily adapted to this format, but picture books or excerpts from longer books can also be effective. Informational trade books like King and Osborne's (1997) *Oh Freedom!: Kids Talk about the Civil Rights Movement with the People Who Made It Happen* or *Owen and Mzee: The True Story of a Remarkable Friendship* (Hatkoff, Hatkoff, & Kahumbu, 2006) are excellent examples of books that can be easily adapted to this format.

What Do I Do?

1. Choose an interesting section of text containing the desired content. (*Optional:* After modeling Readers Theatre, involve students in selecting books and scenes from which they can develop their own Readers Theatre scripts. Through this activity, students develop critical thinking skills, make decisions, work cooperatively, and engage in the process of revision.)

2. Reproduce the text.

3. Delete lines not critical to the content being emphasized, including those indicating that a character is speaking. The narrator's role is often important in informational texts.

4. Decide how to divide the parts for the readers. Dialogue can be assigned to appropriate characters. With some texts, it will be necessary to rewrite text as dialogue or with multiple narrators. Changing the third-person point of view to the first-person point of view ("I" or "we") can create effective narration.

5. Add a prologue to introduce the script in storylike fashion. If needed, a post-script can be added to bring closure to the script.

6. Label the readers' parts by placing the speaker's name in the left-hand margin, followed by a colon.

7. Encourage students to add voice to their scripts. (*Optional:* Discuss how voice adds tone and mood.)

8. When the script is finished, ask others to read it aloud. Listening to the script may make it easier to make appropriate revisions.

9. Give students time to read and rehearse their parts.

10. *Optional:* Allow students to use technology to enhance their presentation. For example, students can create a backdrop using images on PowerPoint. Students can create a playlist for their script by creating mood music. Students can also film and upload their presentations for viewing. (Be sure to get permission from parents before posting anything online.)

Example

Third-grade teacher Bonnie Mulvey decided to introduce her students to using a Readers Theatre script she developed based on *Abe's Honest Words: The Life of Abraham Lincoln* (Rappaport, 2008). She had already read this text aloud to the students. She introduced the script using a KWHL (Strategy 6) and involved her students in reading the script as a group. After her students read the script and discussed it, she assigned each student a part. At this point, the students formed pairs and practiced their parts using paired reading. After each student had ample time to practice, the students worked as a class to read the entire script. Bonnie wanted to model this process for the students so that they could create their own scripts.

She read aloud *Lincoln Tells a Joke: How Laughter Saved the President (and the Country)* (Krull & Brewer, 2010). As Bonnie read the text, she stopped and noted the parts where the authors inserted voice. She discussed how this made the content more enjoyable to readers. She modeled how to insert voice into scriptwriting.

References

Griffith, L. W., & Rasinski, T. (2004). A focus on fluency: How one teacher incorporated fluency with her reading curriculum. *The Reading Teacher, 58*(2), 126–133.

Hatkoff, I., Hatkoff, C., & Kahumbu, P. (2006). *Owen and Mzee: The true story of a remarkable friendship.* New York: Scholastic. (P)

King, C., & Osborne, L. B. (1997). *Oh freedom!: Kids talk about the civil rights movement with the people who made it happen.* New York: Knopf. (YA).

Sample Readers Theatre Script

Narrator 1: Lincoln and Mary finally got married.

Narrator 2: But it wasn't always rainbows and sunshine for the couple.

Lincoln: I'm moody!

Mary: Your moodiness is driving me into a rage!

Lincoln: Good thing we're devoted to each other.

Narrator 1: Lincoln was 16 inches taller than Mary.

Narrator 2: Sixteen inches! Opposites really do attract!

Mary: Yep. Lincoln thinks he's funny. He likes to make jokes about our height differences.

Lincoln: Here I am, and here is Mrs. Lincoln. And that's the long and short of it.

Narrator 1: That's a knee-slapper, Mr. President.

Krull, K., & Brewer, P. (2010). *Lincoln tells a joke: How laughter saved the president (and the country)*. New York: HMH Books for Young Readers. (P)

Miner, K., Follette, P., Rasinski, T., & Yildirum, K. (2014). Scriptwriting: Exploring the use of mentor texts to extend the readers theater experience. *Journal of Teacher Action Research, 1*, 16–30.

Rappaport, D. (2008). *Abe's honest words: The life of Abraham Lincoln*. New York: Hyperion. (P)

Young, C. J., & Rasinski, T. (2009). Implementing Readers Theatre as an approach to classroom fluency instruction. *The Reading Teacher, 63*(1), 4–13.

Young, C. J., & Rasinski, T. (2011). Enhancing author's voice through scripting. *The Reading Teacher, 65*(1), 24–28.

Young, T. A., & Vardell, S. M. (1993). Weaving Readers' Theatre and nonfiction into the curriculum. *The Reading Teacher, 46*, 396–406.

Your Turn!

Select an informational trade book and guide students in developing a Readers Theatre script around it. Follow the steps outlined on pages 230–231, or, for more information, consult Young and Vardell's (1993) article listed in the references. The handout on the facing page provides a "first step" in the process of scriptwriting. Students can record the speaker's name on the short line on the left and what the person will say on the lines on the right.

Readers Theatre Script

Instructions: Think about how you will turn the text into a script. Decide who the speakers will be. Decide what each speaker will say. Record the names of the speakers on the short lines and the words they will say on the longer lines.

Title: _____

Speakers: _____

_____

_____ : _____

_____

_____

_____ : _____

_____

_____

_____ : _____

_____

_____

_____ : _____

_____

_____

_____ : _____

_____

_____

Strategy 35

Paragraph Writing Frames

GRADE LEVELS: 2–12

Getting Started
Building Background
Vocabulary
Reading Closely
Comprehension
Discussion
Writing

CCSS Anchor Standards: Writing

➤ **CCSS.ELA-Literacy.CCRA.W.1** Write arguments to support claims in an analysis of substantive topics or texts using valid reasoning and relevant and sufficient evidence.

➤ **CCSS.ELA-Literacy.CCRA.W.2** Write informative/explanatory texts to examine and convey complex ideas and information clearly and accurately through the effective selection, organization, and analysis of content.

➤ **CCSS.ELA-Literacy.CCRA.W.4** Produce clear and coherent writing in which the development, organization, and style are appropriate to task, purpose, and audience.

➤ **CCSS.ELA-Literacy.CCRA.W.9** Draw evidence from literary or informational texts to support analysis, reflection, and research.

What Is It?

Paragraph Writing Frames are an excellent way to scaffold student writing of informational texts (Armbruster, Anderson, & Ostertag, 1989). They are equally effective with young children or older children who struggle with writing. Originally designed for use with textbook material, Paragraph Writing Frames can be easily adapted for use with informational trade books and magazine or newspaper articles. These frames help students to further their understanding of the most frequently encountered informational text patterns, which include description, sequence, comparison–contrast, cause–effect, and problem–solution (see Strategy 26 for more information about text structures).

Paragraph Writing Frames employ the cloze procedure, providing sentence starters that include signal words or phrases. When these are completed, students have written a paragraph that follows one of the informational text structures. These frames provide an excellent follow-up to the Text Structures graphic organizers presented in Strategy 26. After learning about each text structure, students can then try their hand at writing paragraphs illustrating each pattern.

What Is Its Purpose?

The Paragraph Writing Frames help students further their understanding of the most frequently encountered informational text patterns. They effectively scaffold students' efforts to use these structures in their own writing. These frames also help students develop academic language skills.

What Do I Do?

1. Introduce the frames one at a time. First, model the writing of a sample paragraph illustrating the organizational pattern being introduced. For example, the teacher could write a paragraph about a topic that illustrates sequence. In this paragraph, he or she would use signal words like *first*, *next*, *then*, and *finally*.

2. Review the sequence of events in the paragraph and with the group.

3. Give students the sentences on sentence strips and have them arrange the sentences in order.

4. Depending on their ability, have students copy the strips in paragraph form onto their papers.

5. Introduce the Paragraph Writing Frames to the whole group. Complete the frame by filling in the students' responses. (It may be helpful for students to have the first sentence of the frame provided for them.)

Example

Pat Hammond worked with seventh-grade English learners who were struggling with writing. Pat had been working to help these students recognize the various informational text structures for some time. It was now time to involve them in writing that used these structures. Pat decided to use the comparison–contrast structure for her focus. She showed the students a written sample of work illustrating the contrast pattern, which would be the lesson focus. She helped them to identify the signal words in the passage and demonstrated for them how an author goes back and forth between two topics when contrasting ideas. She then introduced the Paragraph Writing Frame for the contrast structure, explaining to students that it was similar to the cloze strategy they had used before. She pointed out to students the signal words associated with writing using the contrast pattern. At this point, Pat read aloud a section from *George vs. George: The American Revolution as Seen from Both Sides* (Schanzer, 2007), a trade book that explores the American Revolution from the points of view of George Washington and George III. She projected the text on the document camera and read aloud the part of the text that compared life in England with life in the colonies.

After students listened to the text, she had them discuss in pairs the similarities and differences between life in England and in the colonies. After that, she had students complete a contrast frame as illustrated below. The students' words are italicized in the example.

References

Armbruster, B., Anderson, T. H., & Ostertag, J. (1989). Teaching text structure to improve reading and writing. *The Reading Teacher, 43*, 130–137.

Schanzer, R. (2007). *George vs. George: The American Revolution as seen from both sides.* Washington, DC: National Geographic. (I)

Your Turn!

Introduce your students to Paragraph Writing Frames using the suggestions outlined above, then have them try out the frames found on pages 237–238. You may wish to modify these, depending on the subject and topic being studied.

Sample Paragraph Writing Frame

Life in England and in the colonies were different in many ways.

First, *many people in England lived in London, Europe's largest city, but most colonists lived on farms.*

Second, *England's wealthy city dwellers spent time in city-based coffeehouses, taverns, and gardens, while most colonists were middle class and included farmers, shopkeepers, teachers, and craftsmen.*

Third, *British cities were polluted with smog, while American towns had beautiful forests, fish, and game.*

Finally, *the poor in England included beggars and pickpockets, while poor colonists were usually laborers, indentured servants, and slaves.*

Paragraph Writing Frames

Instructions: Figure out the text structure. Select the correct writing frame. Complete the writing frame with content you learned from the text you read.

Description Frame

_____ have many interesting features. First, they have _____,

which allow them to _____. Second, they have _____, which

are _____.

Last, they have _____,

which _____.

Sequence Frame

The first step in making a _____ is to _____.

After that, you must _____

_____. Third, you need to

_____

_____. Finally, you

_____

_____.

Comparison Frame

_____ are alike in many ways. First, both are _____ and

_____. Second, they have similar _____. Finally, they both

_____.

(continued)

Contrast Frame

_____ were different in many ways. First, they differed because _____,

while _____. A second difference was that _____.

A third difference was _____.

Finally, another difference was _____.

Cause–Effect Frame

Because of _____,

_____ happened. Therefore,

_____.

This explains why _____

_____.

Problem–Solution Frame

The problem was that _____

_____.

This problem happened because _____

_____.

The problem was finally solved when _____

_____.

Strategy 36

I Used to Think . . . but Now I Know . . .

GRADE LEVELS: 2–12

Getting Started
Building Background
Vocabulary
Reading Closely
Comprehension
Discussion
Writing

CCSS Anchor Standards: Writing

➤ **CCSS.ELA-Literacy.CCRA.W.2** Write informative/explanatory texts to examine and convey complex ideas and information clearly and accurately through the effective selection, organization, and analysis of content.

➤ **CCSS.ELA-Literacy.CCRA.W.4** Produce clear and coherent writing in which the development, organization, and style are appropriate to task, purpose, and audience.

➤ **CCSS.ELA-Literacy.CCRA.W.9** Draw evidence from literary or informational texts to support analysis, reflection, and research.

What Is It?

I Used to Think . . . but Now I Know . . . (Koch, 1990) is a poetic sentence frame that can be used in any content area. This strategy is best used before and after reading an informational text or at the beginning and end of a unit of study in conjunction with KWHL (Strategy 6). It provides a clear structure for students to state their preconceptions about a topic. Through the reading of informational texts, students will develop the abilities to question these preconceptions and to refer to the text for confirmation or to replace it with fact.

This strategy is also a way to combine poetry and informational texts. These two genres are generally thought of as being opposites, since poetry typically elicits aesthetic, or feeling-type responses, while informational texts elicit more efferent, or factual-type responses (Rosenblatt, 2004). By completing a series of I Used to Think . . . but Now I Know . . . frames, students are essentially creating poems about informational topics.

What Is Its Purpose?

The purpose of the I Used to Think . . . but Now I Know . . . sentence frame is to enhance students' appreciation for poetry, to access their prior knowledge, and to measure what students have learned from a particular text or unit of study. In order to successfully complete the strategy, students must be able to comprehend the text and reflect on how their thinking about the topic may have changed. This strategy aims to solidify and further deepen students' content knowledge. In addition, this strategy allows students an opportunity to think critically about their preconceptions, as the idea is to refute, affirm, or adjust current thinking.

What Do I Do?

1. Model the strategy. For example, in introducing a unit of the American Revolution, you could think aloud the following (adapted from Koch, 1990):

- I used to think   *that there were 15 colonies,*

- But now I know   *there were 13 original colonies.*

- I used to think   *the Americans and British were the only countries fighting in the war,*

- But now I know   *the French were our allies and helped American colonists win.*

2. Begin a class discussion about the topic of study. Have students share what they think they know about the topic.

3. Have students write some of their preconceptions following the sentence frame "I used to think. . . . " Have the students write six to nine of them, as some frames may not be used if they are true. For example, a student could write "I used to think *that George Washington was a general in the Revolutionary War. . . .* " This sentence would be true, so there would be no need to finish the frame. This student would eliminate this particular frame from his or her poem.

4. Select an informational text about the topic under study. The topic should be one about which students have limited prior knowledge.

5. Read the text aloud. Set a purpose for reading by telling the students to listen for whether their "facts" are correct or whether they need to be changed.

6. For younger groups, you might want to scaffold and list some facts learned from the story on chart paper. Students can refer to this collection of learned facts to confirm their preconceptions or refute their misconceptions.

7. Have students complete the "But now I know . . . " sentence frame with the appropriate fact.

8. Have students share their poems with a partner.

9. *Optional:* For the sentences that were correct, instead of eliminating them, the students could change their frames to "I used to think . . . AND now I know that I was right!" This might be a good opportunity to explicitly teach the students the use of the conjunctions *and* versus *but*.

Example

Marilyn Ware, an eighth-grade science teacher, taught a unit on the chemistry of living things. Before starting the unit, she did a KWHL (Strategy 6) with her students. After completing the KWH sections as a whole group, she paired the students up. (Because Marilyn teaches in a school with a large population of English learners, she made sure to partner a proficient or native speaker with a beginning or intermediate speaker.)

Marilyn wrote the following vocabulary words and concepts on the board: *cell*, *mitochondria*, *DNA*, *RNA*, *ribosomes*, and *enzymes*. She had each pair talk about what they thought each of the six terms meant; they were instructed to complete the sentence frame "We used to think. . . . " (They left the "But now we know . . . " sentence frame blank at this point.)

Then Marilyn projected the text for a read-aloud. She read the first chapter, titled "Building Blocks" from *Biology: Life as We Know It* by Dan Green (2008). As she read, she had the pairs complete their sentence frames: "But now we know. . . ." For example, one pair came up with "We used to think *that mitochondria was something that plants produced*, but now we know *that mitochondria are like power plants working inside cells to burn food in order to make ATP, or energy.*"

Marilyn gave each pair a large piece of poster paper and had them record their sentence frames on the paper along with appropriate illustrations. The next day, she hung the posters up around the room and to review, she had the students walk around and read each poster; this strategy is often referred to as a Gallery Walk.

References

Green, D. (2008). *Biology: Life as we know it*. New York: Kingfisher. (YA)

Koch, K. (1990). *Rose, where did you get that red? Teaching great poetry to children*. New York: Vintage.

Rosenblatt, L. (2004). The transactional theory of reading and writing. In R. B. Ruddell & N. J. Unrau (Eds.), *Theoretical models and processes of reading* (5th ed., pp. 1363–1398). Newark, DE: International Reading Association.

Your Turn!

Select an informational trade book from the Appendix at the back of this book or one of your own choosing. This strategy works best when your students have limited knowledge about the subject. Distribute the worksheet on the facing page and model an example.

Writing Strategies

242

"I Used to Think . . . but Now I Know . . ." Sentence Frames

Instructions: Complete each frame by telling what you used to think (prior knowledge) and what you know now (evidence from the text).

Topic: _____

I used to think _____

_____

but now I know _____

_____.

I used to think _____

_____

but now I know _____

_____.

I used to think _____

_____

but now I know _____

_____.

I used to think _____

_____

but now I know _____

_____.

I used to think _____

_____

but now I know _____

_____.

Summary Writing

GRADE LEVELS: 3–12

Getting Started

Building Background

Vocabulary

Reading Closely

Comprehension

Discussion

Writing

CCSS Anchor Standards: Writing

➤ **CCSS.ELA-Literacy.CCRA.W.2** Write informative/explanatory texts to examine and convey complex ideas and information clearly and accurately through the effective selection, organization, and analysis of content.

➤ **CCSS.ELA-Literacy.CCRA.W.4** Produce clear and coherent writing in which the development, organization, and style are appropriate to task, purpose, and audience.

➤ **CCSS.ELA-Literacy.CCRA.W.9** Draw evidence from literary or informational texts to support analysis, reflection, and research.

What Is It?

The Summary Writing strategy (adapted from Klinger & Vaughn, 1998) involves distilling information to its most essential components. A good summary uses as few words as possible to provide a brief overview of a text or section of a text. Effective summaries include only the main ideas from a text; they do not include extraneous details. Summary writing is an essential skill for college and career success. Writing informational text summaries demands some different skills from summarizing a narrative, since it often involves the ability to use appropriate vocabulary terms and key concepts and details, rather than story events.

Writing Strategies

What Is Its Purpose?

The purpose of the Summary Writing strategy is to help students distinguish between important and interesting details. This strategy aims to help students articulate the gist of a text. It helps students to produce a brief overview of a longer piece of work. The ability to summarize in writing requires students to condense, analyze, and synthesize information and to look beyond details to big ideas in a text. Students who can capably summarize demonstrate deep understanding of the most important ideas in a text.

What Do I Do?

1. Present an informational text to your students. Select a text that students are already familiar with.

2. Explain to students that it is often easier to know the main points from a text than to have to remember all of the details. When you write a summary, you have a record of the most important points from a text.

3. Show students a sample summary of a text they have already read. Point out to them that the summary is short, contains only the main points from the text, and condenses these points into very few words.

4. Explain that a main idea consists of two component parts: the *who* or *what* and the most important information about the *who* or *what*. To create a summary students must combine these components into a sentence of no more than 20 words.

5. Read the first paragraph of the text aloud. Think aloud as you identify the *who* or *what* and the most important information about the *who* or *what*. Record this information on the board. Then show students how to combine this information into a statement of no more than 20 words. Record this statement on the board.

6. Continue with this procedure for the rest of the text. Then show students how to combine each statement into a summary statement of no more than 20 words.

7. Then ask students to work with a partner to read a short text. Have them stop at specific points to complete the chart on page 248 as they think about the required information and condense it into a limited number of words. Then give them time to create a 20-word statement for their final summary of the book.

Writing Strategies

Example

Third-grade teacher Molly Bernstein's students were studying a unit on mammals. In order to teach her students about animal life cycles and how to summarize information, she decided to use the National Geographic book *Life Cycles: Giant Pandas* (Reeder, 2005). Molly began the lesson by reviewing with students what they know about mammals. She then asked them what they know about pandas and why they are mammals.

Molly began the lesson on summarizing by showing students the section of the book on panda life cycles. She projected the book and read aloud the first section of the text, titled "Birth." She thought aloud as she noted what the section was about and what was important about the birth of pandas. She recorded this on the Summary Writing Chart (see the facing page). At this point, she created a 20-word summary of the information and recorded it on the chart. She then had students complete the last two sections, "Growth" and "Reproduction," with a partner, following the same format. They summarized these two sections at the bottom of the chart. Following this, students discussed the kind of thinking they had to do to complete the summary.

References

Klinger, J. K., & Vaughn, S. (1998). Using collaborative strategic reading. *Teaching Exceptional Children, 30*(6), 32–37.

Reeder, T. (2005). *Life cycles: Giant pandas.* Washington, DC: National Geographic. (I)

Your Turn!

Select an informational text from the Appendix at the end of this book or one of your own choosing. After you model Summary Writing, have the students use the form on page 248 to summarize key sections and then combine those summaries for the section at the bottom.

Sample Summary Writing Chart

Title of Book: _Life Cycles: Giant Pandas_   **Author:** _Tracey Reeder_

What was the title of this section? _Growth_	What was the title of this section? _Reproduction_
Who or what was this section about? _How pandas grow up and what they do._	Who or what was this section about? _How pandas get babies._
What was the important information about who or what this was about? • _Cubs can see at 6–8 weeks old._ • _Walks at 12 weeks._ • _8–9 months stops drinking milk and eats bamboo._ • _Lives on its own at 18 months._ • _Adult at 4–6 years._	What was the important information about who or what this was about? • _The female egg and male sperm come together._ • _The egg is fertilized._ • _A new baby grows in the mother's body._ • _After 160 days the baby is born._
Write a main idea sentence of no more than 20 words. _Pandas see at 6 weeks, walk at 12 weeks, eat bamboo at 8 months, and become adults at 4 years._	Write a main idea sentence of no more than 20 words. _Pandas reproduce when an egg and sperm join, creating babies that grow in the mother's body and are born after 160 days._

Now combine your main idea sentences to create a summary of no more than 20 words for the entire text.

Baby pandas grow up and become adults at 4 years, when they reproduce to create babies born after 160 days.

Summary Writing Chart

Instructions: Record the title and author in the top row. For each section, record your responses in the box provided. In the bottom row, write your summary using all the information you noted on this handout.

Title of Book: _____   **Author:** _____

What was the title of this section?	What was the title of this section?
Who or what was this section about?	Who or what was this section about?
What was the important information about who or what this was about? • • • • •	What was the important information about who or what this was about? • • • • •
Write a main idea sentence of no more than 20 words.	Write a main idea sentence of no more than 20 words.
Now combine your main idea sentences to create a summary of no more than 20 words for the entire text.	

Strategy 38

CLIQUES

GRADE LEVELS: 6–12

Getting Started
Building Background
Vocabulary
Reading Closely
Comprehension
Discussion
Writing

CCSS Anchor Standards: Writing

➤ **CCSS.ELA-Literacy.CCRA.W.1** Write arguments to support claims in an analysis of substantive topics or texts using valid reasoning and relevant and sufficient evidence.

➤ **CCSS.ELA-Literacy.CCRA.W.2** Write informative/explanatory texts to examine and convey complex ideas and information clearly and accurately through the effective selection, organization, and analysis of content.

➤ **CCSS.ELA-Literacy.CCRA.W.7** Conduct short as well as more sustained research projects based on focused questions, demonstrating understanding of the subject under investigation.

➤ **CCSS.ELA-Literacy.CCRA.W.8** Gather relevant information from multiple print and digital sources, assess the credibility and accuracy of each source, and integrate the information while avoiding plagiarism.

➤ **CCSS.ELA-Literacy.CCRA.W.9** Draw evidence from literary or informational texts to support analysis, reflection, and research.

What Is It?

The CCSS push students to support their thinking and analyses with evidence from the text. Making evidence-based claims about texts is a critical proficiency that all students must develop (Pegg & Adams, 2012). Greater attention is being paid to the importance of textual evidence in writing and discussions. Textual evidence includes but is not limited to facts, statistics, examples, and quotations. Students often don't know how to integrate such evidence effectively into their writing.

Students seem to have a really difficult time using quotations as supporting evidence. They tend to quote too much or too little and to not explain their use of quotations. The CLIQUES strategy (Loh-Hagan, 2015) was developed to help students contextualize quotations when writing expository texts. Adapting Taylor's (2014) simple structure for helping beginning writers compose a supporting paragraph using a quotation, the CLIQUES strategy provides a tool for teachers to explicitly teach students how to incorporate quotations into their expository writing.

The chart below provides an overview of the strategy.

What Is Its Purpose?

The purpose of the CLIQUES strategy is to help students more effectively include quotations in their expository writing. This strategy supports students in writing a supporting body paragraph. Students must learn to make quotations a substantial part of their logical reasoning process. If writing a complete paper, students will need additional scaffolds to write introductory and concluding paragraphs.

What Do I Do?

1. Have students read and study several informational texts about a topic. Make sure students have enough content knowledge to write about the topic and enough sources from which to draw.

Overview of the CLIQUES Strategy

CL	Claim	State your claim. This is the topic sentence, the main idea of your paragraph. It's the argument or the explanation.
I	Introduction of quotation	Prepare to present your evidence. Provide a reason that supports your claim. Build readers up to your quotation by providing some context. If applicable, describe who, to whom, when, and where the quotation appears.
QU	Quotation	State your quotation. Use signal phrases such as *For example . . . , According to . . . ,* _____ *states . . .*
E	Explanation of quotation	Explain how your quotation supports your claim. Explain why you chose this quotation.
S	So what?	Explain your point again. Analyze your position in light of the evidence you included.

2. Have students generate a claim. (*Optional:* Provide students with a claim or a prompt.)

3. Have students find quotations from the text to support their claim. (*Optional:* Discuss different ways to use quotations including paraphrasing, citing completely, or citing parts of the quotations.)

4. Introduce the CLIQUES strategy. (*Optional:* Model the strategy before having students implement it on their own.)

5. Have students complete the handout on page 253. This will serve as their writing organizer.

6. Check students' understanding and allow them to write their paragraphs. (*Optional:* Encourage students to edit and revise before submitting a final copy.)

Example

Sam Revitte teaches ninth-grade social studies. He is teaching a unit on women's roles in American wars. Sam eventually wants his students to write a paper on this topic, but he knows that his students are struggling with writing expository texts. Based on previous student writing samples, Sam knows that his students are specifically having a difficult time using quotations, so he decides to use the CLIQUES strategy and focuses specifically on quotations. He spends some time discussing quotations as a source of evidence as well as how to paraphrase and how to directly quote.

He focused on Chapter 4, titled "Nurses Under Fire," from Mary Cronk Farrell's (2014) *Pure Grit: How American World War II Nurses Survived Battle and Prison Camp in the Pacific*. He had the students read the chapter and complete a Two-Column Journal (Strategy 40) for homework.

In class, Sam modeled the CLIQUES strategy for his students. He picked a quotation from the chapter and completed the template, then performed a think-aloud so that students could follow along with this thought process. Then he had students choose a different quotation from their Two-Column Journals and complete the CLIQUES Template on their own. He walked around and provided assistance as needed. See the student sample on page 252.

References

Farrell, M. C. (2014). *Pure grit: How American World War II nurses survived battle and prison camp in the Pacific*. New York: Abrams. (YA)

Loh-Hagan, V. (2015). Use CLIQUES to make quotations click. Annenberg Learner Log.

Writing Strategies

Sample CLIQUES Template

CL	State your **CL**aim.	Nurses were important to the war effort. Just like soldiers, they put themselves in danger in order to fight for their country.
I	**I**ntroduce your quotation.	Nurses worked at and near battlefields. No place was safe from enemy fire, including hospitals. At the U.S. Army Hospital in Manila during World War II, Japanese bombers attacked.
QU	Include your **QU**otation.	Farrell (2014) states, "Nurses moved other patients under their beds for protection and then leaped into the nearest foxhole themselves" (p. 27).
E	**E**xplain your quotation.	This quotation shows how nurses thought of their patients first before themselves. Even faced with bombs, nurses refused to leave anyone behind.
S	**S**o what?	Both men and women fight in the war. Women should be just as celebrated for their work. They assume the same risks.

Retrieved October 15, 2015, from *http://learnerlog.org/literatureandlanguagearts/use-cliques-to-make-quotations-click*.

Pegg, J., & Adams, A. (2012). Reading for claims and evidence: Using anticipation guides in science. *Science Scope, 36*(2), 74–78.

Taylor, C. B. (2014, November). *The secret recipe—Evidentiary-based writing and analysis made easy.* Paper presented at 104th Annual Convention of the National Council of Teachers of English, Washington, DC.

Your Turn!

Select a topic of study and have students read several informational texts (refer to the Appendix at the back of this book for text ideas). Assign students to write a paragraph that uses a quotation as a source of evidence. Have students complete the template on the facing page. Make sure students know that this strategy is designed to help them write a supporting paragraph; they should not necessarily use this format for writing papers or essays, as they will need introduction and conclusion paragraphs.

The CLIQUES Strategy Template

Instructions: Complete this template and use it as a writing organizer for using quotations. Make sure to cite your evidence using the correct format.

CL	State your **CL**aim.	
I	**I**ntroduce your quotation.	
QU	Include your **QU**otation.	
E	**E**xplain your quotation.	
S	**S**o what?	

EPIC

GRADE LEVELS: 5–12

Getting Started
Building Background
Vocabulary
Reading Closely
Comprehension
Discussion
Writing

CCSS Anchor Standards: Writing

➤ **CCSS.ELA-Literacy.CCRA.W.1** Write arguments to support claims in an analysis of substantive topics or texts using valid reasoning and relevant and sufficient evidence.

➤ **CCSS.ELA-Literacy.CCRA.W.2** Write informative/explanatory texts to examine and convey complex ideas and information clearly and accurately through the effective selection, organization, and analysis of content.

➤ **CCSS.ELA-Literacy.CCRA.W.8** Gather relevant information from multiple print and digital sources, assess the credibility and accuracy of each source, and integrate the information while avoiding plagiarism.

➤ **CCSS.ELA-Literacy.CCRA.W.9** Draw evidence from literary or informational texts to support analysis, reflection, and research.

What Is It?

The EPIC strategy is a method for helping students generate evidence-based claims. EPIC is an acronym; each letter stands for a step in the strategy, described in the chart on the facing page.

We developed the EPIC strategy based on Hillocks's (2010) work. Hillocks (2010) contends that argument is "at the heart of critical thinking and academic discourse, the kind of writing students need to know for success in college" (p. 25). He believes that students should be encouraged to generate their own claims by "looking at the data that are likely to become the evidence in an argument and that give rise to a thesis statement or major claim" (p. 26).

The Four Steps of the EPIC Strategy

E	Step 1: **E**vidence	Pull evidence from the text. What seems important and/or interesting to you?
P	Step 2: **P**atterns	What patterns do you see? What connections seem to exist among these important ideas and details?
I	Step 3: **I**nquiry	What questions do you have about what you just learned?
C	Step 4: **C**laims	What claims can you make about the topic/texts based on the evidence? What conclusions can you make that would be supported by the evidence?

What Is Its Purpose?

The purpose of the EPIC strategy is to guide students toward real-world critical thinking by helping them make their own claims about the evidence they are given. The EPIC strategy challenges teachers to not give students claims or prompts, but rather allow students to create their own ideas based on the texts. In many ways, this approach prepares students to think like researchers, scientists, and historians who analyze data in order to generate new conclusions.

What Do I Do?

1. Select informational texts that will deepen students' knowledge. (Ideally, students should have read at least three different texts from which to gather information.)

2. Review the EPIC strategy using the chart provided above. Make sure students understand the gist of the strategy.

3. Model the strategy by going through the steps. (Consider using topics studied in previous units so that students are familiar with the content knowledge.)

4. Pull evidence from the text by recording important and/or interesting details from the text.

5. Determine patterns or connections from the evidence presented in the previous step. Record on template.

6. Share your thoughts about the evidence presented on the template thus far. Stress to the students the importance of writing this part in their own words.

7. Generate and record some claims. Make sure claims are valid and can be supported by evidence.

8. Allow students the opportunity to practice the strategy independently.

Example

Molly Brecken is an eighth-grade science teacher doing a unit on diseases. She wants her students to learn how to write a five- to eight-page review of the literature. Before she has the students work independently, she explicitly teaches the EPIC strategy to model how to conduct inquiry into data found in texts.

She models a close reading of the introduction and first chapter of Patricia Newman's (2015) *Ebola: Fears and Facts,* then models how to apply the EPIC strategy to what students just read. She tells students that this will serve as a starting point for their research topic. She completes the EPIC Template with them and reviews each step of the strategy. A sample chart is on the facing page.

For homework, Molly has students read at least three online articles on a scientific topic of their choice and complete the EPIC strategy the next day in class. She has them pick one claim from Step 4 to guide their research. She works with the students to refine the claim and she tells them that this is the central idea of their literature review paper. Molly asks students, "Why is this an effective claim?" and charts students' responses. From these responses, she works with students to create a checklist of effective claims and encourages them to use this checklist when reviewing their claims. She tells students that claims need further research in order to be confirmed. She lets them know that some of them may change their claim after conducting more research. That's how real scientists work!

References

Hillocks, G. (2010). Teaching argument for critical thinking and writing: An introduction. *English Journal, 99*(6), 24–32.

Newman, P. (2015). *Ebola: Fears and facts.* Minneapolis, MN: Millbrook Press. (M)

Your Turn!

Select informational texts from the Appendix at the end of this book, or choose your own texts. Model the strategy and then allow students to practice the EPIC strategy after you ensure they understand the process. Make sure students understand that they are generating their own claims based on evidence. As a follow-up, you can have students perform a writing task using their claims.

Sample EPIC Template

E	**Step 1:** **Evidence**	Pull evidence from the text. What seems important and/or interesting to you?	• First outbreak in 1976. Five Ebola outbreaks between 1976 and 1996 in central Africa.
			• Scientists trace the path of the disease and find those who have been exposed. They notice patterns in symptoms and transmission process.
			• Ebola is a river. It means "Black River" in Lingala. But there's no connection between the river and the disease. The Ebola River isn't even the river closest to the first outbreak location. Scientists named the disease in a "tired state" (p. 7).
			• Lots of bleeding. Kills quickly. Half of the patients die.
			• 1996 outbreak: Villagers ate chimpanzee carcass; meat infected 18 people. People who helped got infected. 31 more people got infected.
			• Victims are still contagious after death.
			• No cures. There are vaccines and treatments in testing phase.
			• Some scientists believe immunity could last 10 or more years; more research needed.
			• Ebola is a virus. Thrives best in humans and apes.
			• Nearly 2/3 of diseases come from animals: malaria, influenza, and rabies.
P	**Step 2:** **Patterns**	What patterns do you see? What connections seem to exist among these important ideas and details?	• Scientists are essential for treating diseases. They spend a lot of time studying outbreaks. Tracing the history or origin of diseases is important.
			• Ebola is one of several diseases carried from animals to humans.
			• Africa seems to be host to diseases.
			• Ebola is a really nasty viral disease with gnarly symptoms. It can be fatal. It's really contagious. It was sad how family and community members died trying to help victims. They didn't know how to protect themselves like the scientists did.

(continued)

Sample EPIC Template (p. 2 of 2)

I	**Step 3:** **Inquiry**	What questions do you have about what you just learned?

- Why Africa?
- Why are some animals carriers and not others?
- What compels scientists to study contagious diseases? Aren't they afraid of being infected?

C	**Step 4:** **Claim**	What claims can you make about the topic/texts based on the evidence? What conclusions can you make that would be supported by the evidence?

- Scientists play a huge role in treating diseases like Ebola. The most important part of stopping diseases like Ebola is learning about its origin and understanding how it spreads. As such, in regard to studying diseases, fieldwork is more important than labwork.

- At least one Ebola outbreak can be traced to chimpanzee meat. Other animals spread diseases to humans as well. This suggests that humans are strongly connected to the animal kingdom. (We are what we eat—make a case for becoming vegan??)

- The beginning stages of an outbreak are scary, not because of the symptoms but because of the unknown variables.

EPIC Strategy Template

Instructions: Read the texts. Complete each step of the handout. Refine your claim as needed.

E	**Step 1** **Evidence**	Pull evidence from the text. What seems important and/or interesting to you?
P	**Step 2** **Patterns**	What patterns do you see? What connections seem to exist among these important ideas and details?
I	**Step 3** **Inquiry**	What questions do you have about what you just learned?
C	**Step 4** **Claim**	What claims can you make about the topic/texts based on the evidence? What conclusions can you make that would be supported by the evidence?

Strategy 40

Two-Column Journal

GRADE LEVELS: K–12

Getting Started
Building Background
Vocabulary
Reading Closely
Comprehension
Discussion
Writing

CCSS Anchor Standards: Writing

➤ **CCSS.ELA-Literacy.CCRA.W.2** Write informative/explanatory texts to examine and convey complex ideas and information clearly and accurately through the effective selection, organization, and analysis of content.

➤ **CCSS.ELA-Literacy.CCRA.W.9** Draw evidence from literary or informational texts to support analysis, reflection, and research.

What Is It?

The Two-Column Journal strategy lets students record and respond to informational texts. It promotes both aesthetic, or emotional, and efferent, or factual, responses. On the left side of a Two-Column Journal, students record facts and information found in a book, magazine, or newspaper article. They record words or phrases directly from the text or restate information in their own words. (This is a great opportunity to teach students how to paraphrase.) On the right side of the journal, students describe their feelings or emotional responses to those facts. They can also make textual connections and/or connections to society at large.

What Is Its Purpose?

The purpose of the Two-Column Journal strategy is to get students to think about their learning more deeply through the act of writing. By reflecting on what they think about what they have read, students are reminded of the need to be actively engaged in their reading and to make connections between the text itself, their own lives, society at large, and other texts. In addition, students are basing their reflections and thoughts on specific points of evidence from the text.

What Do I Do?

1. Select an appropriate book, magazine, or newspaper article.

2. Have students fold a piece of paper in half vertically.

3. On the left side of the paper, have students write "According to the Text . . . " on the top line.

4. On the right side of the paper, have students write "What I Thought . . . " on the top line.

5. Ask students to identify a specified number of interesting facts from the reading material. Have them record each fact on the left side of the paper. Next to each fact, have students record their reactions or feelings about each fact on the right side of the paper.

6. Have students discuss their facts and reactions with the whole group.

Example

Fifth-grade teacher Colin Danes involved his students in a unit of study on immigration. As part of that study, his students read *Immigrant Kids* (Freedman, 1995). After they completed their reading, Colin asked the students to complete Two-Column Journals related to the book. He divided students into small groups and had them review specific chapters, then instructed student groups to identify four important facts they learned from the book. Groups were required to reach consensus on which four facts were most important to their assigned sections. Next, they recorded them on the left side of their Two-Column Journals under "According to the Text. . . . " In addition, students were instructed to record their reactions to each fact under "What I Thought . . . " on the right side of the paper (see an example of one student's work on page 262). After completing their journals, each group shared their completed Two-Column Journal on the document camera, discussing their facts and their responses with the entire group. Other students were encouraged to challenge each group's choices of important facts. In this way, each group had to provide evidence for selecting the facts that they did.

Sample: Two-Column Journal

According to the Text . . .	What I Thought . . .
1. Children back then had to work to support their families.	1. I don't think kids should have to work to support their families.
2. Children back then were interested in baseball.	2. I love baseball too, just like the kids back then.
3. Kids back then formed gangs that fought with sticks and stones.	3. Kids today sometimes form gangs, but they fight with guns.
4. Immigrant kids back then had to memorize facts in school.	4. Kids today still have to memorize in school, so I guess schools haven't changed that much.

Reference

Freedman, R. (1995). *Immigrant kids*. New York: Puffin. (I)

Your Turn!

Select a text from the Appendix at the end of this book, or one of your own choosing. After students have read, have them record four or five facts about what they have read under "According to the Text . . . " and their reactions to those facts under "What I Thought. . . . " The handout on the facing page provides a template for their answers.

Two-Column Journal Template

Instructions: Record information from the text in the left column. Record your thoughts in the right column.

According to the Text . . .	What I Thought . . .

Appendix

Recommended Materials

Quality Informational Trade Books

Note: When listed under the references for each strategy, children's trade books are labeled as follows:

- Primary grades K–3 (P)
- Intermediate grades 4–6 (I)
- Middle grades 7–8 (M)
- High school grades 9–12 (YA [young adult])

Primary Grade Books (Grades K–3) (P)

Ancona, G. (2013). *It's our garden: From seeds to harvest in a school garden*. New York: Candlewick.

Appelt, K. (2014). *Mogie: The heart of a house*. New York: Atheneum.

Arnosky, J. (2008). *All about alligators*. New York: Scholastic.

Aston, D. H. (2006). *An egg is quiet*. New York: Chronicle Books.

Aston, D. H. (2007). *A seed is sleepy*. New York: Chronicle Books.

Auch, A. (2002). *Tame and wild*. Minneapolis, MN: Compass Point Books.

Bang, M., & Chisholm, P. (2014). *Sunlight* series. New York: Scholastic.

Berne, J. (2013). *On a beam of light: A story of Albert Einstein*. New York: Chronicle.

Bishop, N. (2007). *Nic Bishop spiders*. New York: Scholastic.

Bishop, N. (2013). *The amazing world of Nic Bishop* series. New York: Scholastic.

Borden, L. (2014). *Baseball is . . .* New York: Margaret K. McElderry Books.

Brown, C. L. (2007). *Beyond the dinosaurs: Monsters of the air and sea*. New York: HarperCollins.

Brown, D. (2004). *Odd boy out*. New York: Houghton Mifflin.

Burleigh, R. (2003). *Amelia Earhart: Free in the skies (American heroes)*. New York: Sandpiper.

Byrd, R. (2012). *Electric Ben: The amazing life and times of Benjamin Franklin*. New York: Dial.

Capstone Press. *Captured history* series. Mankato, MN: Author.

Curtis, J. K. (2015). *Primate school*. Mt. Pleasant, SC: Arbordale.

Davies, N. (2008). *Surprising sharks*. New York: Candlewick.

Deans, K. (2015). *Swing sisters: The story of the international sweethearts of rhythm*. New York: Holiday House.

Dorros, A. (1987). *Ant cities*. New York: Crowell.

Earle, A. (2009). *Zipping, zapping, zooming bats*. New York: HarperCollins.

Ehlert, L. (2014). *The scraps book: Notes from a colorful life.* San Diego, CA: Beach Lane.

Floca, B. (2009). *Moonshot: The flight of Apollo 11.* New York: Atheneum.

Floca, B. (2013). *Locomotive.* New York: Atheneum.

Garland, S. (2004). *Voices of the Alamo.* New York: Pelican.

Ghandi, A., & Hegedus, B. (2014). *Grandfather Gandhi.* New York: Atheneum.

Gibbons, G. (1997). *Nature's green umbrella: Tropical rain forests.* New York: Morrow Junior Books.

Gibbons, G. (2000). *Bats.* New York: Holiday House.

Gibbons, G. (2015). *The fruit we eat.* New York: Holiday House.

Gibbons, G. (2015). *It's raining.* New York: Holiday House.

Golenbock, P. (1992). *Teammates.* San Diego, CA: Harcourt Brace Jovanovich.

Hatkoff, I., Hatkoff, C., & Kuhumbu, P. (2006). *Owen & Mzee: The true story of a remarkable friendship.* New York: Scholastic.

Holland, M. (2015). *Animal mouths.* Mt. Pleasant, SC: Arbordale.

Jenkins, S. (1998). *Hottest, coldest, highest, deepest.* Boston: Houghton Mifflin.

Jenkins, S. (2014). *Eye to eye: How animals see the world.* Boston: Houghton Mifflin Harcourt.

Jordan, H. J. (2000). *How a seed grows (Let's read and find out science 1).* New York: HarperCollins. (P)

Krull, K. (2008). *Hilary Rodham Clinton: Dreams taking flight.* New York: Simon & Schuster.

Krull, K. (2014). *A zippy history of zoos: What's new? The zoo!* New York: Arthur A. Levine Books.

Krull, K., & Brewer, P. (2010). *Lincoln tells a joke: How laughter saved the President (and the country).* New York: HMH Books for Young Readers.

Kudlinski, K. V. (2008). *Boy, were we wrong about dinosaurs!* New York: Puffin.

Leedy, L., & Schuerger, A. (2015). *Amazing plant powers: How plants fly, fight, hide, hunt, and change the world.* New York: Holiday House.

Loh-Hagan, V. (2015). *21st century basic skills library: Splash! Discover sea animals.* North Mankato, MN: Cherry Lake.

Markel, M. (2013). *Brave girl! Clara and the shirtwaist makers' strike of 1909.* New York: Balzer & Bray.

Markle, S. (2004). *Great white sharks.* New York: Carolrhoda.

Martin, B., & Sampson, M. (2003). *I pledge allegiance.* Boston: Candlewick Press.

Martin, J. (2009). *Snowflake Bentley.* Boston: Houghton Mifflin.

Newman, M. (2010). *Polar bears.* New York: Holt.

Pfeffer, W. (2014). *Light is all around us (Let's-read-and-find-out science).* New York: Harper/HarperCollins.

Posada, M. (2002). *Ladybugs: Red, fiery, and bright.* New York: Carolrhoda.

Rappaport, D. (2001). *Martin's big words: The life of Dr. Martin Luther King, Jr.* New York: Hyperion.

Rappaport, D. (2008). *Abe's honest words: The life of Abraham Lincoln.* New York: Hyperion.

Robertson, R. (2015). *Hiawatha and the peacemaker.* New York: Abrams.

Rosenstock, B. (2013). *Thomas Jefferson builds a library.* Honesdale, PA: Calkins Creek.

Shea, P. D. (2009). *Noah Webster: Weaver of words.* Honesdale, PA: Calkins Creek.

Stewart, J., & Salem, L. (2003). *Toad or frog?* New York: Continental Press.

Stone, T. L. (2013). *Who says women can't be doctors? The story of Elizabeth Blackwell.* New York: Holt.

Tonatiuh, D. (2014). *Separate is never equal: Sylvia Mendez and her family's fight for desegregation.* New York: Abrams.

Waters, K. (2008). *Sarah Morton's day: A day in the life of a Pilgrim girl.* New York: Scholastic.

Woelfe, G. (2014). *Mumbet's Declaration of Independence.* New York: Carolrhoda.

Intermediate Grade Books (Grades 4–6) (I)

Albee, S. (2014). *Bugged: How insects changed history.* New York: Walker/Bloomsbury.

Arnold, C. (1993). *On the brink of extinction: The California condor.* New York: Harcourt Brace Jovanovich. (also M)

Arnosky, J. (2011). *Thunder birds*. New York: Sterling.

Ball, J. (2005). *Go figure! A totally cool book about numbers*. New York: DK Children.

Bausum, A. (2014). *Stubby the war dog: The true story of World War I's bravest dog*. Washington, DC: National Geographic.

Burns, L. G. (2012). *Citizen scientists: Be a part of scientific discovery from your own backyard*. New York: Holt.

Charles, O. (1990). *How is a crayon made?* New York: Aladdin.

Cherry, L. (2002). *A river ran wild: An environmental history*. Queensland, Australia: Sandpiper.

Clements, G. (2009). *The picture history of great explorers*. New York: Frances Lincoln.

Collard, S. (2015). *Firebirds: Valuing natural wildfires and burned forests*. Missoula, MT: Bucking Horse Books.

Colson, R. S. (2013). *Bone collection: Animals*. New York: Scholastic.

Cooper, M. L. (2014). *Fighting fire!: Ten of the deadliest fires in American history and how we fought them*. New York: Holt.

Deem, J. (2006). *Bodies from the ash: Life and death in ancient Pompeii*. New York: Houghton Mifflin.

Di Fiore, M. (2013). *Elephant man*. Toronto: Annick Press.

Eamer, C. (2013). *Before the world was ready: Stories of daring genius in science*. Toronto: Annick Press.

Freedman, R. (1995). *Immigrant kids*. New York: Puffin.

George, J. C. (2000). *How to talk to your dog*. New York: HarperCollins.

Gibbons, G. (1990). *Sunken treasure*. New York: HarperCollins.

Greenberg, J. (2008). *Christo and Jeanne-Claude: Through the gates and beyond*. New York: Roaring Brook Press.

Hoyt-Goldsmith, D. (2001). *Celebrating Ramadan*. New York: Holiday House.

Iggulden, C., & Iggulden, H. (2007). *The dangerous book for boys*. New York: HarperCollins.

Jeffrey, L. S. (2004). *Dogs: How to choose and care for a dog*. New York: Enslow.

Jenkins, S., & Page, R. (2003). *What do you do with a tail like this?* Boston: Houghton Mifflin.

Kalman, B. (2004). *The life cycle of an earthworm*. New York: Crabtree.

Keenan, S. (2007). *Animals in the house: A history of pets and people*. New York: Scholastic.

Krull, K. (2005). *Giants of science* series. New York: Puffin.

Krull, K. (2015). *Women who broke the rules* series. New York: Bloomsbury.

Llewellyn, C. (2005). *Crafts and games around the world*. New York: Pearson.

Loh-Hagan, V. (2015–16). *Nailed it! Extreme sports* series. New York: 45th Parallel.

Loh-Hagan, V. (2015–16). *Odd jobs* series. New York: 45th Parallel.

Loh-Hagan, V. (2016). *Do-it-yourself* series. New York: 45th Parallel.

Loh-Hagan, V. (2016). *Extreme animals* series. New York: 45th Parallel.

Markle, S. (2012). *The case of the vanishing golden frogs: A scientific mystery*. New York: Millbrook Press.

Parsons, A. (1993). *Eyewitness juniors: Amazing snakes*. New York: Dorling Kindersley. (also P)

Patent, D. H. (2003). *Slinky, scaly, slithery snakes*. New York: Walker.

Patent, D. H. (2012). *Dogs on duty: Soldiers' best friends on the battlefield and beyond*. New York: Walker.

Powell, P. H. (2014). *Josephine: The dazzling life of Josephine Baker*. New York: Chronicle.

Raum, E. (2014). *A World War II timeline*. Mankato, MN: Capstone.

Reeder, T. (2005). *Giant pandas*. Washington, DC: National Geographic.

Reeder, T. (2005). *Poison dart frogs*. Washington, DC: National Geographic.

Reeve, N. (1993). *Into the mummy's tomb*. New York: Scholastic/Madison Press. (also M)

Ride, S., & Okie, S. (1995). *To space and back*. New York: Lothrop, Lee & Shepard.

Rife, D. (2009). *Letters for freedom: The American Revolution*. New York: Kids Innovative.

Rusch, E. (2013). *Volcano rising*. New York: Charlesbridge.

Ryan, P. M. (2002). *When Marian sang: The true recital of Marian Anderson*. New York: Scholastic.

Schanzer, R. (2007). *George vs. George: The American revolution as seen from both sides*. Washington, DC: National Geographic.

Schlitz, L. A. (2007). *Good masters! Sweet ladies! Voices from a medieval village.* New York: Candlewick.

Schroeder, A. (2015). *Abe Lincoln: His wit and wisdom from A–Z.* New York: Holiday House.

Scott, E. (2007). *When is a planet not a planet?: The story of Pluto.* New York: Clarion.

Sill, C. P. (2003). *About reptiles: A guide for children.* New York: Peachtree.

Sinclair, J. (2005). *Eye openers: All about the body.* New York: Pearson.

Smith, D. J. (2014). *If: A mind-bending new way of looking at big ideas and numbers.* New York: Kids Can Press.

Tanaka, S. (2010). *The buried city of Pompeii.* New York: Black Walnut/Madison Press. (also M)

Tanaka, S. (2010). *Graveyard of the dinosaurs.* New York: Black Walnut/Madison Press. (also M)

Tanaka, S. (2010). *On board the Titanic: What it was like when the great liner sank.* New York: Black Walnut/Madison Press.

Thimmesh, C. (2013). *Scaly spotted feathered frilled: How do we know what dinosaurs really looked like?* Boston: Houghton Mifflin.

Tonatiuh, D. (2015). *Funny bones: Posada and his Day of the Dead Calaveras.* New York: Abrams.

Twist, C. (2007). *The book of stars.* New York: Scholastic.

Wallmark, L. (2015). *Ada Byron Lovelace and the thinking machine.* Berkeley, CA: Creston Books.

Walsh, K. (n.d.). *Time for Kids: Our world.* New York: Time for Kids.

Webb, S. (2011). *Far from shore: Chronicles of an open ocean voyage.* Boston: HMH Books.

Winters, K. (2008). *Colonial voices: Hear them speak.* New York: Dutton.

Yoo, P. (2014). *Twenty-two cents: Muhammad Yunus and the village bank.* New York: Lee and Low Books.

Middle Grade Books (Grades 7–8) (M)

Atkin, S. B. (2000). *Voices from the fields: Children of migrant workers tell their stories.* New York: Little, Brown. (also YA)

Ayer, P. (2015). *Foodprints: The story of what we eat.* Toronto: Annick Press.

Bash, B. (2002). *Desert giant: The world of the saguaro cactus.* San Francisco: Sierra Club Books for Children.

Charleyboy, L., & Leatherdale, M. (2014). *Dreaming in Indian: Contemporary Native American voices.* Toronto: Annick Press.

Cone, M. (2001). *Come back, salmon: How a group of dedicated kids adopted Pigeon Creek and brought it back to life.* San Francisco: Sierra Club Books for Children.

Deem, J. M. (2005). *Bodies from the ash.* New York: Houghton Mifflin.

Freedman, R. (1989). *Lincoln: A photobiography.* New York: Clarion Books.

Freedman, R. (2002). *Confucius: The golden rule.* New York: Arthur Levine Books.

Freedman, R. (2002). *Give me liberty!: The story of the Declaration of Independence.* New York: Holiday House. (also YA)

Hopkinson, D. (2004). *Shutting out the sky: Life in the tenements of New York, 1880–1924.* New York: Orchard Books.

Jiang, J. L. (2008). *Red scarf girl: A memoir of the cultural revolution.* New York: HarperCollins.

Knox, L. M. (2015). *The storyteller: My years with Ernest Thompson Seton.* Minneapolis: Langdon Street Press.

Krull, K. (2012). *Lives of the athletes: Thrills, spills (and what the neighbors thought).* Boston: HMH Books for Young Adults. (also YA).

Krull, K. (2013). *Lives of extraordinary women: Rulers, rebels (and what the neighbors thought).* Boston: HMH Books for Young Adults (also YA).

Krull, K. (2013). *Lives of the musicians: Good times, bad times (and what the neighbors thought)*. Boston: HMH Books for Young Adults (also YA).

Krull, K. (2014). *Lives of the artists: Masterpieces, messes (and what the neighbors thought)*. Boston: HMH Books for Young Adults. (also YA).

Kyi, T. L. (2015). *DNA detective*. Toronto, ON: Annick Press.

Lauber, P. (2001). *Hurricanes: Earth's mightiest storms*. New York: Houghton Mifflin Press. (also I).

Levine, E. (1995). *A fence away from freedom*. New York: Putnam Juvenile.

Macaulay, D. (2008). *The way things work*. Boston: Houghton Mifflin.

Mannis, C. D. (2003). *The queen's progress: An Elizabethan alphabet*. New York: Viking.

Montgomery, S. (2004). *The man-eating tigers of Sundarbans*. Boston: Houghton Mifflin.

Murphy, J. (2012). *Invincible microbe: Tuberculosis and the never-ending search for a cure*. New York: Clarion.

Nelson, K. (2008). *We are the ship: The story of Negro league baseball*. New York: Hyperion.

Nelson, S. D. (2015). *Sitting Bull: Lakota warrior and defender of his people*. New York: Abrams.

Newman, P. (2014). *Plastic ahoy!: Investigating the great Pacific garbage patch*. Minneapolis, MN: Millbrook Press.

Newman, P. (2016). *Ebola: Fears and facts*. Minneapolis, MN: Millbrook Press.

Pringle, L. (2011). *Billions of years, amazing changes: The story of evolution*. Honesdale, PA: Boyds Mill Press.

Pringle, L. (2001). *Global warming*. New York: Seastar.

Reeves, N. (1993). *Into the mummy's tomb*. New York: Scholastic/Madison Press.

Ride, S., & O'Shaughnessy, T. (2009). *Mission: Planet earth: Our world and its climate—and how humans are changing them*. New York: FlashPoint (also YA).

Rusch, E. (2012). *The mighty Mars rovers: The incredible adventures of* Spirit *and* Opportunity. Boston: Houghton Mifflin.

Rusch, E. (2013). *Eruption! Volcanoes and the science of saving lives*. Boston: Houghton Mifflin.

Sattler, H. R. (1995). *Our patchwork planet: The story of plate tectonics*. New York: Lothrop, Lee & Shepard.

Schlitz, L. (2008). *Good masters! Sweet ladies! Voices from a medieval village*. New York: Candlewick. (also I)

Scott, E. (1998). *Close encounters: Exploring the universe with the Hubble space telescope*. New York: Hyperion Books for Children. (also YA)

Scott, E. (2007). *When is a planet not a planet?: The story of Pluto*. New York: Clarion. (also I)

Stanley, J. (1993). *Children of the dust bowl: The true story of the school at Weedpatch Camp*. New York: Crown Books for Young Readers.

Stanley, J. (1998). *I am an American: A true story of Japanese internment*. New York: Scholastic.

Tanaka, S. (2005). *Mummies: The newest, coolest, and creepiest from around the world*. New York: Abrams.

Thimmesh, C. (2002). *Girls think of everything: Stories of ingenious inventions by women*. Boston: Houghton Mifflin.

Thimmesh, C. (2006). *Team moon: How 400,000 people landed Apollo 11 on the moon*. New York: Houghton Mifflin.

Van der Rol, R., & Verhoeven, R. (1993). *Anne Frank: Beyond the diary—A photographic remembrance*. New York: Viking.

Walker, S. M. (2013). *Written in bone: Buried lives of Jamestown and colonial Maryland*. New York: Carolrhoda.

Wulffson, T. (2000). *Toys! Amazing stories behind some real inventions*. New York: Holt. (also I)

Yousafzai, M., & Lamb, C. (2013). *I am Malala: The girl who stood up for education and was shot by the Taliban*. New York: Little, Brown.

High School Grade Books (Grades 9–12) (YA)

Aliki. (2000). *William Shakespeare and The Globe*. New York: HarperCollins. (also M).

Ali-Karamali, S. (2012). *Growing up Muslim: Understanding Islamic beliefs and practices*. New York: Delacorte.

Aronson, M. (2000). *Sir Walter Raleigh and the quest for El Dorado*. New York: Clarion Books.

Aronson, M., & Mayor, A. (2014). *The griffin and the dinosaur: How Adrienne Mayor discovered a fascinating link between myth and science*. Washington, DC: National Geographic.

Bartoletti, S. C. (2001). *Black potatoes: The story of the great Irish famine, 1845–1850*. Boston: Houghton Mifflin.

Bartoletti, S. C. (2014). *They called themselves the KKK: The birth of an American terrorist group*. Boston: Houghton Mifflin.

Bascomb, N. (2014). *The Nazi hunters: How a team of spies and survivors captured the world's most notorious Nazi*. New York: Levine/Scholastic.

Beah, I. (2007). *A long way gone: Memoirs of a boy soldier*. New York: Farrar, Straus & Giroux.

Blumenthal, K. (2005). *Let me play!: The story of Title IX: The law that changed the future of girls in America*. New York: Atheneum.

Bodanis, D. (2001). *E = mc²: A biography of the world's most famous equation*. New York: Berkley Trade.

Brimner, L. D. (2014). *Strike! The farm workers' fight for their rights*. Honesdale, PA: Calkins Creek.

Brimner, L. D. (2015). *The rain wizard: The amazing, mysterious, true life of Charles Mallory Hatfield*. Honesdale, PA: Calkins Creek.

Cohen-Janca, I. (2015). *Mister doctor: Janusz Korczak and the orphans of Warsaw ghetto*. Toronto: Annick Press.

D'Aluisio, F. (2008). *What the world eats*. New York: Tricycle Press.

Farrell, J. (1998). *Invisible enemies: Stories of infectious disease*. New York: Farrar, Straus & Giroux.

Farrell, J. (2005). *Invisible allies: Microbes that shape our lives*. New York: Farrar, Straus & Giroux.

Farrell, M. C. (2014). *Pure grit: How American World War II nurses survived battle and prison camp in the Pacific*. New York: Abrams.

Fleischman, J. (2004). *Phineas Gage: A gruesome but true story about brain science*. New York: Houghton Mifflin.

Fleischman, P. (2014). *Eyes wide open: Going behind the environmental headlines*. New York: Candlewick.

Fleming, C. (2014). *The family Romanov: Murder, rebellion, and the fall of imperial Russia*. New York: Schwartz & Wade.

Fradin, D. (2013). *Stolen into slavery: The true story of Solomon Northrup, free black man*. Washington, DC: National Geographic.

Frank, M. (2005). *Understanding the Holy Land: Answering questions about the Israeli–Palestinean conflict*. New York: Viking.

Freedman, R. (2010). *The war to end all wars: WWI*. New York: Clarion.

Green, D. (2008). *Biology: Life as we know it*. New York: Kingfisher.

Hall, S., & Wysocky, L. (2014). *Hidden girl: The true story of a modern-day child slave*. New York: Simon & Schuster.

Hoose, P. (2001). *We were there too! Young people in U.S. history*. New York: Farrar, Straus & Giroux.

Jenkins, S. (2002). *Life on earth: The story of evolution*. New York: Houghton Mifflin.

Johnson, G. (2009). *Animal tracks and signs*. Washington, DC: National Geographic.

King, C., & Osborne, L. B. (1997). *Oh freedom!: Kids talk about the civil rights movement with the people who made it happen*. New York: Knopf.

Lobel, A. (2008). *No pretty pictures: A child of war*. New York: HarperCollins.

Lowinger, K. (2015). *Give me wings: How a choir of former slaves took on the world*. Toronto: Annick Press.

McPherson, J. (2002). *Fields of fury: The American Civil War*. New York: Atheneum.

McWhorter, D. (2005). *A dream of freedom: The civil rights movement from 1954–1958*. New York: Scholastic.

Myers, W. D. (2001). *The greatest: Muhammed Ali*. New York: Scholastic.

Partridge, E. (2002). *This land was made for you and me: The life and songs of Woody Guthrie*. New York: Viking.

Partridge, E. (2005). *John Lennon: All I want is the truth*. New York: Viking.

Rappaport, D. (2012). *Beyond courage: The untold story of Jewish resistance during the Holocaust*. New York: Candlewick.

Sandler, M. W. (2013). *Imprisoned: The betrayal of Japanese Americans during World War II*. New York: Walker.

Sheinkin, S. (2012). *The notorious Benedict Arnold: A true story of adventure, heroism, and treachery*. New York: Flash Point.

Sherrow, V. (1996). *Violence and the media. The question of cause and effect*. New York: Millbrook Press.

Siegel, S. C. (2006). *To dance: A ballerina's graphic novel*. New York: Atheneum/Richard Jackson.

Stone, T. L. (2009). *Almost astronauts: 13 women who dared to dream*. New York: Candlewick.

Thomson, S., Mortenson, G., & Relin, D. O. (2007). *Three cups of tea: One man's journey to change the world . . . One child at a time*. New York: Puffin.

Warren, A. (2001). *Surviving Hitler: A boy in the Nazi death camps*. New York: HarperCollins.

Welden, A. (2001). *Girls who rocked the world: Heroines from Sacajawea to Sheryl Swoopes*. Hillsboro, OR: Beyond Words. (also M)

Quality Informational Magazines

Ask

Cobblestone

Faces

Kids Discover

Know

National Geographic Kids

Odyssey

Ranger Rick

Sports Illustrated Kids

Time for Kids

Yes Magazine

Zoobooks

Quality Informational Text Websites

All About Explorers
www.allaboutexplorers.com/explorers

California Department of Education Recommended Literature List K–12
www.cde.ca.gov/ci/sc/ll

California Reading Association's Eureka! Nonfiction Children's Book Award
www.californiareads.org/display.asp?p=awards_eureka

CommonLit
www.commonlit.org

Discovery Channel School
www.school.discoveryeducation.com

Library of Congress Teacher Resources
www.loc.gov/teachers

National Council for the Social Studies Notable Trade Books for Young People
www.ncss.org/resources/notable

National Library of Virtual Manipulatives
http://nlvm.usu.edu/en/nav/vlibrary.html

National Science Teachers Association Outstanding Science Trade Books for Students
K–12
www.nsta.org/bs04

NewsELA
https://newsela.com

PBS Kids
http://pbskids.org

ReadWorks
www.readworks.org

StarWalk Kids Media
https://starwalkkids.com

Vicki Cobb's Science Page
www.vickicobb.com

Index

Accuracy of the text
   Shared Reading and Text Feature Search strategy, 33
   Understanding and Evaluating Information Texts
       strategy, 14–15
Active reading, 138–142
After-reading experiences, 7–8
Analysis skills. *See also* Critical literacy
   CLIQUES strategy, 249–253
   Creator, Assumptions, Audience/User, Time and Place,
       and Significance (CAATS) strategy, 165–172
   Evidence, Patterns, Inquiry, and Claims (EPIC) strategy,
       254–259
   I-Chart strategy, 158–164
   Summary Writing strategy, 244–248
   Two-Column Journal strategy, 260–263
Anchor Standards for Reading, Speaking and Listening,
   and Writing, ix, 4. *See also individual strategies*
Annotation of texts
   I-Chart strategy, 158–164
   Text Annotation strategy, 115–118
Anticipation Guide strategy, 39–43
   forms for, 42–43
Appeal of the text, 14–15
Appropriateness of text, 14–15
Argumentation skills
   Intra-Act strategy, 202–207
   Text-Dependent Questions (TDQs) strategy, 124–131
Argumentative texts, 13
Artistry of the material, 14–15
Assessing Text Complexity strategy, 19–30
   forms for, 22–23, 25–30
Assessments
   Close Reading strategy, 102, 103
   Close Thinking strategy, 112, 114
Audience, 165–172
Authority of the author, 14
Author's purpose, 124–131

Background knowledge. *See* Building Background
   category of strategies; Prior knowledge
Before-reading experiences, 7–8
Biased information, viii
Brainstorming, 82–86

Building Background category of strategies
   Anticipation Guide strategy, 39–43
   Imagine, Elaborate, Predict, and Confirm (IEPC)
       strategy, 60–64
   KLEW strategy, 50–54
   KWHL strategy, 44–49
   overview, ix
   Table of Contents Prediction strategy, 55–59

CAATS. *See* Creator, Assumptions, Audience/User, Time
   and Place, and Significance strategy
Cause–effect map, 175, 182. *See also* Graphic organizers
Cause–effect text structure. *See also* Text structures
   Paragraph Writing Frames strategy, 234–238
   Text Structures strategy, 173–183
CLIQUES strategy, 249–253
   forms for, 252, 253
Close Reading
   Assessing Text Complexity strategy, 19–30
   Close Reading strategy, 99–108
   Close Thinking strategy, 109–118
   Text Annotation strategy, 115–188
   text complexity, 7, 14, 19–30
   Text-Dependent Questions (TDQs) strategy, 124–131
Close Reading strategy, 99–108
   forms for, 105–108
Close Thinking strategy, 109–118
   forms for, 115–118
Cluster map, 175, 179. *See also* Graphic organizers
Common Core State Standards (CCSS), vii, ix, 4. *See also*
   individual strategies
Compare–contrast text structure. *See also* Text
   structures
   Paragraph Writing Frames strategy, 234–238
   Text Structures strategy, 173–183
Complexity, text. *See* Text complexity
Comprehension
   Interactive Notebooks strategy, 184–188
   Text-Dependent Questions (TDQs) strategy and,
       124–131
   Thinking Aloud strategy, 134
   Understanding and Evaluating Information Texts
       strategy, 12–18

Comprehension category of strategies
  Creator, Assumptions, Audience/User, Time and Place, and Significance (CAATS) strategy, 165–172
  Four-Box Comment Card strategy, 150–157
  I-Chart strategy, 158–164
  overview, ix
  Study Guide strategy, 145–149
  Text Structures strategy, 173–183
Context clues, 71–76
  SLAP strategy, 71–76
Creator, Assumptions, Audience/User, Time and Place, and Significance (CAATS) strategy, 165–172
  forms for, 169–172
Critical literacy. *See also* Analysis skills
  Evidence, Patterns, Inquiry, and Claims (EPIC) strategy, 254–259
  Four-Box Comment Card strategy, 150–157
  overview, viii

Degree of challenge, 19–30
Descriptive text structure. *See also* Text structures
  Paragraph Writing Frames strategy, 234–238
  Text Structures strategy, 173–183
Details, 124–131
Discussion category of strategies
  Discussion Web strategy, 191–195
  4–3–2–1 Discussion Guide strategy, 196–201
  Intra-Act strategy, 202–207
  overview, ix
  Talking Points strategy, 208–215
  3-Minute Pause strategy, 221–226
  Three-Step Interview strategy, 216–220
Discussion Web strategy, 191–195
  forms for, 193, 195
During-reading experiences, 7–8

Evidence, Patterns, Inquiry, and Claims (EPIC) strategy, 254–259
  forms for, 257–259
Expository texts, 13

Features of text. *See* Text features
Forms
  Anticipation Guide form, 42–43
  CAATS Template, 169–172
  Cause–Effect Map, 182
  CLIQUES strategy Template, 252, 253
  Cluster Map form, 179
  Discussion Web form, 193, 195
  EPIC Template, 257–259
  Evaluating Informational Texts for Complexity Form, 22–23, 25–30
  Four-Box Comment Card form, 155, 157
  4–3–2–1 Discussion Guide form, 197, 199, 201
  "I Used to Think … but Now I Know …" Sentence Frames, 243
  I-Chart form, 161, 163–164
  IEPC Chart, 61–62, 64
  Informational Text Close Reading Planning Guide, 105–108
  Informational Text Close Thinking Planning Guide, 115–118

Informational Text Evaluation Form, 15, 18
Informational Text Feature Search, 34, 35–36
Informational Text Lesson Planning Guide, 10–11
Interactive Notebook form, 186, 188
Intra-Act Template, 205, 207
KLEW Chart, 51, 53–54
KWHL Chart, 45, 47, 49
List–Group–Label Chart, 84, 86
Paragraph Writing Frames form, 237–238
Problem–Solution Outline form, 183
Readers Theatre Script form, 232, 233
Root Wheel form, 79, 80–81
Semantic Feature Analysis Matrix, 94, 95
Series of Events Chart, 177, 180
SLAP Chart, 74, 76
Sticky Notes Bookmarks form, 142
Study Guide form, 147, 149
Summary Writing Chart, 247–248
Table of Contents Prediction form, 57, 59
Talking Points Template, 210, 211–212, 214–215
Text Annotation Planning Guide, 122, 123
Text-Dependent Questions Template, 129, 131
Think-Aloud Listening Guide, 133, 137
3-Minute Pause Planning Guide, 225–226
Three-Step Interview Notes Template, 220
Two-Column Journal Template, 262–263
Venn Diagram form, 181
Word Map form, 69, 70
Word Sort form, 89, 91
Four-Box Comment Card strategy, 150–157
  forms for, 155, 157
4–3–2–1 Discussion Guide strategy, 196–201
  forms for, 197, 199, 201
Functional/procedural texts, 13

Getting Started category of strategies
  Assessing Text Complexity strategy, 19–30
  overview, ix
  Planning a Lesson with Informational Texts strategy, 3–11
  Shared Reading and Text Feature Search strategy, 31–36
  Understanding and Evaluating Information Texts strategy, 12–18
Graphic organizers
  Discussion Web strategy, 191–195
  Interactive Notebooks strategy, 184–188
  Text Structures strategy, 173–183
Guided reading
  Planning a Lesson with Informational Texts strategy, 4
  Text-Dependent Questions (TDQs) strategy, 125

"**I** Used to Think … but Now I Know …" strategy, 239–243
  forms for, 243
I-Chart strategy, 158–164
  forms for, 161, 163–164
Imagine, Elaborate, Predict, and Confirm (IEPC) strategy, 60–64
  forms for, 61–62, 64
Inferences, 124–131
Informational magazines, ix, 271

nal texts, 13–14, 265–272
harts, 158–164
ve Notebooks strategy, 184–188
s for, 186, 188
xtual connections, 124–131
Act strategy, 202–207
ms for, 205, 207

EW strategy, 50–54
rms for, 51, 53–54
wledge demands, 22
HL strategy, 44–49
forms for, 45, 47, 49

Language use, 22
Layouts, 21
Lesson planning, 3–11
Lexiles, 20, 23
Listening, 109–118
List–Group–Label strategy, 82–86
  forms for, 84, 86
Literary nonfiction, 13

Notebooking, 184–188
Note-taking skills
  Interactive Notebooks strategy, 184–188
  Talking Points strategy, 208–215
  Two-Column Journal strategy, 260–263

Opinions
  Intra-Act strategy, 202–207
  Text-Dependent Questions (TDQs) strategy, 124–131
Oral reading, 229–233
Organization of text, 21

Paragraph Writing Frames strategy, 234–238
  forms for, 237–238
Partnership for Assessment of Readiness for College and
    Careers (PARCC), viii
Peer interactions, 208–215
Performance tasks, 102
Perspectives, 191–195
Persuasive texts, 13
Planning a Lesson with Informational Texts strategy, 3–11
  forms for, 10–11
Portfolios, 184–188
Preconceptions, 239–243
Prediction guides, 39–43
Predictions
  Anticipation Guide strategy, 39–43
  "I Used to Think … but Now I Know …" strategy,
    239–243
  Imagine, Elaborate, Predict, and Confirm (IEPC)
    strategy, 60–64
  List–Group–Label strategy, 82–86
  Shared Reading and Text Feature Search strategy, 32
  Table of Contents Prediction strategy, 55–59
Prefixes, 77–81
Prior knowledge. See also Building Background category
    of strategies
  Close Reading strategy, 100
  Close Thinking strategy, 110

"I Used to Think … but Now I Know …" strategy,
    239–243
  I-Chart strategy, 158–164
  List–Group–Label strategy, 82–86
  Table of Contents Prediction strategy, 56
  Thinking Aloud strategy, 134
  3-Minute Pause strategy, 221–226
Problem–solution outline, 175, 183. See also Graphic
    organizers
Problem–solution text structure. See also Text structures
  Paragraph Writing Frames strategy, 234–238
  Text Structures strategy, 173–183

Qualitative features, 20–23. See also Text features
Quantitative features, 20. See also Text features

Readability formulas, 20
Read-alouds
  Close Thinking strategy, 109–118
  formats for, 6
  Planning a Lesson with Informational Texts strategy, 4
Reader concerns, 22
Readers Theatre strategy, 229–233
  forms for, 232, 233
Reading closely, 132–142
Reading Closely category of strategies
  Close Reading strategy, 99–108
  Close Thinking strategy, 109–118
  overview, ix
  Sticky Notes Bookmark strategy, 138–142
  Text Annotation strategy, 119–123
  Text-Dependent Questions (TDQs) strategy, 124–131
Reading Quest, 196–201
Reasoning skills, 158–164
Reflection
  Talking Points strategy, 208–215
  Two-Column Journal strategy, 260–263
Relationships among informational ideas, 21
Research skills, 158–164
Resources and materials, 265–272
Root Wheels strategy, 77–81
  forms for, 79, 80–81
Roots, 77–81

Semantic Feature Analysis strategy, 92–95
  forms for, 94, 95
Sequence/order text structure. See also Text structures
  Paragraph Writing Frames strategy, 234–238
  Text Structures strategy, 173–183
Series of events chart, 175, 177, 180. See also Graphic
    organizers
Shared reading
  Planning a Lesson with Informational Texts strategy, 4,
    7–8
  Shared Reading and Text Feature Search strategy, 31–36
  Text-Dependent Questions (TDQs) strategy, 125
Shared Reading and Text Feature Search strategy, 31–36
  forms for, 34, 35–36
SLAP strategy, 71–76
  forms for, 74, 76
Small-group activities
  Four-Box Comment Card strategy, 150–151, 153

Small-group activities (*continued*)
    Planning a Lesson with Informational Texts strategy, 4
    Three-Step Interview strategy, 216–220
Smarter Balance assessments, viii
Sticky Notes Bookmark strategy, 138–142
    forms for, 142
Structures, text. *See* Text structures
Study Guide strategy, 145–149
    forms for, 147, 149
Style, 21
Suffixes, 77–81
Summarizing
    Summary Writing strategy, 244–248
    Talking Points strategy, 208–215
    Thinking Aloud strategy, 134
Summary Writing strategy, 244–248
    forms for, 247–248
Synonyms, 72, 73

Table of Contents Prediction strategy, 55–59
    forms for, 57, 59
Talking Points strategy, 208–215
    forms for, 210, 211–212, 214–215
Task concerns, 22
Text analysis. *See* Analysis skills
Text Annotation strategy, 115–118
    forms for, 122, 123
Text complexity
    Assessing Text Complexity strategy, 19–30
    Planning a Lesson with Informational Texts strategy, 7
    Understanding and Evaluating Information Texts strategy, 14
Text-Dependent Questions (TDQs) strategy, 124–131
    forms for, 129, 131
Text features
    Shared Reading and Text Feature Search strategy, 31–36
    Text-Dependent Questions (TDQs) strategy and, 127
Text structures
    Paragraph Writing Frames strategy, 234–238
    Text-Dependent Questions (TDQs) strategy and, 124–131
    Text Structures strategy, 173–183
    Thinking Aloud strategy, 134
Text Structures strategy, 173–183
    forms for, 177, 179–183
Textual evidence, 249–253
Theme, 22
Thinking aloud, 12–18, 72
Thinking Aloud strategy, 132–142
    forms for, 133, 137
Think–Pause–Share, 221–226

3-Minute Pause strategy, 221–226
    forms for, 225–226
Three-Step Interview strategy, 216–220
    forms for, 220
Tone, 21
Two-Column Journal strategy, 260–263
    forms for, 262–263

Understanding, 12–18, 124–131. *See also* Comprehen
Understanding and Evaluating Informational Texts strategy, 12–18
    forms for, 15, 18
    Thinking Aloud strategy, 134

Validity of content, 33. *See also* Accuracy of the text
Venn diagram, 175, 181. *See also* Graphic organizers
Visual supports
    Assessing Text Complexity strategy, 21
    Shared Reading and Text Feature Search strategy, 33
    Text Structures strategy, 173–183
Vocabulary
    Text-Dependent Questions (TDQs) strategy, 124–131
    Thinking Aloud strategy, 134
Vocabulary category of strategies
    List–Group–Label strategy, 82–86
    overview, ix
    Root Wheels strategy, 77–81
    Semantic Feature Analysis strategy, 92–95
    SLAP strategy, 71–76
    Word Map strategy, 67–70
    Word Sort strategy, 87–91

Website recommendations, 271–272
Whole-class discussion, 151
Word Map strategy, 67–70
    forms for, 69, 70
Word Sort strategy, 87–91
    forms for, 89, 91
Writing activities
    Close Reading strategy, 103
    Close Thinking strategy, 114
Writing category of strategies
    CLIQUES strategy, 249–253
    Evidence, Patterns, Inquiry, and Claims (EPIC) strategy, 254–259
    "I Used to Think … but Now I Know …" strategy, 239–243
    overview, ix
    Paragraph Writing Frames strategy, 234–238
    Readers Theatre strategy, 229–233
    Summary Writing strategy, 244–248
    Two-Column Journal strategy, 260–263